City Schools

City Schools

Leading the Way

Patrick B. Forsyth
Marilyn Tallerico

Editors

CORWIN PRESS, INC.
A Sage Publications Company
Newbury Park, California

For information address:

SAGE Publications, Inc.
2455 Teller Road
Newbury Park, California 91320

SAGE Publications Ltd.
6 Bonhill Street
London EC2A 4PU
United Kingdom

SAGE Publications India Pvt. Ltd.
M-32 Market
Greater Kailash I
New Delhi 110 048 India

Printed in the United States of America

Library of Congress Cataloging-in-Publication Data

Main entry under title:

City schools: leading the way / edited by Patrick B. Forsyth, Marilyn
Tallerico.
    p.   cm.
    Includes bibliographical references and index.
    ISBN 0-8039-6065-4.—ISBN 0-8039-6066-2 (pbk.)
    1. Urban schools—United States. 2. School management and
organization—United States. 3. Educational leadership—United
States. I. Forsyth, Patrick B. II. Tallerico, Marilyn.
LC5131.C53 1993
370.19′348′0973—dc20   93-12058

93 94 95 96 10 9 8 7 6 5 4 3 2 1

Corwin Press Production Editor: Marie Louise Penchoen

Contents

Acknowledgments

Participants in the Select Conference selflessly devoted their time, energy, and expertise to this project. We salute them and their respective sponsoring school districts/agencies for their contributions and continuing support:

Principals:
Fermin Burgos, Kosciuszko Middle School, Milwaukee, WI
Robert L. Bussmann, Elliott Elementary School, Lincoln, NE
Ruby Cremaschi-Schwimmer, Abraham Lincoln Preparatory High School, San Diego, CA
Betty J. Hines, Southwestern High School, Detroit, MI
Arthur Lebowitz, Trevor Browne High School, Phoenix, AZ
Robert L. Miller, Maxfield Magnet School, St. Paul, MN
Gyuri Nemeth, Ronald E. McNair Senior High School, Atlanta, GA
Yolanda Rocha, Dobie Middle School, Austin, TX
Pamela D. Thomas, John Marshall High School, Oklahoma City, OK
Frances Williams, G. W. Childs Elementary School, Philadelphia, PA

Youth Serving Agency Representatives:
Kevin Buckley, Consulting Psychologist, Phoenix, AZ
Deborah Dillon, Education Director, City of Phoenix, AZ
Raul Espericueta, Director, Youth & Family Services, The Friendly House, Phoenix, AZ
Joe Mendoza, Director of Juvenile Court Program, Chicanos Por La Causa, Phoenix, AZ
Rose Newsome, Director of Equal Opportunity Department, City of Phoenix, AZ
Mary Ann Perez, Head Start Director, Cartwright School District, Phoenix, AZ

Task Force Members:
James Bliss, Associate Professor, Rutgers University
Richard M. Englert, Associate Vice President for Administration, Temple University
Patrick B. Forsyth, Executive Director, UCEA
William J. Kritek, Associate Professor, University of Wisconsin-Milwaukee

Laurence Parker, Associate Professor, Temple University
Marilyn Tallerico, Associate Professor, Syracuse University
Linda F. Winfield, Visiting Professor, UCLA Graduate School of
  Education

We likewise express our sincere appreciation to Bruce Anderson
and The Danforth Foundation for the generous financial commitments
to this endeavor, and to the members of the Advisory Board for the
Urban Initiative Project:
Eugene C. Campbell, Newark Public Schools
Thomas B. Corcoran, Research for Better Schools Robert
Timothy J. Dyer, Phoenix Union High School
John Ellis, Austin Independent Schools
Samuel Husk, Council of Great City Schools
Arthur Jefferson, Detroit Public Schools
Gladys S. Johnston, Arizona State University
K. Forbis Jordan, Arizona State University
William M. Kendrick, Seattle Public Schools
Karen Seashore Louis, University of Minnesota
S. Peterkin, Milwaukee Public Schools
Hugh Petrie, SUNY-Buffalo
Ruth E. Randall, Minnesota Department of Education
Victor Rodriguez, San Antonio School District
Lonnie Wagstaff, University of Cincinnati
Max Weiner, Fordham University
Everett J. Williams, New Orleans Public Schools

Finally, we thank members of the UCEA staff, especially Jeanette
Hausman, who coordinated the project during its final year, Jan Nuetzel,
who helped in manuscript preparation and did the typesetting, and
Holly Price and Bobbi Jo Bennett, who performed numerous production tasks.

Preface

City Schools: Leading the Way is intended to be useful to both current and prospective principals of urban schools, as well as to professors of educational administration. It is grounded in the current realities of urban education, and organized around nine significant "problems of practice" identified by a specially selected group of successful city principals, metropolitan youth-serving professionals, and urban university faculty.

The term problem of practice refers not to the countless details and crises that monopolize principals' daily worklives, but rather to focal issues that are of a middle-range level of abstraction (Silver, 1983) and have long-term consequences for students. Individual chapters review, organize, and integrate information around these focal issues and provide examples of possible interventions appropriate to the unique context of urban schools. An important goal of this work is to help practitioners better understand and manage complex problems, by identifying and presenting in a scholarly but nontechnical format the theory, research, analytic tools, and administrative strategies relevant to each issue. An additional goal is that the unanswered questions raised in each chapter will become the foci of future inquiry and analysis by practitioners and professors interested in the improvement of urban schools through applied research.

Origins of the Problems of Practice

It is important to underscore that the nine problems of practice addressed in this volume were not arrived at arbitrarily. In fact, they emerged from a systematic application of the research approach known as *nominal group technique*. In this case, the "nominal group" was an invited gathering (the Select Conference) of 10 principals of urban schools (nominated by their respective superintendents, from Austin, Oklahoma City, San Diego, Lincoln, Detroit, Milwaukee, St. Paul, Phoenix, Philadelphia, and Atlanta), six representatives of metropolitan youth-serving agencies (for example, Youth and Family Services, Head Start, Equal Opportunity Office, Chicanos Por La Causa), and eight educational administration faculty members from universities serving urban communities (Temple, Rutgers, Johns Hopkins, Arizona State, Syracuse, and the University of Wisconsin-Milwaukee). The racial, ethnic, and gender diversity of the group was 25% African American, 21% Hispanic, and 42% female.

The technique for engaging Select Conference participants in the problem-identification task involved multistep processes of independent reflection, issue clarification, discussion, formal balloting, and prioritization of concerns, in both small and large groups. Professor-participants served as observers, recorders, and group facilitators, while principals and youth-serving agency professionals provided the substance and direction of the task of distilling a set of key problems of practice affecting today's urban schools.

The Select Conference, held in a retreat setting in Mesa, Arizona, lasted two days. It resulted in the identification of the following critical problems of practice, which have been translated in this volume into foci for the organization of a knowledge-base relevant to the work of urban school principals:

1. Understanding the urban context and conditions of practice
2. Motivating urban children to learn
3. Managing instructional diversity
4. Building open climates in urban schools
5. Collecting and using information for problem solving and decision making
6. Acquiring and using urban resources
7. Governing urban schools
8. Effecting change in urban schools
9. Establishing mission, vision, and goals

It should be noted that the sequencing of the above (and that of the ensuing chapters) is not intended to convey relative importance. It is clear that current and prospective city principals require an integrated and informed command of each of these focal issues and tasks, in order to effect improvements in the education of urban youth.

The Broader Context

It is also important to note that this compendium is but one product of a broader, multiyear, national endeavor to improve the preparation and development of school administrators in general, to tie urban administrator preparation more closely to administrative practice, and to create a cadre of scholars with expertise in, and commitment to, issues important to urban school leadership. That endeavor, formally titled "The Urban Initiative Project," was begun in 1989, under the joint sponsorship of the Danforth Foundation and the University Council for Educational Administration (UCEA).

The Project's underlying assumptions (Stout, 1989) were: (a) urban schools should be a focus of national attention; (b) school principals are a key to general school improvement; (c) the extant knowledge-base is not organized or presented in such a way as to be accessible and useful to urban school principals; (d) preparation programs for urban educational administrators can and should be improved; and (e) UCEA and The Danforth Foundation can serve as catalysts in all of these regards. To date, key outcomes prompted by those catalysts have been: (a) the successful completion of the Select Conference's charge to distill a set of urban school problems of practice that could serve as foci for the organization of a relevant knowledge-base, and (b) the resultant publication and dissemination of this volume.

Where to Next?

The purposes, processes, and outcomes described above represent the accomplishment of just one phase of the UCEA-Danforth Urban Initiative Project. The second phase uses the contents of this volume as the baseline knowledge for developing or improving urban educational administration curriculums in universities serving urban communities throughout the United States.

Interest and expertise in such curricular revisions will be generated by bringing together Invited Fellows for a series of special summer institutes. Fellows will be selected from the ranks of promising university faculty of urban universities that prepare school administrators. Before fellowships are offered, a commitment to addressing the need to emphasize professional preparation for urban school administration will be required from the sponsoring college of education and its dean.

The objectives of the summer institutes will be to outline research agendas related to urban school administration and to encourage scholars to develop specialties in the area of urban school administration. It is expected that these specialists will influence future curriculum development in the universities, complete research on the subject, teach courses on the subject, lend technical assistance to urban schools, and assure that attention to these focal issues is sustained in the decades to come.

Organization of Text

The volume begins with Richard Englert's chapter (chapter 1) describing the environmental context of today's urban schools. His discussion is based on the premise that classroom interactions in city schools are shaped to some extent by the urban setting, and that this special context gives rise to a number of unique conditions of practice for school administrators. The main point of the chapter is that by understanding the salient features of the urban environment and the key conditions of practice, principals can both better cope with the obstacles, and take better advantage of the opportunities, that urban settings present. A comprehensive framework and review of the literature are included to help principals better understand the complex set of relationships that influence urban schools. Several of the issues introduced by Englert are revisited and expanded in subsequent chapters (for example, resource acquisition, climate, and governance structures).

Patrick Forsyth's chapter (chapter 2) on motivating urban children to learn likewise establishes a theme that flows throughout the remainder of the text: the student-centeredness of these nine critical problems of practice. Forsyth focuses on the concept of student "engagement," and how principals can investigate and intervene to improve learner engagement in urban contexts. He argues for mobilizing school energies and resources to build systems supporting the broad, long-term goal of student connectedness and involvement, rather than building programs to address specific symptoms of student disengagement.

Linda Winfield, Ruth Johnson, and JoAnne Manning's chapter (chapter 3) continues Forsyth's focus on students and the core educational tasks of learning and instruction. The authors draw a critical connection between learning outcomes and organizational structures, by underscoring how administrative decisions about allocating resources affect access to knowledge by students from diverse populations. In order to help current and prospective urban principals recognize and understand inequities in educational opportunities, Winfield et al. provide a comprehensive review of the research on traditional attempts to deal with student diversity in urban settings. They explain how differential access to knowledge is related to student grouping practices, teacher beliefs, personnel assignments, and other inequities in the curriculum. The authors emphasize four functional categories of possible intervention by school administrators: coordinating instructional programming and related services, adapting curriculum and instruction, generating social service and community support, and facilitating the development and renewal of staff.

In Chapter 4, James Bliss takes a broad view of the nature of urban "school climates," which frame student learning and engagement. He illustrates the multidimensionality of school climate and argues for attention to both relationships *within* schools and relationships *between* home and school. While offering principals suggestions for ways to build more open urban school climates, the author underscores the importance of a network of interrelationships among four key stakeholder groups: students, parents, teachers, and administrators. According to Bliss, the challenge to urban principals (and conventional thinking) is that schools have not one, but many climates. The strategies for interventions, therefore, must likewise be multifaceted.

In Chapter 5, Robert Slater focuses on two phases of a continuous process that is key to the exercise of leadership not only in urban but in *all* schools: problem solving and decision making. He argues convincingly for improving the quality of information used in this two-stage process, as a means of influencing student learning and school effectiveness. His selected review of research and theory provides useful background information on the nature and acquisition of information and their relationship to problem solving and decision making in schools. While Slater offers principals an easily understandable, five-step approach, he carefully contrasts his ideal, rational model with others available in the literature. Along with this general strategy, the author includes numerous specific techniques for improving the acquisition, use, and management of information for collaborative problem solving and participative decision making.

Laurence Parker in chapter 6 signals a subtle shift in the volume's progression from largely *within-school* variables to the broader financial-political contexts of schooling and efforts to capitalize on *external* sources of support. Parker raises provoking questions and argues persuasively for a critical perspective on the leadership and advocacy functions of urban school principals. This chapter reinforces some of the inner-city environmental factors described in Chapter 1, as a means of providing a vivid contextual frame for the discussion of the unique (and often ignored) resource needs of children of poverty. The author describes four different approaches used by city principals to marshall additional funds/human capital for their schools, including partnerships with business, with parents, with universities, and with community cultural resources. Unlike conventional treatments, however, Parker includes pointed caveats and critical analyses of the advantages and disadvantages of these strategies. He concludes by underscoring the long-term futility of any such approaches, absent serious attention to the broader societal and economic inequities that affect the lives of urban school students.

Like Parker's, Marilyn Tallerico's chapter (chapter 7) focuses on districtwide and external-to-individual-school-site issues, this time specific to urban educational governance. Her chapter centers on the pervasive tension that exists between school-level autonomy and systemwide uniformity and coordination in urban districts. The student-centeredness of this problem of practice concerns issues of *where* and *how* decisions are made that affect teaching and learning, thus concepts such as power, control, and authority over decision making are central to her discussion. She organizes the chapter into four major sections: (a) what is understood about this problem of practice, in terms of relevant theory and conceptual frameworks; (b) what is known about the problem, including its historical underpinnings and research findings from urban studies; (c) specific implications for the work of city school principals; and (d) selected examples of intervention strategies utilized by several urban districts currently experimenting with innovative approaches to educational governance.

In Chapter 8, William Kritek provides a comprehensive review of the knowledge-base relevant to effecting change in urban schools by synthesizing three separate but interrelated strands of research and theory: (a) school effectiveness; (b) the process of change; and (c) school culture. A focus on principals "working together" with *teachers* serves as a major theme woven throughout the author's discussions of each of these distinct literatures. Kritek explains his rationale for this focus in pragmatic terms: Quite simply, urban principals will be unable to effect change "without the active cooperation of the school's teachers." He intentionally avoids how-to's and cookbook-recipes for the complex task of school improvement, as "there is no guarantee that what worked for one principal will work for another, or that what worked for a principal in one school will work for that same principal when he or she moves to another building." Instead, Kritek concludes by suggesting four integrative concepts that should enhance principals' understandings of effecting change in complex and unpredictable environments.

Like Kritek's, Robert Stout's chapter (chapter 9) refrains from simplistic prescriptions, this time within the context of establishing the mission, vision, and goals for urban schools. Stout also avoids what he calls "complex or academic" definitions and language, thus the general *tone* of this chapter may strike the reader as quite different from the others. (For example, he begins by quoting several nontraditional sources, including bumper stickers.) Yet the content of this chapter is quite serious and important. Stout discusses the problem of vision-, goal-, and mission-establishment as an "imbedded problem of the larger social order." He provides a critical historical perspective, discussing America's perennial ambivalence over questions of social justice and equal opportunity as they relate to schooling. He illustrates how urban schools' mission and goals are influenced by sets of both external and internal forces, and how schools can be understood as a special class of organizations. And he relates these discussions to urban school practice in several ways: (a) by applying seven generalizations about leadership, organizations, and organization goals; (b) by describing five prerequisite conditions for effective mission-setting; and (c) by raising a provocative set of questions that can help guide principals in the political process of establishing mission and goals.

References

Silver, P. B. (1983). *Professionalism in educational administration*. Victoria, Australia: Deakin University Press.

Stout, R. T. (1989, April). *Charge to the Select Conference*. Paper presented at the opening meeting of the Select Conference on Urban Educational Administration, Mesa, AZ.

About the Editors

Patrick B. Forsyth, is Executive Director of the University Council for Educational Administration and Associate Professor at The Pennsylvania State University. After teaching in New York City and New Jersey, he completed his doctoral study at Rutgers University in 1977. Forsyth's research interests are in the sociology of organizations and urban school administration. In 1983, he became the first recipient of the Jack A. Culbertson Award for outstanding contributions by a junior professor to the field of school administration for his research on professionalization process. Among his writings are: *Effective Supervision: Theory into Practice*, (Random House), with Wayne K. Hoy, and *Leaders for America's Schools: The Report and Papers of the National Commission on Excellence in Educational Administration*, (McCutchan), with Daniel E. Griffiths and Robert T. Stout, editors. In 1989-90, Forsyth chaired the study group for the National Policy Board for Educational Administration that produced *Improving the Preparation of School Administrators: An Agenda for Reform*.

Marilyn Tallerico, Associate Professor of Educational Administration, earned her Ph.D. from Arizona State University and joined the Syracuse University faculty in 1988. Her professional interests center on both school board research and gender issues in educational leadership. Her most recent publications have appeared in *The Journal of Educational Administration, Qualitative Sociology, Urban Education, The Journal of School Leadership, Planning & Changing*, and *The Journal of Staff Development*. Her teaching interests at Syracuse include the politics and governance of education, instructional supervision, staff development, women and educational leadership, and the principalship. She brings to her university work 12 years of experience as a teacher and administrator in the public schools.

About the Contributors

James R. Bliss received his Ph.D. from Cornell University. Currently an Associate Professor at Rutgers University, he is Co-editor of *Rethinking Effective Schools: Research and Practice* (with William A. Firestone and Craig E. Richards). Recent articles have appeared in *Educational Administration Quarterly, Planning and Changing,* and *High School Journal* (with C. John Tarter and Wayne K. Hoy). His research interests focus on organizational issues in schooling such as the challenges of organizing for a quality education in New Jersey's urban schools. He has participated in other UCEA-related publications including *Leaders for America's Schools* (edited by Daniel E. Griffiths, Robert T. Stout, and Patrick B. Forsyth), and serves on the editorial board of *Educational Administration Quarterly.*

Richard M. Englert is Associate Vice President for Administration and Professor of Educational Administration at Temple University, where he is also Senior Research Associate in the Center for Research in Human Development and Education. He serves as the Co-director of the Pennsylvania Leadership in Educational Administration Development (PA-LEAD) Institute.

A graduate of the Educational Administration doctoral program of the University of California, he has a master's degree from Pepperdine University. He has extensive experience both in basic education as a classroom teacher and in higher education as a university administrator, including Dean of the College of Education at Temple University. His research, writing, and teaching emphases are in the areas of urban education, the politics of education, teacher collective bargaining, and the administration of higher education.

Ruth Johnson is Associate Professor of Educational Administration at California State University, Los Angeles, and received her Ed.D. from Rutgers University. Prior to her current position, she held a variety of positions in K-12 education, including classroom teaching and consulting, assistant superintendent in curriculum and business administration, and superintendent of schools.

Her major research interest is on processes related to changing the academic culture of urban schools. While directing the California based Achievement Council's comprehensive urban school improvement initiative, she is developing instruments to measure qualitative indicators of change in underachieving schools. She has co-authored two reports for the Independent Analysis Unit of the Los Angeles School District; one on achievement patterns in elementary schools and the other on the actual college-going rates by ethnicity. Ruth Johnson serves on national, state, and local advisory boards and committees, makes frequent presentations, and serves as a consultant to schools and districts throughout the nation.

William J. Kritek is Associate Professor in the Department of Administrative Leadership at the University of Wisconsin, Milwaukee, where he has been for 16 years and has served as Director of the School Service Center as Department Chair and as Associate Dean of the School of Education. He has also been a high school mathematics teacher and principal. His most recent publications include a chapter on teachers and principals in the Milwaukee Public Schools for the forthcoming *Seeds of Crisis: Public Education in Milwaukee Since 1920* and "Whatever Happened to Project RISE" in the *KAPPAN*. The latter is a retrospective look at one of the country's first school-effectiveness programs. He has been university coordinator of the formal collaboration between UWM and the Milwaukee Public Schools and was the author of a report for the Ford Foundation, "Obstacles to University/ School Collaboration in an Urban Setting" based on a study of university-school collaboration in cities across the country.

JoAnne B. Manning is Assistant Superintendent for the William Penn School District. She is also a Research Associate at Temple University's Center for Research in Human Development and Education and an Adjunct Professor at Penn State University. Her publications and areas of research are in leadership development and service delivery for students with diverse needs.

Laurence Parker is an Associate Professor in the Department of Educational Leadership and Policy Studies at Temple University. He is currently on the editorial board of *Educational Administration Quarterly*, and is the Program Chair for the AERA SIG on Research on Race, Class, and Gender. His most current works include the co-authored article "Where is the Discussion of Diversity in Educational Administration Programs? Graduate Students Voices Addressing an Omission in Their Preparation", in the January 1992 issue of the *Journal of School Leadership*.

Robert O. Slater, formerly Senior Research Associate with the U.S. Department of Education's Office of Educational Research and Improvement, is currently a Professor of Educational Administration at Texas A & M University, where he is also Associate Director of the Principals' Center. Professor Slater does research and provides technical assistance in the areas of problem-solving, school restructuring, site-based management and leadership, and comparative educational administration.

Robert T. Stout is a Professor in the Division of Educational Leadership and Policy Studies, Arizona State University. He has been on the faculty of the University of California, Berkeley, The Claremont Graduate School, California State University, Fullerton, and Arizona State University. His interests include the politics of education and the sociology of schools. He has published in the areas of politics of education, leadership and values, leadership training, education reform, school desegregagation and race, social class, and gender equity. Although he has never been a public school teacher or administrator, he has been quite active in working in and for public schools. His students are leaders in school systems throughout the United States.

Linda F. Winfield is Visiting Professor, UCLA Graduate School of Education/CRESST, formerly Principal Research Scientist, Center for Research on Effective Schooling for Disadvantaged Students at Johns Hopkins University; Co-director, "Special Strategies for Educating Disadvantaged Students", a congressionally-mandated, national study of promising practices in Chapter I elementary and secondary schools. She earned her Ph.D. and her master's degrees from the University of Delaware. Dr. Winfield was also a Visiting Scholar, National Assessment of Educational Progress, Educational Testing Service, Princeton, NJ.

Prior to Johns Hopkins, Winfield was a faculty member in the Graduate School of Education at Temple University in the Department of Educational Leadership and Policy Studies. She has served as Director of Research/Evaluation for a consortium of school districts in New Castle County, Wilmington, Delaware (1981-1985) and has received support from the Rockefeller Foundation and the National Science Foundation for her work on literacy proficiency among black young adults.

Winfield's current research examines the implementation and evaluation of school change in compensatory education as a result of Hawkins-Stafford amendments (1988) and other alterable practices which impact student achievement in urban settings. Other research focuses on the assessment of racial/ethnic minority students and equity. She is Chairperson of American Educational Research Association, Special Interest Group on Research using NAEP data and is a former AERA Palmer O. Johnson Memorial Award Recipient (1992).

1

Understanding the Urban Context and Conditions of Practice of School Administration

RICHARD M. ENGLERT

The city school interacts continuously with its urban environment. Some principals—the most successful ones—understand this interaction and thus are able to take full advantage of a vast array of urban resources, buffer the school and its students from some of the negative environmental influences, and provide educational and other services that help to offset these factors placing students at risk. Other, less successful principals are virtually immobilized by the seemingly overwhelming forces of city life and thus are unable to combat, let alone influence, the myriad of dysfunctional and pathological pressures on the school and its students.

Ackoff (1974) described four types of planners confronting a changing environment. These same types could easily be applied to the role of urban school principal. The *inactive* principal does nothing with respect to the future, either not recognizing external threats or hoping they simply will go away. The *reactive* principal yearns for the "good old days" when things were allegedly better and tries to resist change and return things to some prior ideal state. The *preactive* principal attempts to anticipate trends and prepare for the most probable future. The *interactive* principal not merely anticipates trends but tries to understand and create the future by a continuous interchange between the school, its context, and a range of possible futures.

An interactive approach to school management and leadership is asserted here. The effective principal understands the urban context in order to create productive interchanges that will tap environmental resources of potential benefit to the school, insulate to some extent the school against unwanted forces, provide services and supports that can help compensate for unalterable negative influences that place students and the school at risk of failure, and generally manipulate those alterable variables at the school's disposal. An adequate understanding of the urban context is a necessary component of the knowledge base of the interactive principal who wishes to take positive action for school success.

This chapter proceeds in five stages. After the introduction, the general nature of the urban context is addressed, including the traditional ambivalence our society (including educational leaders) has toward our urban schools and several salient features of the urban context of schools. Then, the focus is on a model for understanding the urban influences on student learning. Its starting point is a conceptualization, developed by the late Paula Silver, involving the conditions and problems of practice that a principal needs to confront as a practicing professional. The emphasis is on the student as the key referent point for a professional's attention. Next, the major ways in which the urban environment affects the key actors and features of the school and of learning are presented. This discussion is based on a framework that asserts that the family, school, and community are in an interactive relationship that directly and indirectly affects student outcomes. Finally, the more important implications this interaction between the school and its environment has for the school principal are reviewed, followed by some unanswered questions and a few concluding remarks. Throughout the chapter, a conscious effort is made to reference a substantial portion of the literature on the school in the urban context; this literature is an invaluable resource for the continuing professional development of the city principal.

The Urban Context

Ambivalence About City Schools

The literature on schools in big cities is ambivalent. On the negative side, the problems seem insurmountable, and big city schools are viewed as failures in their central functions. City-school students achieve at lower levels than nonurban students (Wolf, 1978). Urban schools have been criticized for being too large, very impersonal, and unconnected to the outside, and for having poorly motivated students, low expectations, terrible attendance patterns, and unsupportive environments (Maeroff, 1988). In the 1960s, the condition of the city schools was depicted as failing (Herndon, 1965; Kohl, 1967; Kozol, 1967). Faced with seemingly hopeless situations, some came to the same conclusion as Halpin (1966) when he wrote:

> The conditions in some of our schools are so bad, and the physical and social environments in which these schools are located are so frightful, that we may have to cross off some of these schools as expendable. This is a shocking statement, I know, but I think that we had better face it. (p. 235)

Yet even more shocking is the observation that city schools have worsened considerably *since* the 1960s (Hill, Wise & Shapiro, 1989; Kasarda, 1989; Wacquant & Wilson, 1989; Kozol, 1991). The prognosis is particularly poor because new teachers hired to teach in urban schools over the next few years actually would prefer suburban schools and are not adequately prepared for the urban context (Grant, 1989). Some big-city school districts have dropout rates in the neighborhood of 40% to 60%, with some schools exceeding 75% to 80% (Hahn, Danzberger & Lefkowitz, 1987). And city-school students score on average below suburban students on standardized tests (Ornstein & Levine, 1989). These problems provoked Maeroff (1988) to observe that "no white suburb in America would long tolerate the low academic achievement taken for granted in urban high schools attended largely by blacks and hispanics" (p. 633).

In spite of such widespread perceptions, the reform movement that was signaled by the publication of *A Nation at Risk* (National Commission on Excellence in Education, 1983) and that continued through the mid-1980s was judged by some experts to be largely irrelevant to urban schools (Carnegie Foundation for the Advancement of Teaching, 1988) and lacking "the voice of urban America" (Council of the Great City Schools, 1987).

At the same time, the literature also paints a *positive* picture of urban schools. Edmonds (1979; 1982) emphasized that there are effective schools in urban areas and that these schools have identifiable characteristics. Urban schools have long been considered pioneers of educational reform and have implemented numerous models of successful programs (Council of the Great City Schools, 1987; 1988). Empirical studies indicate that urban school systems and individual schools can be successfully reformed provided certain factors are addressed (Brookover, Beady, Flood, Schweitzer& Wisenbaker, 1977; Clark, Lotto & McCarthy, 1980; Hill, Wise & Shapiro, 1989; Purkey & Smith, 1983; 1985). And city schools can draw on a multiplicity of resources in their urban environments (Hill, Wise & Shapiro, 1989).

Too often, in spite of the problems city schools have, critics neglect to notice the great achievements that our city schools have wrought. For example, Ravitch (1974) painted an impressive portrait of the New York City school system when she wrote:

> Critics of the public schools in each generation have emphasized failure and inefficiency. What is inevitably lost sight of is the monumental accomplishments of the public school system of New York City. It has provided free, unlimited educational opportunities for millions, regardless of language, race, class, or religion. It has pioneered in the creation of programs for children with special gifts or special handicaps. It has willingly accepted the responsibility for solving problems which were national in scope, the result of major demographic shifts. The descendants of the miserably poor European immigrants who overflowed the city schools in the nineteenth and early twentieth century are today the prosperous middle class of the city and its suburbs. Without the public schools, despite their obvious faults, this unprecedented social and economic mobility would be inconceivable. (p. 403)

Similarly, Chase (1978), who conducted a study of urban schools, summarized the positive approach to urban schools as follows:

> Urban education has an inner vitality which is generating innovative programs of great potential even in the midst of extremely adverse conditions. Despite well-documented testimony on the low achievement in urban schools and recent statistics purporting to show the schools as the most dangerous

place to be, we are discovering many administrators, teachers, and other staff members who are demonstrating ability to rouse zest for learning in students from diverse backgrounds, including those whose histories have been marked by failure, loss of hope, and/or antisocial behaviors. (pp. 35-36)

In short, the literature amply supports both the negative and the positive aspects of schools in the cities. In fact, the considerable literature on different aspects of urban education probably signals what Wacquant and Wilson (1989) called the ghetto's "stunning comeback into the collective consciousness of America" (p.9). In line with this awakening consciousness and in recognition that early reform did not adequately deal with the problems of education in the cities, a spate of national reports emerged in the late 1980s that addressed the unique problems of city schools along with a number of proposals for action. In 1990, Lytle provided a comprehensive review of these reports, along with a comment and analysis of their context. His overall conclusion, however, is that "the prospects for significant improvement seem bleak" (p. 219). He goes on to state that these reports "lack the sense of outrage that their student constituents deserve" (p. 219).

Against this backdrop of ambivalent views in the face of very real urban problems, the principal is called on to serve as the designated school leader. If the urban principal is to be effective, she or he needs to go beyond simplistic stereotypes of the city and to understand the various facets of urban life, of which the school is an integral part.

Salient Features of the Urban Context

Gordon (1982) correctly noted that many people have the mistaken notion that *urban* issues are nothing more than the problems associated with ethnic, racial, and low-socioeconomic minorities. Such a view has the connotation of placing the blame for urban problems on the shoulders of those who are modern society's greatest victims. This view also is simplistic, grossly overlooking the fundamental complexities that underlie the modern city.

According to Gordon (1982), urbanization involves a set of interactive characteristics. As he wrote:

> Urban areas are characterized by large numbers of people, by
> high densities, by great diversity and heterogeneity of charac-
> teristics and concerns of people; by high degrees of mobility, a
> relatively high incidence of anonymity; by conflicting lifestyles
> in close proximity; by cultural richness; by a concentration of
> material resources; by ease of communication and geographic
> mobility; and by the coexistence of fluidity and rigidity in
> institutional and personal behavior. (p. 1973)

At the core of these characteristics are size, density, diversity, and
technological development permitting mobility of transportation and
rapid communications. Because cities are big and densely populated,
a variety of interests are in constant contact and competition. Highly
bureaucratic institutions are necessary to maintain a certain level of
stability and control, yet those bureaucracies create a rigidity that
conflicts with the rich diversity inherent in cities. Simultaneously, cities
provide both a rich, stimulating environment and the potential for
"isolation, deprivation and overstimulation," what Gordon (1982) refers to as a "developmental paradox of contradiction" (p. 1974).

The urban context thus has a direct effect on the individuals who
are a large city's inhabitants. Fantini and Weinstein (1968) conceptualized the central features of cities in terms of three structural factors
interacting with three psychological variables. Since cities have large,
high-density populations, an individual necessarily forms many impersonal relationships. Ultimately, there is a tendency for vast size and
density to result in a loss of personal identity as each individual
becomes just another face in the crowd. At the same time, large cities
are very complex and require immense bureaucracies. Bureaucratic
complexity often causes an individual to feel a loss of control over his
or her own identity, resulting in a sense of individual powerlessness.
Also, diversity, which Fantini and Weinstein called "one of the most
unique aspects of an urban environment" (1968, p. 9), leads to an
individual's loss of affiliation with like-minded people and a sense of
disconnectedness from a homogeneous group. According to Fantini
and Weinstein, the essential characteristics of the city (namely, size/
density, bureaucratic complexity, and diversity) are "social realities
which persistently lay stress on the individual's concern for identity,
power, and connectedness" (p. 10). To the extent that these social
realities are extreme and dysfunctional, they force the individual to feel
worthless, powerless, and unconnected.

Fantini and Weinstein's discussion of social realities does not go far enough in depicting some other salient features of the urban environment. Moreover, the depiction above only emphasizes the negative corollaries of the characteristics of cities. There are also positive ones that an interactive principal needs to understand. Consequently, some additional variables that have significance for the urban school deserve attention.

For example, population size, density, and diversity also mean that there is a greater tolerance for atypical behavior, a greater richness of different cultures, and greater opportunity to build powerful coalitions of like-minded interests. Similarly, bureaucratization and specialization imply that rule-driven systems exist that, if one knows the appropriate codes, can be unlocked and accessed in predictable ways.

Political variables also merit scrutiny. Invariably, a city has many essential relations with other political jurisdictions. There is competition for power and resources between a city and its surrounding suburbs as well as attempts by a city to exercise autonomy vis-á-vis state control. Population density gives a city concentrations of votes in state and national elections as well as concentrations of legislators in state and national legislatures. These power blocs can further the aims of the city in other arenas. At the same time, city unity is splintered by a proliferation of interest groups, each with the power to veto but few with the power to enact and implement a proposal alone. Also, suburban and rural coalitions at the state level often form to produce an anti-urban sentiment in many states.

In addition, a city has socioeconomic systems that provide a broad economic base and a wide range of goods, services, resources, and opportunities. At the same time, loss of industry and jobs to competing suburbs and regions, loss of the middle class to suburbs, an older and eroding infrastructure, greater cost of services, concentration of an underclass, social/ethnic segregation, and a concentration of pathologies (drugs, crime, gangs) create a continuous need for intervention and social change.

The works of Gordon (1982) and Fantini and Weinstein (1968) as well as the listing of additional variables above identify very well the most significant *theoretical* features of the urban context of schools. Two other features of American cities derive from the *historical* development of urban areas: (1) a heavy concentration of minority populations, especially African Americans and Latinos, in our cities and (2) the extreme concentration of poverty in our inner cities. Each historical development greatly influences our urban schools.

One of the major migration patterns of 20th century America was the movement of many African Americans from the rural South into the cities (Lemann, 1986). In addition, more recently, Latinos have been migrating into urban areas in increasing numbers (Wilson, 1987). As a result, 40% of all African Americans in the United States are concentrated in 11 central cities, and 77% of all African Americans live in urban areas (Action Council on Minority Education, 1990). Similarly, Latino populations inhabit urban areas in large numbers. For example, more than 50% of all Mexican Americans live in the five largest metropolitan areas, thereby making them "more urbanized than any other major demographic group" (Hill, 1990, p. 399). Moreover, such concentrations could be expected to intensify. Fertility rates vary widely by populations subgroup. Hodgkinson (1988) reported:

> Generally, in order for a population to be stable, women must produce 2.1 children each, 2 to replace mom and dad and .1 to cover infant mortality. Currently, in the U.S., Mexican-Americans produce 2.9 children per female; blacks, 2.4; Puerto Ricans, 2.1; whites, 1.7; Cubans, 1.3. (p. 11)

The overall growth rate of Mexican Americans to the year 2000 is projected to be 46% and that of African Americans is projected to be 23%, in comparison with a 7% increase for white Americans (Hill, 1990).

This growing diversity is also evident in national immigration rates. Whereas the 1920s witnessed the immigration of about 14 million people almost exclusively from Europe, the 1980s had over 14 million immigrants with 80% of them originating in South America and Asia (Hodgkinson, 1988). Since cities are the major portals through which immigrants enter the United States, the implications of diverse cultures and languages and changing neighborhoods are enormous for schools.

One additional demographic factor is relevant: the age of our population. Overall, our population is rapidly aging. Hodgkinson (1988) reported:

> In 1983, we crossed a major watershed; we had, for the first time, more people over 65 than we had teenagers. This will be true as long as you live. The consequences for education will be momen-

tous. Dependent youth need expensive educational services; dependent elderly need expensive medical services. (p.12)

Since the average white American is about 24% older than the average African American and about 40% older than the average Latino American, the age distribution varies by population subgroup. An aging white population in need of medical support will compete for scarce dollars and political support with a younger minority population, much of it concentrated in the cities. Moreover, the city-based minority population is also heavily poor.

Over the past 30 years, American cities have experienced a growing concentration of poverty and an increasing isolation of central-city concentrations from the mainstream of society. The period from 1970 to 1980 especially witnessed a severe decline. For example, as Wilson (1987) demonstrated:

Although the total population in [the] five largest cities decreased by 9 percent between 1970 and 1980, the poverty population increased by 22 percent. . . . Furthermore, the population living in poverty areas grew by 40 percent overall, by 69 percent in high poverty areas and by a staggering 161 percent in extreme poverty areas. . . . (p. 46)

Also, urban minorities have been especially affected adversely by structural changes in the economy in the past two decades (Wilson, 1987). A study by Ricketts and Sawhill (1986) emphasized the economic plight of urban areas. They analyzed U.S. census tracts to determine which had large concentrations of dropouts, welfare recipients, female heads of households, unemployed males, and incomes below the poverty line. They identified 880 census tracts that simultaneously had high levels of the first four variables, 874 of which had average income levels below the established poverty line. Of the 880 tracts, which they termed "underclass" areas, 99% of them were located in urban areas. Within these census tracts, African Americans made up 58% of the population, white Americans 28%, and Latino Americans 11%. An alarming 36% of the population of these 880 tracts was made up of children (Schorr & Schorr, 1988).

This study by Ricketts and Sawhill exemplifies a critical feature of the inner city: the concentration of factors related to poverty, especially for some minorities. Wilson (1987) emphasized the importance of the concentration effects within our cities:

> If I had to use one term to capture the differences in the experiences of low-income families who live in inner-city areas from the experiences of those who live in other areas in the central city today, that term would be *concentration effects*. The social transformation of the inner city has resulted in a disproportionate concentration of the most disadvantaged segments of the urban black population creating a social milieu significantly different from the environment that existed in these communities several decades ago. (p. 58)

Economic decline has had its severest effects on African Americans, who are disproportionately represented among our innercity poor. More and more, poor African Americans are "becoming increasingly concentrated in dilapidated territorial enclaves that epitomize acute social and economic marginalization" (Wacquant & Wilson, 1989, p. 9). Intense concentration has led to another key feature of U.S. inner-city life: social isolation. Inner-city residents have become more and more isolated socially from the mainstream. In the context of high rates of joblessness and economic deterioration of the central cities, the result is a "hyperghettoization" in which concentrations of poverty and extreme social isolation emerge as stable working and middle classes (which would normally serve as buffers in the midst of economic downturns) have largely disappeared (Wacquant & Wilson, 1989). Without the buffers of the working and middle classes, the residents of extreme poverty areas have a lower volume of social capital available. Therefore, "today's ghetto residents face a closed opportunity structure" (Wacquant & Wilson, 1989, p. 10). Moreover, structural changes in the economy of the city lead to a reduction in the number of lower-skilled and blue-collar jobs, an exodus of white middle-class residents from the city, and a disappearance of the neighborhood business establishments serving those departing residents. Such factors lead in turn to a further weakening of the city economy and an exacerbation of the problems of those who are economically deprived in the city.

By way of summary, a number of salient features of the urban context have been highlighted in the literature. A principal who wishes to understand that context should start with a knowledge of these underlying features. This is only the beginning, however. A full understanding needs to extend into how these features and the entire context affect the mission and day-to-day workings of the school, including the effects on the students the schools serve.

Understanding the Context

Focus on Students

An understanding of the urban context is actually a subset of the entire knowledge base a school administrator needs to have in order to operate effectively and efficiently. Traditionally, school administrators are prepared in such areas as personnel administration, plant management, legal issues, supervision, and the like. What is often unclear, however, is how the traditional areas of expertise relate to the success of students in the school.

Silver (1983) called for the field of educational administration to refocus its attention from traditional areas to student outcomes. In doing so, she noted that other practical professions normally employ a knowledge base constructed on the kinds of problems faced by the clients served by the profession. Instead of being focused on the day-to-day discomforts encountered by the practicing professional, the professions properly direct their attention to solving problems in order to enhance client success. For the education professional, this entails knowing about

> how schools or organizations affect students' cognitive, affec-
> tive, and psychomotor learnings and, more to the point, how
> administrators can organize those learning environments to
> both maximize student learning in all those domains and
> minimize learning inequities in all those domains. (Silver,
> 1983, p. 12)

Such areas of concentration become for the school administrator the appropriate *problems of practice* of administration.

However, a school administrator always works within a wider context of variables, some of which are alterable by the administrator's action and others of which are entirely uncontrollable. Many aspects of the school environment establish basic *conditions* within which the principal practices. These conditions often have direct impact on the student's ability to succeed and the school's capacity for assisting in that success. The principal who understands those conditions will understand better how to mount interventions that will either change some negative aspects of the environment or serve as a buffer to offset those negative forces that cannot be directly changed. Consequently, for any principal who wishes to enhance student outcomes, a basic problem of practice is to be able to identify and understand the conditions within which that practice occurs. These conditions of practice are intertwined with the salient features of the urban context addressed above. For the principal, the basic question becomes: How do the various elements of the urban context affect the major components that combine to influence student learning?

Urban Influence on Student Learning: A Framework

Using the work of Silver (1983) as a starting point, a framework can be constructed to organize the main factors of the urban context that are related to student learning in schools and that need to be understood by the school principal (see Fig. 1.1). As Silver suggested, the student is the centerpiece of the framework because the student is the chief client served by the education profession. A student's behavior is strongly influenced by her or his own capabilities and achievements, as well as by three general categories of factors: the home and family, the community, and the school. These three categories are in turn influenced by state and school district factors as well as by the condition of the overall society (for example, the current status of the economy). These categories form the major elements of the organizing framework of this chapter.

This framework is a modification of a model developed by the Temple University Center for Research in Human Development and Education (1990), which serves as the basis for the work of the Center for Education in the Inner Cities, one of the national research centers established by the U.S. Department of Education. This chapter's framework also adopted elements from Wang, Haertel, and Walberg's (1990) conceptional framework, which was based on a synthesis of 179 scholarly works (also cf. Wang & Peverly, 1986).

A few brief comments are in order regarding this framework. Student behavior (in terms of learning outcomes) is the ultimate focus.

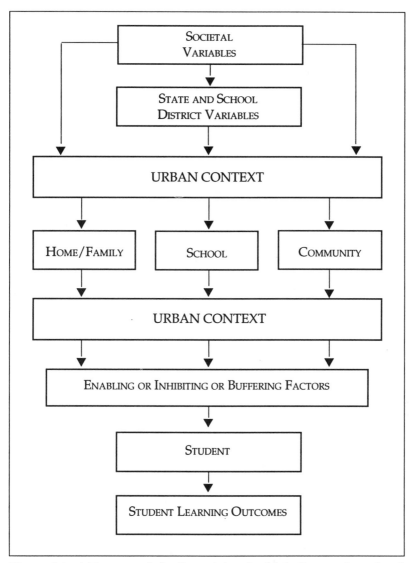

Figure 1.1. A Framework for Organizing the Main Factors Associated With the Urban Context and Influencing Student Learning.

This behavior is the result of a number of very important interactions that occur among the student, the home, the school, and the community. These interactions are mediated by the urban context, insofar as various aspects of that context affect each of the major categories of variables. In addition, the home, the school, and the community are affected by the state, the school district, and the wider society, and these interactions are also mediated by the urban context. The many interactions affecting the student are generally of three types: those that enable the student to learn (for example, family encouragement to read), those that inhibit a student from learning (for example, peer pressures to take drugs), and those that buffer or block the inhibiting pressures (for example, a neighborhood recreation program to combat drug use).

In this regard, Schorr and Schorr's (1988) conception of the exponential effects of risk factors is especially relevant. Building on the work of Escalona (1982), Rutter (1980), and others, the Schorrs described graphically how the addition of factors that tend to place a child at risk of failure in life actually has an exponential effect on that child's life. This is because the individual risk factors interact with each other to create an effect larger than their additive sum. The Schorrs' illustration depicts how such interactions occur:

> The child in a poor family who is malnourished and living in an unheated apartment is more susceptible to ear infection; once the ear infection takes hold, inaccessible or inattentive health care may mean it will not be properly treated; hearing loss in the midst of economic stress may go undetected at home, in day care and by the health system; undetected hearing loss will do long-term damage to a child who needs all the help he can get to cope with a world more complicated than the world of most middle-class children. When this child enters school, his chances of being in an overcrowded classroom with an overwhelmed teacher further compromises his chances of successful learning. Thus risk factors join to shorten the odds of favorable long-term outcomes. (p. 30)

At the same time, as Schorr and Schorr (1988) pointed out, each risk factor that is buffered or removed has an exponential effect in the positive direction. As they documented:

No one circumstance, no single event, is the cause of a rotten outcome. School failure, delinquency, teenage pregnancy-none is dependent on a single devastating risk factor. But each risk factor vanquished does enhance the odds of averting later serious damage. A healthy birth, a family helped to function even though one parent is depressed and the other seldom there, effective preparation for school entry-all powerfully tip the scales toward favorable outcomes. (p. 32)

Consequently, the model used in this chapter emphasizes the positive (enabling and buffering) and negative (inhibiting) effects of various factors in the urban context, as expressed through the family, school, and community.

In this model, the home and family category includes a number of variables, especially as related to the school. As Ogbu (1981) has indicated, each family needs to be understood in terms of its cultural ecology. In this chapter, attention is drawn to the educative functions of the home and ways in which various structural and dynamic elements of the family serve to create an atmosphere conducive to learning, to mediate learning, and to serve as a buffer for various factors that tend to place the student at risk of failure in school.

The school category includes a number of key elements associated with student learning, from the viewpoint of the school principal. These elements include the makeup of the student body, the faculty, the curriculum and instruction of the school, the overall school climate and culture, the adequacy of financial resources and physical facilities, and the overall school leadership, organization, and governance structures. The emphasis in this chapter is on how these elements are influenced by the urban context.

The community category includes a number of variables both of the immediate neighborhood and of the broader urban community. Of special concern here are the social-political-economic systems of the city, the socioeconomic status of the neighborhood, the social services available for the student, the nonschool education systems (library, mass media, museums), and the peer group. Since the perspective of this chapter is almost entirely from the viewpoint of the public school principal, the availability of private and parochial schools is also an ingredient in this category.

The state and district variables include a number of factors affecting student learning, including school district governance and organizational structures as well as general policies and laws that regulate the practices of the school. Similarly, the category of societal variables includes a number of possible influences. The state of the general economy is an example. This chapter is concerned specifically with those factors at the societal, state, or district levels that differentially affect urban contexts and consequently urban schools.

Finally, a few caveats must be raised about this framework. First, the factors or variables are meant to be suggestive rather than exhaustive. The aim of this chapter is to sensitize the principal to the variety of ways in which the urban context might affect learning. The mention of some factors is intended to empower the principal to extend the analysis to additional factors, especially ones in her or his own idiosyncratic situation. In addition, the categories in the framework are not hard-and-fast ones. For example, the community variable involves a number of elements, both citywide as well as local neighborhood. Furthermore, one could argue that the school district is really a part of the wider community (or city). Nonetheless, *from the principal's viewpoint*, it does make some degree of sense to differentiate the two. Also, it needs to be stressed that this framework is not intended to be anything more than a convenient and shorthand way to organize the complex interactions that occur in the real world. This is not intended to be an explanatory model or a predictive theory about the cause-and-effect relationships that actually occur. The most important criterion for this framework to meet is one of utility: Does it help organize this chapter and does it help the principal create her or his own structure to understand better the complex set of relationships in the urban school? Does it facilitate understanding of the ways in which the urban context generates conditions of practice that the principal needs to address in order to enhance student learning in the school?

Conditions of Practice

As a result of the salient features of the urban context mentioned earlier in this chapter, the urban principal must encounter a number of conditions of practice. Although causal relationships are not entirely clear, certain conditions tend to emerge in urban areas, especially in large cities. These conditions are organized here according to the framework outlined above.

Students

Urban school systems have greater variability within their student populations than do nonurban systems. For example, there are a larger concentration of disadvantaged individuals (Hill, Wise & Shapiro, 1989) and a greater number of special-needs students in urban schools than in nonurban schools. An urban student is twice as likely to be achieving at a low level than is that student's nonurban peer (Wolf, 1978). The urban student is also twice as likely to drop out of school or be charged with a crime (Hill, Wise & Shapiro, 1989).

Urban schools have a high concentration of "at-risk students." As Kagan (1990) pointed out, at-risk students often are described according to a general profile, which she depicted as follows:

At-risk students have low educational aspirations, low self-esteem, an external locus of control, and negative attitudes toward school along with a history of academic failure, truancy, and misconduct, with no indication that they lack requisite aptitudes. (pp. 105-106)

As Kagan further notes, this profile is consistent "over several decades and across varied urban sites" (p. 106). Levin (1989) reported that such at-risk students "are concentrated among minority groups, immigrants, non-English speaking families, families headed by single mothers and economically disadvantaged groups" (p. 47), that is, precisely the groups that disproportionately inhabit our inner cities (Council of the Great City Schools, 1987; 1988).

Numerous data indicate a crisis in urban schools, as reflected in the low achievement of many urban students. The Carnegie Foundation for the Advancement of Teaching in its special 1988 report entitled *An Imperiled Generation: Saving Urban Schools* cited a number of instances of low achievement, including the following:

At a Chicago high school, only 10 percent of the entering tenth graders were able to read effectively. In New Orleans, the average high school senior was reading at a level exceeded by 80 percent of the students in the country. In a Houston elementary school, half the students had to repeat a grade because of unsatisfactory academic progress.

During school visits, we found that 75 percent of the high school freshmen in Chicago had reading test scores below the national average, and only five of that city's sixty-four public high schools had averages approaching national reading norms. Only 229 of the 1,918 students at one Los Angeles high school scored at grade level in reading.

A particularly sobering appraisal was offered by the City-wide Educational Coalition in Boston, which concluded: "Not only do 44 percent of [Boston's] high school students drop out before they reach 12th grade, but over 40 percent of those who do reach 12th grade score below the 30th percentile on a standardized reading test. They may graduate, but they are functionally illiterate." (p. xiii)

The reality behind these statistics and reports reflects the depth of the problem. Watson (1987) wrote:

The problems seem so complex, the statistics so overwhelming, the magnitude of the proposed remedies so costly, that too many Americans have become paralyzed. The whole scene immobilizes us. But behind those statistics are real people. Each one of the dropouts is an individual, so is each graduate. Each young black man who is killed is somebody's son, just as the person who did the killing is someone's son or daughter. Each of those young people who fails to learn to read or write, to acquire skills, or a diploma, is a person, a person who at some time probably aspired and dreamed of a better life, of participation in the American Dream. They are real flesh and blood; vulnerable, feeling human beings who cannot and should not be dismissed or buried as part of some statistical subset. (p. x)

In the face of such a depressing picture, the principal of an urban school might be tempted to develop a stereotype of the urban student. With so many at-risk children entering school, how can success be anything but limited for the urban school?

Yet, it is precisely this notion of at-risk student that some educators reject. Cuban (1989a) criticized the at-risk concept because in his view it places the blame for failure on the student (or the family or culture of the student). Clayton (1989) similarly attacked the "at-risk rhetoric" as a misnomer because it connotes that a problem resides in the student or the family. Rather, Clayton proposed, the formulation should be in terms of children of value, "affirming the worth and dignity of the children" (p. 135). She espoused an aggressive advocacy on behalf of children, and based her view on the work of Edmonds, especially his statement that "[w]e can, whenever and wherever we choose, successfully teach all children whose schooling is of interest to us" (p. 135).

Both Cuban and Clayton argue a position that has been emerging among some of the top educators addressing urban education: Make the student the focus of our activities in schools and other social services and do not assume that the problem lies with the student. This posture is echoed by Hodgkinson (1989) who described the necessity for us to view the educational system and other social services from the vantage point of the student/client who moves through them. Similarly, Kirst, McLaughlin, and Massell (1990) argued that school administrators "need a better grasp of the educational implications of the everyday lives of children" (p. 69).

Successful principals carry high expectations for their students, even when those students sometimes face seemingly insurmountable odds. They recognize that different students learn in many different ways and at different rates. Indeed, there is an emerging emphasis on the resilience of students who have been able to succeed in life in spite of multiple factors placing them at risk of failure (Temple University Center for Research in Human Development and Education, 1990). There is a need to place the student at center stage, understand his or her unique patterns of behavior and the context in which they emerged, advocate aggressively on the student's behalf, and hold out models of achievement of other students who have been able to succeed.

The Urban Community

When school people talk about the "community," they generally include virtually the entire local environment outside of the family, the school, and the school district. For the purposes of this chapter, the same general meaning is retained. Thus, community includes both citywide systems and services as well as the neighborhood and immediate environs of the local school site. Earlier, under the section entitled Urban Context, I discussed the major system features of cities, including concentrations of poverty, minority populations, and social isolation. The following section focuses on the more immediate community constituting the school's neighborhood and the delivery of city services with special emphasis on how school and students are affected by the urban context.

The urban community, especially in the large cities, involves a complex set of interactions, institutions, and actors. In the 1990s, several characteristics are especially noteworthy of the community. Deteriorating economic conditions and long-time migration patterns in most cities have been such that poverty and joblessness are concentrated in certain pockets, thereby isolating large groups from the mainstream of American life. Combined with the historical segregation of some racial/ethnic and language minorities, this isolation creates difficult conditions within which our schools must work and has an especially adverse impact on our children. An erosion of the sense of community, services and systems that are fragmented and ineffective, and severe safety health, housing, transportation, and early education problems—all interact to place enormous stress on the city's residents, especially its young.

At the same time, urban communities have major resources, including financial, economic, cultural, religious, and nonschool educative institutions. As Hill, Wise, and Shapiro (1989) pointed out, these urban resources are considerable:

> Every city possesses such major assets as an educated middle class, black and white; large, well-managed businesses; important financial institutions; powerful research universities; and potentially generous local foundations. All have sophisticated political, religious and social leaders capable of uniting to solve a problem if they consider it significant. (p. 4)

These resources can be tapped to help offset and buffer the dysfunctional elements and pathologies that exist in certain areas of the large cities. For the sake of brevity, the following will highlight the pathologies in the areas of neighborhood social capital, transportation, housing, health inadequacies, and crime. These exemplify the kinds of community forces that can affect the education of our young and over which our schools have relatively low levels of influence.

As explained earlier, *severe concentration of poverty and social isolation* of the inner-city from the mainstream of American life have created a hypersegregation of deprived populations. One particularly poignant manifestation of the impact of these forces on a local neighborhood is the diminished social capital available after working-class and middle-class families depart from the neighborhood. Schorr and Schorr (1988) quoted one neighborhood leader in the Harlem section of New York City, who said that of 454 families in a particular block, there were 600 children and no more than 10 to 15 men. The Schorrs observed:

> A boy being brought up by a mother alone, even a poor mother alone, need not necessarily suffer damaging effects. . . . But when single parenting is not only a family fact but a community fact, the effect-especially on boys-can be highly disruptive of normal development. When the whole neighborhood is made up of families without fathers or a consistent male presence, not only the income but also the discipline and role models that fathers traditionally have provided are missing. Boys are left to learn about manhood on the streets, where the temptation is strong to demonstrate powers through lawbreaking, violence, and fathering a child. (p. 20)

What is true for the need of male models is likely true also for the need for models of working and middle class adults able to demonstrate regular employment and entrepreneurship and the behavior patterns associated with them. Especially needed are models who are able to show a connection between educational achievement in school and success in later life.

Transportation also has implications for city students. Hodgkinson (1989) wrote:

> Our school bus fleet is mainly suburban, leaving students in inner-city schools with more walking to subway or commercial bus routes, more travel through dangerous streets. Even with reduced or free fares, the danger level is still considerably higher for city schools. On the other hand, increased population density in many cities means a short walk or ride to school, even though the short trip may be risky. (p. 11)

Moreover, unlike suburban bus transportation, the dependence of inner-city youth on pubic transportation often means that they are in transit without adult supervision. Not only does this contribute to safety problems, it also likely has a role in tardiness and school truancy. At the same time, transportation poses a special problem for those in the lowest income levels, often without a reliable car. The family headed by a single mother is especially affected:

> The educationally related transport problem most in need of repair is that of low income families with children, in which the mother must get the kids to day care and herself to work. Without a car, these trips can be a most excruciating combination of buses and subways, held together by a fragile thread. If the ride consists of four buses in sequence, one miss can mean a major delay, and that's just to get the kids to day care. Then another complicated sequence to get yourself to work, followed by the reverse at the end of day. If a child is sick, you add to that recipe the problem of getting to medical services by public transportation *before* you get yourself to work. (Hodgkinson, 1989, p. 10)

Similarly, the mother in this situation will find it extremely difficult to get to school during the workweek for conferences, school meetings, and the like. This places serious constraints on the single parent's ability to participate in the school and to stay informed about her child's progress as a student.

The education of urban students is also seriously affected by the availability and quality of *housing*. Hodgkinson (1989) provided data on the problems of housing for the poor:

- The costs of housing have increased three times more rapidly than income over the past 15 years thereby putting home ownership even more out of the reach of low income families.

- From 1984 through 1986, the availability of low-income housing decreased by over one million units nationally. During the same period, the number of households with an income below $5,000 annually actually increased by 55%.

- The costs of rent equal 81% of the income of young single parents with children in 1988.

- Over 50% of the homeless in cities are made up of families.

- About 43% of homeless children have developmental problems.
  (pp. 6-7)

Also, housing inadequacy is more prevalent among African American children (Council of the Great City Schools, 1987). The problems of housing inadequacy are captured in Hodgkinson's (1989) portrait of a low-income family with limited room:

> In a one-bedroom apartment, the child's "room" is likely to be a convertible sofa in the living room, including the television, the phone and other distractions, right next to a busy, noisy kitchen.... In addition, rents are such a high percentage of this family's income that *any* crisis-repairs on the car, for example— can tip the family into the street as additional homeless. (p. 8)

Hodgkinson concluded that housing is a major factor affecting failure in school.

The problems of housing in poverty-stricken, inner-city neighborhoods are certainly exacerbated and probably caused to some extent by unfair home mortgage lending practices. In 1988, a Pulitzer Prize-winning investigative series in *The Atlanta Journal/The Atlanta Constitution* described in detail how such practices discriminated against African Americans in the city. Analysis of the neighborhoods in which most African Americans lived and the ones in which home loans were made by Atlanta's banks and savings and loans institutions indicated "race-not home value or household income-consistently determines the lending patterns of metro Atlanta's largest financial institutions" (Dedman, 1988a, p. 1). These investigative articles went on to demonstrate how such lending practices fit into the history of racial discrimination in the patterns of lending in the United States. For example, Homer Hoyt who was "hired by the federal government to develop the first underwriting criteria-who is a good credit risk and who is not-for the new Federal Housing Administration (FHA)" (Dedman, 1988b, p. 12), had the following history:

> In 1933, a respected economist at the University of Chicago, Homer Hoyt, published a list of racial groups, ranking them from positive to negative influence on property values:

1. English, Scotch, Irish, Scandinavians

2. North Italians

3. Bohemians or Czechs

4. Poles

5. Lithuanians

6. Greeks

7. Russians, Jews (lower class)

8. South Italians

9. Negroes

10. Mexicans (Dedman, 1988b, p. 12)

Dedman went on to show how such stereotypes became embodied in lending practices. It is no coincidence then that the Federal Housing Authority in 1939 took the position that "[i]f a neighborhood is to retain stability, it is necessary that properties shall continue to be occupied by the same social and racial classes" (Jackson, 1985, p. 208). Such an attitude continues to be prevalent among some real estate brokers and lending institutions and contributes to the isolation of many of our urban neighborhoods.

Dedman (1988b) also demonstrated how the concentration of loans guaranteed by the federal government (the Federal Housing Authority and the Veterans Administration) and the lack of conventional loans are associated with the decline of a neighborhood. He wrote:

> However, FHA and VA loans can have disadvantages for the neighborhood. If an area has many FHA and VA loans, bank and savings and loans may not make conventional loans there. . . . Whatever the cause and effect home buyers and homeowners in black neighborhoods can be trapped in an endless Catch-22.
>
> • Bank loan officers have become conditioned to steer clear of neighborhoods with a preponderance of FHA and VA loans.
>
> • Without a good mix of credit to fuel it, including conventional lenders, the housing market in the neighborhood sputters and property values stall.

• Stagnant property values discourage investment and reinforce bank skepticism about the neighborhood, and the cycle begins again. (Dedman, 1988b, p. 16)

Such a downward spiral works against the urban neighborhoods and reinforces racial stereotyping and isolation.

Poverty is clearly related to higher rates of *health problems* (Kirst, McLaughlin & Massell, 1990). The crisis in the quality of health in the inner city is shockingly evident in the 1990 study of mortality in Harlem reported in the *New England Journal of Medicine*. Stating that the "pattern of medical care in Harlem is similar to that reported for the other poor and black communities" (p. 173), McCord and Freeman (1990) analyzed death rates for the population between the ages of 5 and 65. They found that for 19 out of 20 categories of cause of death, the death rates were higher than for the white population as a whole. (The only exception being the category of suicide). They concluded that "a male born in Harlem has only a 40 percent chance of living to age 65" and that this probability is worse than for a resident of Bangladesh (Maykuth, 1990, p. 3-A). Other statistics are similarly alarming for urban populations. Infant deaths in the United States are higher in the central cities (Council of the Great City Schools, 1987). The rates of infant mortality among African Americans are two times higher than those of white Americans (Hodgkinson, 1989). Lead poisoning is a particular scourge of the inner-city poor. One researcher estimated that "55 percent of poor, black urban children under the age of 6 have elevated levels of lead in the blood" (Schmidt, 1990, p. 32). He also concluded, on the basis of a long-term study, that teenage students who had been exposed to lead early in their lives were much more likely to have reading disabilities and drop out of school. The problem stems from the widespread presence of lead paint on older, inner-city houses. The paint crumbles and oxidizes and becomes airborne. Even the soil of some portions of a city are contaminated. It is estimated that, for children aged six months through five years old, 62% in Philadelphia, 74% in New York City, and 69% in Boston have blood levels of lead above the point at which researchers have established that learning and central nervous system dysfunctions occur (Jaffe, 1990a; 1990b).

Especially frustrating is the fact that many of the health problems afflicting urban youth are preventable. Schorr and Schorr (1988) told the story of youngsters whose undiagnosed medical problems led to serious conditions resulting in significant behavioral dysfunctioning. These cases occurred because of a series of factors related to poverty. The case of a child named Gail

> illustrates the fact that most health care works best for families with the means and knowledge to monitor their own care, identify their needs, and see to it that they are met. Gail's family had little education, was overwhelmed by other problems, and had no idea what Gail's examination had shown or that follow-up neurological tests had been recommended. . . . [N]o single professional had a continuing responsibility for making sense of the many complicated factors in Gail's background. . . .
>
> But Gail's family was dependent on episodic care in a local hospital clinic, where patients typically see physicians they have never seen before and do not expect to see again. In such circumstances accurate diagnosis is difficult, and the prospects for proper treatment and management of complex conditions are low (pp. 90-91).

Another of the most serious problems for students in inner-cities is the concern for *safety*. During the decade of 1977 through 1987, violent crimes rose by 43% in the 59 largest U.S. cities (Irwin, 1989, p. 9-A). The neighborhoods surrounding some inner-city schools create a dangerous environment for our youth. For example, Menacker, Weldon, and Hurwitz (1989) studied four inner-city elementary schools in Chicago. They reviewed the files of the city police over a two-year period and discovered the following:

> Police records showed that the area surrounding two of those schools had been the scene of five murders, one manslaughter, 17 aggravated assaults, five criminal assaults, 48 simple assaults, 116 armed robberies, 108 strong-arm robberies, 103 batteries with a weapon, 115 batteries with no weapon, 121 burglaries, 58 thefts of more than $300, 193 thefts of less than $300, 11 cases of arson, 67 cases of property damage, and 23 cases of unlawful possession of a handgun. (p. 40)

During the year 1990, reports of killings of young children appeared in our newspapers as drug-related violence in cities claimed innocent victims caught by stray bullets (Terry, 1990). Not surprisingly, some of these problems spill over into the schools. The *Safe Schools-Violent Schools* study found that 40% of the robberies and 36% of the assaults on urban youth occurred in the schools (U.S. Department of Health, Education, and Welfare and National Institute of Education, 1978). The Menacker, Weldon, and Hurwitz (1989) study found that more than 50% of students had at least one theft occur during a year, 32% carried a weapon to school, and 15% reported hitting a teacher. Zinsmeister (1990) estimated that, nationally, there are about 3 million incidents of street crime (assault, rape, robbery, or theft) on school property annually and that about 338,000 students had carried a hand-gun to school at least once in 1987, with an alarming number (about 100,000) carrying a gun *daily!*

These problems are accompanied by a proliferation of gang violence in some urban areas (Garrison, 1989). Moreover, the presence of illegal drugs in our cities not only spawns violence but also forces our schools to deal with children who have been exposed to drugs, many prenatally, and who thus come to school at serious risk of failure (Viadero, 1989). Wilson (1987) hypothesized that some of the high rates of crime and gang activity might be explainable by the dense concentrations of large numbers of urban youth. He wrote that

> there may be a "critical mass" of young persons in a given community such that when that mass is reached or is increased suddenly and substantially, "a self-sustaining chain reaction is set off that creates an explosive increase in the amount of crime, addiction, and welfare dependency." (p. 38; also, Wilson, 1975, pp. 17-18)

Even in the face of such statistics, Menacker, Weldon, and Hurwitz (1989) found that the public school is an "island of relative safety in an ocean of danger that surrounds the school" (p. 39). They argued that only a comprehensive, coordinated safety approach in which the school is one element in a total community effort can be successful in combating crime and violence. An effective disciplinary code could be developed, they found, along with a community involvement whereby community members developed a psychological ownership over security matters.

Over and above the pathologies associated with transportation, housing, health inadequacies, and crime in urban neighborhoods, there are also problems with the *delivery of the city services* that are supposed to address these pathologies. Kirst, McLaughlin, and Massell (1990) identified two sets of problems of services for children, especially those children who have multiple special needs. First are problems of underservice. Substantial numbers of needy children do not receive sufficient support. For example, funding for such programs as Aid to Families with Dependent Children (AFDC), an important source of minimal support for the very needy, has been diminishing over the years. As Kirst, McLaughlin, and Massell (1990) reported for 1985-1986, the parents of only one-half of all children defined as poor received AFDC income; 39% of those children who met the eligibility requirements of the free or reduced-price lunch programs actually received such lunches; and only 38% of eligible poor families actually received food stamps (p. 74). Such considerable underservice denies the minimal levels of services that poor families, heavily concentrated in urban areas, need.

Yet, a second problem of social service delivery is its severe fragmentation. For example, "in California, over 160 programs located in thirty-five agencies and seven departments exist to serve children and youth, an array which is certainly not unique to that state" (Kirst, McLaughlin & Massell, 1990, p. 75). Such fragmentation, however well intentioned each program might be in its own right, can be dysfunctional when viewed from the vantage point of the individual student receiving the service. Comer (1988) told of the following case in a school in New Haven, Connecticut "we ran into a situation where one child at one of the schools we were in was being seen by seven different people, and taken in and out of the classroom for help, and they did not talk to each other" (p. 55).

What kind of effects would such a situation have on a student? Which professional would bring some sense of continuity and unity of service for the student? As Kirst, McLaughlin, and Massell (1990) wrote, the substantial fragmentation of services to students have at least five negative consequences. Individual problems are viewed in their isolation and the student is labeled according to the problem. There is a discontinuity of care as a student moves from one jurisdiction to another. Different service agencies have different goals, and those goals can be conflicting; for example, one agency's approach to child care might be custodial while another's is developmental in nature. A lack of communication among service providers can mean an inability to bring available resources to bear on a student's problems. And fragmentation leads ultimately to a disempowered youth, since no one takes the overall view of the student and since the student perceives herself or himself to be a pawn of the many systems providing unconnected services. Kirst, McLaughlin, and Massell (1990) also noted that schools, which over the years have deliberately developed structures and practices separate from county and city governments, are a key element in this overall problem of service fragmentation. They suggested that we need to rethink our service delivery systems from the viewpoint of our children and that educators, especially administrators, need to be more attentive to the everyday lives of youth. Similarly, Hodgkinson (1989) argued that the student/client must be viewed as the centerpiece and most important element of our service organizations. He quoted from the 1930 report of the White House Conference on Children and Youth, and the words are still relevant 60 years later:

> To the doctor, the child is a typhoid patient; to the playground supervisor, a first baseman; to the teacher, a learner of arithmetic. At times, he may be different things to each of these specialists, but rarely is he a whole child to any of them. (opposite p. 1)

Over and above the problems and pathologies already discussed, other problems exist that have relevance to the school. The urban principal needs to use the problems presented above as suggestive of the kinds of ways in which the neighborhood is affected by the urban context and how the school can be influenced. What is clear is that such problems derive from fundamental factors at work in society as a whole. The effect is that the neighborhood is buffeted as much as, or even more than, the school.

At the same time, the city is a source of numerous *resources and services*, even if they are highly fragmented. There are businesses and corporations that have the ability to support a local school and that themselves provide education to employees. There are numerous examples of business-school partnerships that increase the school's capacity to provide a quality education (Justiz & Kameen, 1987). Cities have an extensive range of health-care facilities, mental health clinics, homeless shelters, social service agencies and other care-giving facilities. Research universities provide direct assistance for schools. Foundations have the potential to provide considerable funding for special projects and initiatives. Cities have extensive youth service agencies, libraries, museums, and media.

Levine and Havighurst (1968) described the extent of an urban area's institutions and services in terms of fourteen social systems: local government, public services (e.g., police), cultural institutions (e.g., museums), recreational systems, social welfare, religious organizations and congregations, economic systems, civic spirit and social betterment associations, political systems, social leisure clubs and groups, health maintenance systems, transportation system, communications, and educational systems. Since another chapter in this book is devoted to the topic of urban resources, this chapter will not address these subsystems. What is important for the urban principal is that each of the subsystems mentioned above is made up of a set of actors, institutions and services that can be of assistance to the school in pursuing its mission. The inter-activist principal is able to analyze the opportunities and identify the ways in which functional linkages can be constructed. The school is one element in an interactive network of problems and opportunities.

One context in which to view the abundant resources of the city is to explore ways in which education occurs and might occur in nonschool settings within the city. Goodlad (1984) asked whether schools are trying to do too much and called for them to refocus their energies on better defined goals. Similarly, Fantini and Sinclair (1985) argued that society has expected that public schools attempt to accomplish too much. They called (1) for other institutions within society to assume greater responsibility for education and (2) for the school to reexamine its mission and to build partnerships with other educative, nonschool institutions. Fantini (1985) believed that in order to prepare adequately for the Information Age, society needs to move away from a school-based system of education, in which the school is responsible for delivering nearly all educational services. Instead, what is needed, according to Fantini, is a community-based, lifelong learning system in which the school orchestrates and coordinates a whole range of educative activities, some of which are delivered directly by the school and others of which come through other educative institutions. This means that current *school reform* efforts are not enough; *education reform* is necessary to reorder priorities and reconstruct relationships within the entire community. Fantini (1986) further called for an urban strategy of reform that includes citywide partnerships, the use of magnet schools, a mobilization of community resources, better use of computers and telecommunications, school-based management structures, and better links between schools and community (including parent) advisory councils. Fantini also stated that such reform needs to embody the following basic principles that have emerged from research and experience and that represent the state of our knowledge about educational excellence:

- All people can learn; there are not learner failures, only program failures.
- Learners should be able to choose among a range of legitimate learning environments.
- There are multiple intelligences and talents among people and they are expressed in different ways.
- A learner should have control over his or her own fate.
- There is a broad range of individual differences.
- Every person has the right to a complete, quality education.
- There is great potential for teaching and learning through telecommunications and new technologies.
- There needs to be a close linkage between school and nonschool learning.
- Testing and evaluation need to become more focused upon diagnosis and assistance to learners and teachers.
- We need to draw upon the best research and development in education.
- The goal is lifelong learning in the educative community, tying together many learning environments, actors and institutions.

Based upon these principles, the school can more effectively relate to the many resources of the city and reconceptualize its role within a broad educative community.

Home and Family

As the primary influence on the life of the child, the family should be the basic institution upon which other socializing institutions within society build. It is amazing, therefore, that the traditional nuclear family, based upon the image of the self-sufficient farm family, continues to be the standard model for Americans (Wagstaff & Gallagher, 1990). The societal institutions that serve young people, including the school, are structured on this model, even though this traditional stereotype actually fits fewer than one-third of all U.S. families (Kirst, McLaughlin & Massell, 1990). In fact, it is estimated that over one-half of all young people will live in a single-parent home at some time (Kirst, McLaughlin & Massell, 1990). Given the nontraditional nature of the vast majority of families, therefore, it makes sense that any given family is best understood within its own context, what Ogbu (1981) termed a "cultural-ecological perspective," rather than by comparison with other groups (Wagstaff & Gallagher, 1990).

Trends in key indicators about the family suggest that many families, especially those in urban areas, are troubled. Female-headed families, many of whom are heavily concentrated in the inner cities, are disproportionately poor. Moreover, single-parent families also vary considerably by race. Of all children in such families, 10% are Asian Americans, 12% white Americans, 24% Hispanic Americans, and 52% African Americans (Kirst & McLaughlin, 1990). In 1985, "20 percent of all children, 54 percent of children in female-headed families and 78 percent of black children in female-headed families lived in poverty" (Wagstaff & Gallagher, 1990, p. 103). Families with two parents and no children and families with single-parent females who have children in need of welfare support are the two fastest-growing family structures (Coleman, 1987; Mitchell, 1990). As Hoffer and Coleman (1990) noted, there is a "pattern of growing inequality of family background which one would expect to find reflected in measures of educational outcomes" (p. 123). If this hypothesis is correct, then school achievement is likely to be adversely affected, as family structures continue to change for urban populations.

Schorr and Schorr (1988) explained how all families need some support, whether formal or informal, at some time to help them raise children. The essential need of a child for "coherence, structure, and predictability" (p. 151) is fundamentally grounded in the early child-rearing practices of the family. But various stresses on the family can place the child at risk if there are not forces to buffer these stresses. As Schorr and Schorr (1988) described:

> Both common sense and research tell us that as family stress, *regardless of its source,* increases, the capacity for nurturing decreases, and the likelihood of abuse and neglect increases. Whether the stress stems from insufficient income, a difficult child, an impaired adult, family violence and discord, inadequate housing, chronic hunger and poor health, or surroundings of brutality, hopelessness, and despair - these are circumstances in which affection withers into hostility, discipline turns into abuse, stability dissolves into chaos, and love becomes neglect. (p. 151)

Such stress on the family can become most dysfunctional in those neighborhoods that have the lowest levels of supportive mechanisms, namely, the poorest of the inner-city neighborhoods. Once again, Schorr and Schorr (1988) noted:

> Social isolation cuts across class lines but is worst in poor neighborhoods, where everyone is stressed and few have energy to spare. James Garbarino and D. Sherman, experts in the social content of child abuse, believe that the increasing incidence of child abuse is directly related to the spread of "socially impoverished environments, denuded of enduring supportive relationships" and the scarcity of people "free from drain" who can afford to be supportive to neighbors because their own needs do not exceed their resources. (p. 154)

Thus, the total social capital available within the neighborhood in which poverty is extreme and concentrated and social isolation is characteristic is not sufficient to support families in need. Other neighborhoods with a greater reservoir of social capital might be able to bolster a family in stress. But inner-city neighborhoods in extreme poverty can not, so child rearing under stress is much more difficult. Where informal supports are not forthcoming, there is a greater dependence on formal supports of social service institutions. When those formal supports are not present or are insufficient in quality or scope, the family under stress is forced to depend on its own resources, which often are simply not enough to insure adequate child rearing.

One stress that inner-city families must face is the absence of fathers and the high incidence of unmarried mothers. Wilson (1989) argued that such an occurrence was based on the effects of joblessness and economic exclusion for inner-city residents. Citing the work of Testa, Astone, Krogh, and Neckerman (1989), Wilson noted that employed fathers are 2 1/2 times more likely to marry the mother of their firstborn child than are unemployed fathers. Therefore, joblessness is central to the fact that many children in the ghetto do not have married parents. This effect of joblessness pertains not only for African Americans but also for Puerto Ricans, Mexican Americans, and white Americans. This is but another indication that dysfunctional elements in the inner city have a systemic basis related to broader forces of the economy and the urban context.

The problems of inner-city families are intensified when there is discontinuity between school and home. According to cultural discontinuity theory, "low-income disadvantaged children arrive at school with a different background in linguistic, cognitive, motivational, and social development than that of middle-class children" (Boyd, 1990, p. 26). Since lower-class students have more restricted language patterns and middle-class students more elaborate ones (Bernstein, 1973; Boyd, 1990), the school, which is based on middle-class patterns, is discontinuous with the family and communities of lower-class students. In the face of such cultural discontinuity, Cazden and Mehan (1989) argued that schools should not deny the significance of the language and culture of the home. Instead, they recommended that both the student and the school need to adapt to each other in a mutual accommodation so that each changes behavior in order to accomplish a common goal. This is consistent with research that has found that the parents of minority students are excluded from school involvement and do not know exactly how to help their children academically even though they want their children to succeed in school and would like to become more involved in helping them to succeed (Wong Fillmore, 1983; Cummins, 1986).

What then constitutes a desirable relationship between the family and the school? According to the research, parental involvement in their children's education is positively correlated with children's school achievement (Epstein, 1989). Even more, such parental involvement appears to be especially important for success in low-income communities (*The Harvard Education Letter*, 1988). Yet, parental involvement is often not high in the inner cities. Is this the fault of the family or the school? Research evidence indicates that the "school's practices to inform and to involve parents are more important than parent education, family size, marital status, and even grade level in determining whether inner-city parents get involved" (Center for Research on Elementary and Middle Schools, 1989, p.10; also, Epstein & Dauber, 1989; Dauber & Epstein, 1989). This means the onus for establishing appropriate levels of parental involvement in inner cities rests with the school.

School

As we have seen, the urban context has a number of implications for the neighborhood community and the family. The context also affects the school, especially its student body, its teaching staff, its curriculum and instructional programs, and its physical facilities and resources. Let me address each of these briefly after first discussing a crucial point: What should be the principal's overall attitude about the school-student interaction in our cities?

The basic attitudinal question that a school leader needs to confront is this: When learning does not occur, who is responsible? A common attitude among school people is to blame the student or the student's cultural background. These are termed, respectively, the student deficit and the cultural deficit models to indicate that there are fundamental lacks within the student or within the cultural background that make learning very difficult. These models are variously portrayed. Goodlad and Oakes's (1988) description captured the basic attitude from a historical perspective:

The more noticeable the differences-as in language, color, dress, and the like-the more likely are negative comparisons. Early in this century, the influx of immigrants speaking languages other than English was accompanied by fear on the part of English-speaking settlers that the culture would be watered down. The use of the Binet test by H. H. Goodard (Harvard University) at Ellis Island led him to the bizarre conclusion that large percentages of the immigrants were feebleminded (in

Gould, 1981). This kind of thinking accompanied the myth that
native indians and blacks were intellectually inferior.

The advent of near-universal schooling and the equating of
education with schooling contributed greatly to misunder-
standing about individual learning differences and about different kinds of intelligence. To be intelligent frequently was
equated with doing well in school.

The school's general failure to provide for, let alone capitalize on, different kinds of intelligence and styles of learning
resulted in clearly prejudicial practices. (p. 18)

Goodlad and Oakes urged educators to rid themselves and their
schools of these kinds of misperceptions of intelligence and to reform
school structures that had been built upon them.

Comer (1988) recounted a similar view from his experience in the
New Haven schools. Based on his work within schools, he came to the
conclusion that most of the behavioral and mental health problems of
the students he encountered in these inner-city schools were "really
created by the climate and conditions of the school" (p. 56). Kagan
(1990) came to the same conclusion about how school practices cause at-
risk students to drop out of school. Citing the work of Edmonds (1986)
on how an effective school could be "so potent that for at least six hours
a day it can override almost everything else in the lives of children " (p.
103), Kagan (1990) developed a model based on the assumption that
"factors within classrooms transform at-risk students into a discrete
subculture that is functionally incompatible with school success" resulting in "alienation, a feeling of isolation and estrangement. . . . and
academic failure" (p. 108). In short, Kagan said that dropping out of
school by at-risk students is a symptom of a pathology of the *institution*
(the school) rather than of the individual student.

The solution at minimum is to make certain that urban schools do
not establish structures that cause at-risk students to become alienated
from school. Even more so, we need to design what Hodgkinson (1988)
called the "right schools for the right kids," making reference to the
pluralism emerging from the demographic trends of the students to be
served by the schools:

Our schools need to be more responsive to the diversity of
students including the challenges that come from the problems

associated with poverty, non-English speaking populations and an increasing number of students with physical and emotional disabilities (p. 14).

In addition to this issue of overall attitude in working with the diversity of urban children and cultures, there are also challenges to the urban school that arise from the nature of its student body, teaching staff, curriculum and instructional program, and physical facilities and resources. Let me turn to a brief review of some of the issues involved in each of these areas. In the interest of brevity, J will mention some issues that are suggestive of the kinds that an urban principal needs to understand rather than attempting to cover all issues comprehensively.

With respect to the *student body*, I have already reviewed major issues from the viewpoint of the student. My concern here is the peer group as it influences the individual student. According to Hoffer and Coleman (1990), the peer group is emerging as a stronger influence on the child, particularly as the family has had a diminishing role in education and as the school is perceived by students as too impersonal. Consequently, peer influence from other students has an increasing effect. Within urban schools, some of this influence has been negative, especially for some minorities. For example, Fordham (1988) described how high-achieving African-American youth sometimes experience a conflict between racial identity with the collective ethos of their community and the individualistic values of the school. One of the strategies some African-American high school students employ when they succeed in school is to become "raceless," that is, to disaffiliate themselves from their collective ethos and to assimilate into the school culture. However, as Fordham (1988) noted, for many African-American adolescents, the sacrifice of cultural affiliation is too high a price. This is especially true for adolescent males:

When compared with the female students, the high-achieving males appear to be less committed to the cultural system of the larger society and far more confused and ambivalent about the value of forsaking their indigenous beliefs and values. Hence, the high-achieving male students mask their raceless personae to a far greater degree than their female counterparts in the school context. (p. 80)

In this way, urban schools have a major challenge: How to encourage high achievement in its students without requiring them to forsake their cultural backgrounds.

With respect to the urban school's *teaching staff*, the school once again is faced with challenges that derive from the nature of the urban context. Urban schools have a great deal of difficulty recruiting and retaining qualified teachers (Council of the Great City Schools, 1988; Haberman, 1987). There continue to be significant shortages in the number of minority teachers as well as teachers in the specialties of mathematics, science, special education, and bilingual education. Whereas once urban teachers had a salary advantage, it is no longer so, as many suburban districts offer lucrative salary and benefit packages. Urban districts are also challenged by inferior working conditions, low teacher morale, high turnover of teachers, and a lack of professional status (Council of the Great City Schools, 1988). Moreover, even when an urban school is able to hire teachers, there is likely to be a high degree of incongruity between the cultural backgrounds of the teachers and those of the students. Cazden and Mehan (1989) described the problem of a mismatch between new teachers and their students: "The typical beginning teacher in the 1990's will be female, in the early to mid-twenties, Anglo, and from a lower-middle income to middle-income family. . . . [These cultural background characteristics] will not match those of their pupils" (p. 47). Grant (1989) observed that these new teachers do not have an interest in teaching in urban areas and would leave to teach in the suburbs if they could. Parkay (1983) depicted the culture shock of a new teacher teaching for the first time in an urban setting. Moreover, new teachers in general are less likely to change even negative school characteristics since they have an inclination to accept traditional school norms without questioning them (Florio-Ruane, 1989). Also, some researchers have found that suburban teachers are engaged in higher levels of academic interaction with their students than are urban teachers (Greenwood, Whorton & Delquadri, 1984). For all of these reasons, some experts have recommended new approaches to recruit and select teachers, including a greater involvement of urban public schools in the preparation of urban teachers (e.g., Haberman, 1987).

With respect to the *curriculum and instructional programs*, Fantini and Weinstein (1968) noted that the urban school curriculum is not relevant to and even works against the "curriculum" of daily urban life.

Consequently, they recommended that urban schools become better integrated with their communities. Schools could do so if they develop curricula that engage pupils in examining the social realities of the city, teach learning skills that will permit them to influence those realities, and provide occasions in which these skills can actually be applied to those realities in real-life situations. Fantini and Weinstein urged urban schools to encourage diversity of all kinds, both individual and cultural. In essence, they called for the richness of the urban setting to be brought into the formal classroom. Comer (1988) likewise stressed a curriculum more relevant to urban students. In the New Haven schools, he asked parents about what they wanted for their children. The result was a social skills curriculum for inner-city children that integrated the learning of academic skills, social skills, and the appreciation of the arts through units on politics and government, business and economics, health and nutrition, and spiritual and leisure time activities. This curriculum, according to Comer, was both meaningful and useful to the students while still being academic in nature. The question of relevance has prompted some educators to propose an Ethnocentric or Afrocentric Curriculum to provide urban students with alternatives to the traditional Eurocentric curriculum (Viadero, 1990).

Critiques of urban schools have extended beyond the curriculum into the instructional practices and structures for teaching and learning. Noting research that stated that urban school systems retain between 15% and 20% of students at each grade level (Gottfredson, 1988), McPartland and Slavin (1990) criticized urban schools' current instructional structures, including retention in grade, teaching, and special-education placements. They proposed a set of alternatives, based on the accumulated research, in order to increase the achievement of at-risk students. Wang, Reynolds, and Walberg (1988) suggested that schools need to stop the practice of labeling special-needs students and removing them from the regular classroom. They proposed the development of new instructional delivery models in the regular classroom. Cuban (1989a) demonstrated how the graded school structure contributes to the failure of at-risk students and recommended restructuring alternatives to make schools more appropriate for those students. Levin (1988) developed an alternative program, termed the *accelerated school program*, which draws on the strengths and talents of disadvantaged students, including:

an interest and a curiosity in oral and artistic expression,
abilities to learn through the manipulation of appropriate
learning materials. . . ., a capability for engrossment in intrinsically interesting tasks, and the ability to learn to write before
attaining competence in decoding skills which are prerequisite
to reading. In addition, such students can serve as enthusiastic
and effective learning resources for other students through
peer tutoring and cooperative-learning approaches. (Levin
1988, p. 216)

Also, there is strong research evidence that *cooperative learning*, as
opposed to traditional classroom instruction, is an effective approach
for teaching at-risk students (Slavin & Madden, 1989). And Cummins
(1986) developed a framework to permit educators and schools to
"redefine their roles with respect to minority students and communities" (p. 19). The framework emphasized the empowerment of students, respect for the students' culture and language in the home,
involvement of family and community, and pedagogical approaches
that permit students to become more active learners.

With respect to *physical facilities*, it is clear that urban schools have
serious problems that need to be addressed. Urban schools are located
in older buildings, and in the largest cities at least one-third of all
buildings are over 50 years old (Council of the Great City Schools, 1987).
Many facilities are in a dilapidated condition, and cleanliness and plant
condition are often rated below average (Carnegie Foundation for the
Advancement of Teaching, 1988). The problems associated with the
upkeep of school buildings and facilities come from a variety of sources:
the large number of buildings needing maintenance, the need to negotiate with many different unions, the regulations of many municipal
and state agencies, the demands of demographic changes and educational reforms, the establishment of numerous building ordinances
since most city schools were originally built (e.g., ordinances regarding
asbestos abatement, fire, electrical wiring, handicapped access), and
the difficulties of new construction because of scarce land, zoning
requirements, and crowded infrastructures beneath city streets (Council of the Great City Schools, 1987). The presence of asbestos and the
laws involving its removal place extraordinary demands on urban
schools (Romano, 1989). All in all, there is need for a massive dedication

of funds to upgrade facilities if students are to get the message "that they and their schools are important" (Picigallo, 1989).

With respect to *financial resources,* urban schools have been shown to be lacking necessary levels, especially in big cities. Because of multiple demands placed on schools and limited means to meet those demands, urban schools have a limited capacity to meet their identified needs, especially those of its diverse populations (Council of the Great City Schools, 1987). External financial support is important; however, it is not enough by itself. Adequate financial resources are necessary, but insufficient for school improvement (Clark, Lotto & McCarthy, 1980). Research has shown that the *ways* in which resources are used are extremely important to school success. It is also worth noting that one reason urban schools are in such need of additional financial resources is because they have such a wide range of individual differences they need to serve, including large numbers of students considered to be at risk of failure in school. As Levin (1989) demonstrated, although the costs of intervention with at-risk students is high, such an investment is cost-effective and "yields high returns to society" (p. 53), especially in comparison to the very high costs to society of failure.

One of the most comprehensive arguments for increased funding for urban schools came from a 1990 decision by the New Jersey Supreme Court to declare New Jersey's Public School Act of 1975 unconstitutional as it applied to poorer urban school districts (*Abbott v. Burke,* 1990). (See also ensuing chapter 6, "Acquiring and Using Resources.") In very clear and sometimes scathing terms, the court espoused the cause of urban school districts vis-á-vis more affluent suburban ones. For example, the ruling very decisively stated "these students in poorer urban districts have not been able to participate fully as citizens and workers in our society. . . . We find the constitutional failure clear, severe, extensive, and of long duration" (p. 408). The court also observed that the problems facing urban populations are broad ones extending to our wider society:

The fact is that a large part of our society is disintegrating, so large a part that it cannot help but affect the rest. Everyone's future is at stake, and not just the poor's. Certainly the urban poor need more than education, but it is hard to believe that their isolation and society's division can be reversed without it. (p. 412)

The court explicitly recognized the plight of students living in urban poverty by noting the following:

> Their cities have deteriorated and their lives are often bleak. They live in a culture where schools, studying, and homework are secondary. Their test scores, their dropout rate, their attendance at college, all indicate a severe failure of education. While education is largely absent from their lives, we get some idea of what is present from the crime rate, disease rate, drug addiction rate, teenage pregnancy rate, and the unemployment rate. (p. 411)

Moreover, the court emphasized that it is New Jersey's duty to provide a thorough and efficient education to poor students and that the past failure to do so has exacerbated the problems of the urban students. The court stated: "Today the disadvantaged are doubly mistreated: first, by the accident of their environment and, second, by the disadvantage added by an inadequate education. The State has compounded the wrong and must right it" (p. 403).

In making its decision, the court reviewed a substantial amount of statistical data on the relationships involving per-pupil expenditures and other indicators of wealth, tax burden, and educational quality. In doing so, the court acknowledged the municipal overburden argument whereby cities levy overall excessive taxes in order to provide for governmental services over and above education:

> The social and economic pressures on municipalities, school districts, public officials, and citizens of these disaster areas-many poorer urban districts-are so severe that tax increases in any substantial amount are almost unthinkable. (p. 394)

Consequently, poor urban districts do not have the ability to raise sufficient funding to support a thorough and efficient education for their populations. The court also pointedly linked educational quality with level of resources and decided that poor urban districts suffered lesser educational quality because of a lack of sufficient resources. The court wrote:

> The record supported the conclusion that the quality of education in poor urban districts was significantly inferior compared

to other school districts within the state, as measured by finances and programs and by student achievement, based on differences in educational opportunities in many areas including exposure to computers, science education, foreign language programs, art and music programs, physical education and physical facilities. (p. 360)

What is truly remarkable about the New Jersey decision is the extent to which the court was willing to enter into the world of professional education in establishing a rationale for its decision. The court gave a strong explanation for why poor urban students needed not merely an adequate education but one that was different from and went beyond traditional education and even the education provided in the wealthier suburbs. The court made the following argument:

This record shows that the educational needs of students in poorer urban districts vastly exceed those of others, especially those from richer districts. Those needs go beyond educational needs, they include food, clothing and shelter, and extend to lack of close family and community ties and support, and lack of helpful role models. They include the needs that arise from a life led in an environment of violence, poverty, and despair. Urban youth are often isolated from the mainstream of society. . . . The goal is to motivate them, to wipe out their disadvantage as much as a school district can, and to give them an educational opportunity that will enable them to use their innate ability. (p. 400)

The Court called for "a significantly different approach to education" to help poorer urban schools succeed (p. 401). Such an approach includes more libraries, guidance programs, alternative educational programs, intensive preschool programs, and all-day kindergartens (p. 402). The court proceeded to go even further and state that urban schools needed even more in their programs than suburban schools:

It is clear to us that in order to achieve the constitutional standard for the student from these poorer urban districts - the ability to function in that society entered by their relatively advantaged peers-the totality of the districts' educational offering must contain elements over and above those found in the affluent suburban district. (p. 402)

All in all, the New Jersey decision is perhaps the most spirited and far-reaching public policy statement on the unique needs of urban schools. It called for an ambitious, comprehensive, and extended commitment by society for our urban schools.

School District and State Level Policies

An urban principal also needs to understand the ways in which urban school districts are unique and how they are affected by state and national policies. A *multiplicity of federal, state, and local mandates and guidelines* creates a morass of compliance requirements for urban school sites. Excessive regulatory requirements especially follow special programs and services targeted to special-needs students (Wang, Reynolds & Walberg, 1988). Moreover, policies aimed at the segmentation of problems and problem solving lead to an artificial separation of related issues that need to be dealt with systemically (Schorr & Schorr, 1988). All of this occurs in the context of a declining role of the federal government, especially a decrease in financial support for cities and city schools (Hinds & Eckholm, 1990). The declining role of federal government in urban education can be seen in those programs which have traditionally been focused on schools with high levels of poverty. Known as "Chapter 1" programs, they have been, for over 25 years, relatively successful in addressing the educational problems of low-achieving, disadvantaged students (Slavin, 1987). Lytle (1990) reviewed the 1988 reauthorization of federal legislation for Chapter 1 programs (1988). He concluded that the legislation included "a contradictory amalgam of highly prescriptive, top-down policies" (p. 211), providing only limited funding for the cities. Moreover, he observed that the future outlook is that "Chapter 1 will continue to be a program driven by bureaucratic compliance concerns rather than concern for more effective and appropriate instruction for low-achieving, disadvantaged children" (p. 211).

At the same time, there is federal legislation that has significant implications for urban schools, even though it is not focused on education. For example, national immigration policy has substantial implications for the demographics of education in our cities (P. Schmidt,

1990). This is but an example of the important ways federal policy differentially affects urban schools, just as in the past federal transportation and housing policies helped create development outside of cities and encouraged an exodus from our urban centers (Kemp & Cheslow, 1976).

Court decisions at the federal and state levels continue to have enormous influence over urban schools. In addition to the New Jersey funding case *(Abbott v. Burke*, 1990; Newman, 1990) mentioned above, more recent examples include decisions directly affecting the reform of Chicago's school district through the establishment of school-site policy councils (Olson, 1990b), the attempts by the state of Wisconsin to establish plans to permit student/parental choice of schools (Lawton, 1990b), and the reform of the financing systems for public schools in Texas (Harp, 1990). In each of these cases, reforms were instituted that were overturned in part or whole by the courts, with substantial impact on city schools.

At the *school district level*, there are numerous factors at work that a school principal needs to understand. The urban school system, with its many complexities, has been depicted as an impersonal system that presents a maze of roadblocks for the principal (Sarason, 1982), as a corporate conglomerate (Hill, Wise & Shapiro, 1989), and as a bureaucracy dominated by noneducation professionals. Urban school districts are also found to be more and more isolated from the civic, political, and economic mainstream of the cities in which they exist (Hill, Wise & Shapiro, 1989). Yet, the school district can also be a major determining factor for the adoption, implementation, and institutionalization of change at the local level, especially the school site (Fullan, 1985). The locus of policy making at the district level sometimes hinders the exercise of leadership at the school site; yet, the existence of supportive policy frameworks at the school-district level is related to the effectiveness of schools and their ability to effect positive change (Fullan, 1982; Purkey & Smith, 1985).

Currently, urban school districts are the locales of numerous experiments in the restructuring of schools. In Chicago, parents and community members are being given substantial power on locally elected school councils, including the authority to hire and fire principals (Wilkerson, 1989). The school district of Chelsea, Massachusetts, has been taken over by Boston University, which manages the district under a special management contract (Watkins, 1990). In Rochester,

New York, the school district and the teachers union entered into an innovative collective bargaining contract granting the teachers substantial professionalism, which subsequently was contested by the school administrators who protested the apparent loss of administrative authority (Bradley, 1989). In Jersey City, New Jersey, the state declared the school district educationally bankrupt and proceeded to take over the district's operation including the installation of an interim superintendent who has aggressively shaken up the district's administration (Olson, 1990a). Milwaukee took the dramatic step of instituting two schools specifically for African-American males in recognition of the fact that urban schools have traditionally done so poorly with young African Americans (Lawton, 1990a).

One proposed solution for the problems of schools in general and inner-city schools in particular is the development of mechanisms (e.g., vouchers) that would enable parents and students to choose the specific schools they wish to attend. Such mechanisms deregulate the monopoly of the public schools and propose a market system of competition sensitive to the needs of consumers (Chubb & Moe, 1990; 1991). Such proposals have been countered by spirited arguments criticizing the limitations of the market to deliver educational equity (Scovic, 1991; Shanker, 1990). The willingness to experiment so radically with the restructuring of schools is indicative of the risks some reformers are willing to take in the face of the poor performance of our schools, especially in the urban setting.

Throughout all of these reform experiments, there is a debate over the appropriate roles of centralization and decentralization of authority within school districts. (This topic is treated in greater detail in the ensuing chapter 7, "Governing Urban Schools.") The current trend is clearly in the direction of the latter-with emphasis on more authority and accountability at the school site level. In the midst of such a trend, it is useful to keep a historical perspective. Ravitch (1974) reminded us that the centralization/ decentralization debate has been a long-standing one. Referring to the history of New York City, she wrote:

> *Neither centralization nor local control has solved the problems of the*
> *school system.* Each has its advantages and disadvantages, which cause a pendulum movement over the years from one form to the other. When school officials have known what they wanted to do and how to do it, then faith in centralization was strong, as in the

early nineteenth century and in the 1890s. But when both the means and the ends of schooling seem confused and uncertain, and when the political legitimacy of the educational authorities appeared doubtful, there has been a trend to decentralize control of the schools, as in the 1840s and 1960s. (p. 401)

Another perennial debate in urban school districts involves the myriad of issues surrounding school desegregation. Bates (1990) indicated that the public schools are actually experiencing a "resegregation." He argued that early efforts focused on ending physical segregation, what he termed "first generation" activities. What is now needed, he proposed, is attention to "the second-generation issue of within-school segregation and the third-generation issue of the achievement gap between minority students and white students" (p. 11). The necessity of addressing desegregation in its many forms represents one of the biggest challenges to urban school leaders.

One final aspect of urban school districts is noteworthy. The tenure of urban school superintendents averages approximately 2.5 years (Daley, 1990). At the time of this writing, the superintendencies of more than 15 major cities are waiting to be filled permanently. In December 1990, more than one-half of the superintendents of the 45 largest school districts were in their first or second year (Allis, 1990). A real crisis of leadership has emerged as districts have had a difficult time trying to attract and identify talented leaders who are willing to face the stress, problems, and uncertainties of running an urban district. The implications for the principal are readily apparent. As Blank (1987) noted, "school leadership in large urban districts is often a product of co-management or co-leadership by the principal and the superintendent" (p.78). Rapid or frequent turnover in the superintendency removes a vital anchor of stability for the principal, leaving the latter to depend more on her or his own political resources for long-term survival.

Implications for the Urban School Principal

The urban context is a complicated one with numerous forces and relationships-both positive and negative. The interactivist principal is one who is able to anticipate trends and also tries to understand and create the future by regulating continuous interchanges between the school, its context, and a range of possible futures. Such an interactivist approach involves a broad and diverse knowledge base as well as a fierce commitment to urban school reform, the courage to lead, and a willingness to set specific directions for the school. The other chapters of this book provide a number of solutions to the problems of practice that the urban principal regularly faces. The following are observations and suggestions derived from the foregoing review of the urban context.

Need to Understand Context

Phi Delta Kappa (1980) conducted a systematic review of case studies and research studies of urban schools as well as interviews with several leading researchers and writers on urban education. The focus was on six clusters of variables (leadership, personnel, finance, curriculum and instruction, resources and facilities, and community). One of the key findings was that the behavior of the school leader (especially the principal) was a critical variable and that the leader's *attitude toward urban education* and *expectations for success* within the school were important determinants of the leader's impact on the school (Phi Delta Kappa, 1980, p. 204; see also Clark, Lotto & McCarthy, 1980).

Sarason (1982) viewed the principal from a different perspective. He noted that principals' expectations about the "system" and anticipation of trouble vis-á-vis the system often determined their ability to effect change. Moreover, principals often have a poor knowledge of the system in large urban districts, so they are more likely to adopt a passive stance rather than an active one. This is unfortunate because in Sarason's view "more than any other single position in the American school hierarchy, the principalship represents the pivotal exchange point, the most important point of connection between teachers, students, and parents. . . . and the educational policy-making structure" (p. 180).

The two works cited above are suggestive of a whole body of literature that indicates that principals who understand the system and context in which they work and who have a positive attitude toward urban schools, the potential of students to learn, and their ability to effect change, will be able to make a difference. The effective principal needs to understand the context of the school in order to be able to work within the limitations of those contextual variables that cannot be changed and to manipulate those that can be. Better understanding provokes new ways to appreciate the students and neighborhood served. For example, familiarity with sociological analyses that tie the formation of an inner-city underclass to the scarcity of jobs and economic exclusion rather than to welfare abuse (Wacquant & Wilson, 1989; Kasarda, 1989) gives a greater appreciation of inner-city poverty.

Students as the Centerpiece

For the interactivist principal, students should be at the center of consideration. The danger is that traditional day-to-day administrative activities distract the principal from the core mission of the school. As Silver (1983) suggested, the administrative profession needs to be reoriented toward student learning outcomes as the principal concern. This reorientation has the following implications.

A successful urban principal needs to have high expectations for the students served. Rather than being labeled *disadvantaged* or *at risk*, urban students should be viewed as "children of worth" (Clayton, 1989). The *at risk* label connotes a cultural deficit model on the side of the student, whereas an alternative view is that schools are not adequately reaching many urban children and may even be too inflexible to accommodate cultural diversity (Cuban, 1989a). The interactivist principal views failure as a deficit of the school, not the student. The urban school principal must be committed to the notion that all children can learn.

The notion of "children of worth" also implies that the principal will be an aggressive advocate on behalf of urban students, constantly "affirming the worth and dignity of the children" (Clayton, 1989, p.135) the school serves. The principal, as a professional, should be concerned first and foremost about the welfare of the school's clients-the students. When that welfare is threatened, the principal needs to act aggressively in the best interests of the client to insure that the educational environment is supportive of children and produces the learning outcomes that are appropriate in the professional's best judgment. Such child advocacy is particularly necessary in the context of an American society that is growing older on average. Children need champions when the political and economic structures more and more favor older populations.

The successful principal needs to view the context of the urban child through the eyes of the child. Kirst, McLaughlin and Massell, (1990) called for a systematic rethinking of the ways in which services for children and youth are designed and implemented. They argued that the school, which historically had separated itself from the social, economic, governmental, and political subsystems of society, needs to understand the context of childhood from the viewpoint of the child. The school needs to place itself at the hub of the array of social services intended to support the child in need and help to coordinate and integrate them on behalf of the child. Such a posture, they suggested, requires also a rethinking of the role of the principal. The principal, in their view, needs to be a leader in orchestrating and mediating the external forces and services affecting our youngsters in modern society.

Linking with the Urban Context

The principal needs to identify local urban resources with which the school can link to better serve its community. These resources include cultural institutions, universities, businesses, financial institutions, private foundations, churches, and the like, as well as various social service agencies. A catalog of these is an indispensable resource. A principal needs to develop a network of contacts with such organizations and agencies in order to develop broad community support for the school and its goals. The principal must recognize that the urban school is entangled with the broader urban community (Hill, Wise & Shapiro, 1989). Consequently, the principal must constantly look for ways to build bridges between school and community. In the literature, there are some innovative models for doing this.

The successful urban principal should have a healthy distrust of the status quo. The principal needs to be able to disrupt routines and ask basic questions, including "What is going on here?" (Florio-Ruanne, 1988). Simply because something has traditionally been done a certain way is not a justification for its continuance. The good leader constantly examines what others take for granted and looks for ways in which the organization can continuously improve itself. This is a necessary characteristic of a reformer.

The principal must learn the rules of the bureaucratic system to avert obstacles and to recognize the pressure points for certain types of decisions. This means taking charge and aggressively expecting positive results, rather than passively anticipating that some impersonal system will block anything one tries to do (Sarason, 1982).

The principal also needs to build a strong positive relationship with the district superintendent. Successful schools in cities are usually the result of co-leadership or co-management by the principal and the superintendent (Blank, 1987). This means that the principal and super-intendent need to work together as a team, with a line relationship connecting them (Hill, Wise & Shapiro, 1989). The successful principal needs a supportive district.

Activist Orientation

The literature on successful programs time and time again empha-sizes that active leadership is a crucial ingredient of success. The principal should take the attitude that she or he can make a difference. As some researchers have observed, "it is well known that administra-tive leadership, particularly on the part of the building principal, frequently is the crucial characteristic associated with successful inner-city schools" (Levine, Levine & Eubanks, 1987, p.84).

There are several strategies that principals can employ to influence the bureaucratic and cultural linkage of schools in order to improve instruction (Firestone & Wilson, 1985). The literature abounds with prescriptions for action at the school level. For example, the Carnegie Foundation for the Advancement of Teaching (1988) emphasized the need for high expectations and good governance, along with a five-point plan for school reform:

> We suggest that every school give priority to the early years; have a clearly defined curriculum; be flexible in its scheduling arrangements; provide a program of coordinated services; and be a safe, attractive place with good equipment and adequate resources for learning. (p. 17)

Substantive Knowledge

The educational leader needs to have a solid grounding in the substance of the educational enterprise: successful systems of teaching and learning. Consequently, successful principals need to be familiar with literature on urban school reform, with special attention to those factors that they are able to manipulate. The recommended literature includes works on factors associated with success (Phi Delta Kappa, 1980), change processes and strategies in schools and school districts (Fullan, 1982; 1985), the effective schools literature (Purkey & Smith, 1983; 1985), working with at-risk students (McPartland & Slavin, 1990;

Cuban, 1989b; Madden, Slavin, Karweit & Livermon, 1989), and examples of successful programs in urban schools (Council of the Great City Schools, 1987). These and similar works are essential elements of a principal's ready-to-use reference library.

General Knowledge of Context

In addition, the knowledgeable principal also needs to be familiar with some broader works that address the underlying features of the urban scene. Let me list a few examples. Schorr and Schorr (1988) provided a superb overview of the complexity of problems associated with poverty and the arsenal of intervention strategies that are "within our reach" as a society. Fantini and Weinstein (1968) gave us the seminal work on the nature of urban schools, and Gordon (1982) provided one of the best logical analyses of the meaning of urban education. Hodgkinson's works (1988; 1989) contain demographic trends and analyses that are helpful in anticipating the needs of the populations the schools will serve in the years ahead. The 1990 yearbook of the National Society for the Study of Education (Mitchell & Cunningham, 1990) explored educational leadership with special attention to the changing context of families, communities, and schools. The January 1989 issue of the *Annals* of the American Academy of Political and Social Science was devoted to social science perspectives on the ghetto underclass. The comprehensive book *The Truly Disadvantaged: The Inner City, the Underclass and Public Policy* (Wilson, 1987) provided an insightful analysis of the structural and human factors contributing to the patterns of inner cities. Each of these works provides the urban principal with a deep appreciation of the workings of the city and the contextual factors impinging on the school and urban inhabitants. The principal who wishes to be a force in the community needs to understand the social, political, sociological, and economic dynamics of the community.

Some Unanswered Questions

Even though we know a great deal about the ingredients of successful programs (Schorr & Schorr, 1988), there are many important unanswered questions. Let me briefly address three interconnected ones and suggest a strategy for addressing them. As Cuban (1989b) pointed out, we understand many of the separate elements associated with effective schools, yet we do not know the precise order in which to arrange them. Moreover, we do not fully understand the steps necessary to turn a failing school into a successful one. Nor do we have adequate explanations for the relationships between resource levels and successful programs. Undoubtedly, the answers to questions such as these are heavily dependent on the situation. Each school is a unique system within a unique environment, and the dynamic interplay of countless variables is not replicable from one situation to the next.

Nevertheless, this does not mean that we cannot develop a better understanding of such questions. In fact, the urban principal might be the key to building a reliable data base from which to formulate answers. As Silver (1983) described, other professions have had to deal with the issue of generating knowledge about how best to solve concrete problems in real-life, complex situations. She wrote that in many professions,

> each practitioner maintains detailed records in accordance with a standard format to document what she or he did in each case and what the outcomes of that action seem to have been. Case histories, hospital charts, legal briefs, blueprints, and job specifications are examples of such standardized case-by-case records of practice. In the conduct of inquiry within the professions, these records maintained by individual practitioners are an invaluable resource for generating both theoretical and technical knowledge about how concrete problems are solved. (p. 14)

Through systematic record-keeping, reflections on the records kept, and discussion with other professionals who are doing the same thing in their unique circumstances, a principal can both understand better the dynamics of her or his school and make a valuable contribution to the entire education profession and its understanding of schools within their urban context.

Conclusion

By systematic recordkeeping and by familiarity with the literature on successful urban schools and on the ways in which the urban context affects schools and students, the urban principal can develop a broad knowledge base on the web of relationships between the school and its urban environment. Such a knowledge base empowers the interactivist principal to understand these relationships, seize the opportunities presented by the resources within the urban context, and insulate the school and its students from the negative contextual factors that place students at risk and interfere with learning.

References

Abbott v. Burke, 575 A.2d 359, N.J., (1990).

Ackoff, R. L. (1974). *Redesigning the future: A systems approach to societal problems.* New York: Wiley.

Action Council on Minority Education. (1990, January). *Education that works: An action plan for the education of minorities.* Quality Education for Minorities Project. Cambridge, MA: Massachusetts Institute of Technology.

Allis, S. (1990, December 3). Grad work for the war zone. *Time,* pp. 91-94.

Bates, P. (1990, September). Desegregation: Can we get there from here? *Phi Delta Kappan, 72* (1), 8-17.

Bernstein, B. (1973). *Class, codes and control.* Vol. 1. London: Paladin.

Blank, R. K. (1987, November-December). The role of the principal as leader: Analysis of variation in leadership of urban high schools. *The Journal of Educational Research, 81* (2), 69-80.

Boyd, W. L. (1990). *What makes ghetto schools work or not work?* Invited paper for conference "The Truly Disadvantaged," sponsored by the Social Science Research Council, Committee for Research on the Urban Underclass, and the Center for Urban Affairs and Policy Research, Northwestern University, Evanston, IL, October 19-21, 1989 (Revised, February 1990).

Bradley, A. (1989, October 18). After two tough years in Rochester, school reformers look to the future. *Education Week,* 10-12.

Brookover, W. B., Beady, C., Flood, P., Schweitzer, J., & Wisenbaker, J. (1977). *Schools can make a difference.* East Lansing, MI: Michigan State University, College of Urban Development.

Carnegie Foundation for the Advancement of Teaching. (1988). *An imperiled generation: Saving urban schools.* Princeton, NJ: The Carnegie Foundation for the Advancement of Teaching.

Cazden, C. B., & Mehan, H. (1989). Principles from sociology and anthropology: Content, code, classroom and culture. In M. C. Reynolds (Ed.), *Knowledge base for the beginning teacher* (pp. 47-57). New York: Pergamon.

Center for Research on Elementary and Middle Schools. (1989, June). Teacher attitudes, parent attitudes, and parent involvement in inner-city elementary and middle schools. *CREMS*, 10-12.

Chase, F. S. (1978). *Urban education studies: 1977-78 report.* Dallas: Council of the Great City Schools.

Chub, J. E., & Moe, T. M. (1990). *Politics, markets and America's schools.* Washington, DC: Brookings Institute.

Chub, J. E., & Moe, M. (1991). Schools in a marketplace: Chubb and Moe argue their bold proposal. *The School Administrator, 1* (48), 18, 20, 22, 25.

Clark, D. L., Lotto, L. S., & McCarthy, M. M. (1980, March). Factors associated with success in urban elementary schools. *Phi Delta Kappan, 61* (7), March 467-470.

Clayton, C. (1989, July 24-31). We *can* educate our children. *The Nation,* pp. 132-135.

Coleman, J. S. (1987, August-September). Families and schools. *Educational Researcher, 16,* 32-38.

Comer, J. P. (1988, October 18). Keynote address. Invitational roundtable " Stress, distress and educational outcomes: Towards ensuring the emotional well-being of our children." Transcript of roundtable (pp.16-77). Philadelphia: School District of Philadelphia.

Council of the Great City Schools. (1987). *Challenges to urban education: Results in the making.* Washington, DC: C.G.C.S.

Council of the Great City Schools. (1988). *Teaching and leading in the great city schools.* Washington, DC: C.G.C.S.

Cuban, L. (1989a, June) The "at-risk" label and the problem of urban school reform. *Phi Delta Kappan, 70* (10), 780-784, 799-801.

Cuban, L. (1989b, February). At risk students: What teachers and principals can do. *Educational leadership, 46* (5), 29-32.

Cummins, J. (1986, February) Empowering minority students: A framework for intervention. *Harvard Educational Review, 56* (1), 18-36.

Daley, S. (1990, December 26). School chiefs dropping out, plagued by urban problems. *The New York Times,* A1, B12.

Dauber, S. L., & Epstein, J. L. (1989, March). *Parent attitudes and practices of parent involvement in inner-city elementary and middle schools.*

Report No. 33. Baltimore, MD: Center for Research on Elementary and Middle Schools, The John Hopkins University.

Dedman, B. (1988a, May 1). Atlanta blacks losing in home loans scramble. *The Atlanta Journal/The Atlanta Constitution.* Altanta, GA: Reprinted in *The color of money: Home mortgage lending practices discriminate against blacks,* 1-6. Reprinted with permission from *The Atlanta Journal* and *The Atlanta Constitution.*

Dedman, B. (1988b, May 2). Southside treated like banks' stepchild? *The Atlanta Journal/The Atlanta Constitution.* Atlanta, GA: Reprinted in *The color of money: Home mortgage lending practices discriminate against blacks,* 11-16. Reprinted with permission from *The Atlanta Journal* and *The Atlanta Constitution.*

Edmonds, R. R. (1979, October). Effective schools for the urban poor. *Educational Leadership, 37,* 15-27.

Edmonds, R. R. (1982, December). Programs of school improvement: An overview. *Educational Leadership, 40* (3), 4-11.

Edmonds, R. R. (1986). Characteristics of effective schools. In U. Neisser (Ed.), *The school achievement of minority children* (pp. 93-104). Hillsdale, NJ: Lawrence Erlbaum.

Epstein, J. L. (1989). Building parent-teacher partnerships in inner-city schools. *Family Resource Coalition Report, 8* (2), 7.

Epstein, J. L., & Dauber, S. L. (1989, March). Teacher attitudes and practices of parent involvement in inner-city elementary and middle schools. Report No. 32. Baltimore, MD: Center for Research on Elementary and Middle Schools, The John Hopkins University.

Escalona, S. K. (1982, November). Babies at double hazard: Early development of infants at biologic and social risk. *Pediatrics, 70* (5), 670-76.

Fantini, M. D. (1985). Stages of linking school and nonschool learning environments. In M. D. Fantini and R. L. Sinclair (Eds.), *Education in school and nonschool settings.* Eighty-fourth yearbook of the National Society for the Study of Education, Part I (pp. 46-63). Chicago: University of Chicago Press.

Fantini, M. D. (1986). *Regaining excellence in education.* Columbus: Merrill.

Fantini, M. D., & Sinclair, R. L. (Eds.) (1985). *Education in school and nonschool settings.* Eighty-fourth yearbook of the National Society for the Study of Education, Part I (pp. 46-63). Chicago: University of Chicago Press.

Fantini, M. D., & Weinstein, G. (1968). *Making urban schools work: Social realities and the urban school.* New York: Holt, Rinehart & Winston.

Firestone, W. A., & Wilson, B. L. (1985, Spring). Using bureaucratic and cultural linkages to improve instruction: The principal's contribution. *Educational Administration Quarterly, 21* (2), 7-30.

Florio-Ruane, S. (1989). Social organization of classes and schools. In M. C. Reynolds (Ed), *Knowledge base for the beginning teacher (pp. 163-172)*. New York: Pergamon.

Fordham, S. (1988, February). Racelessness as a factor in black students' school success: Pragmatic strategy or Pyrrhic victory? *Harvard Educational Review, 58* (1), 54-84.

Fullan, M. (1982). *The meaning of educational change*. New York: Teachers College Press.

Fullan, M. (1985, January). Change processes and strategies at the local level. *The Elementary School Journal, 85* (3), 391-421.

Garrison, R. W. (1989, Fall). Gangsters: Back to the future. *School Safety*, 20-22.

Goodlad, J. I. (1984). *A place called school: Prospects for the future*. New York: McGraw-Hill.

Goodlad, J. I., & Oakes, J. (1988, February). We must offer equal access to knowledge. *Educational Leadership, 45* (5), 16-22.

Gordon, E. W. (1982). Urban education. In H. E. Metzel (Ed.), *Encyclopedia of educational research*. Fifth edition. Vol. 4 (pp. 1973-1980). New York: The Free Press.

Gottfredson, G. D. (1988, April). *You get what you measure -you get what you don't: Higher standards, higher test scores, American retention in grade*. Paper presented at the 1988 annual meeting of the American Educational Research Association in New Orleans.

Gould, S. (1981). *The mismeasure of man*. New York: Norton.

Grant, C. A. (1989, June). Urban Teachers: Their new colleagues and curriculum. *Phi Delta Kappan, 70* (10), 764-770.

Greenwood, C. R., Whorton, D., & Delquadri, J. L. (1984).Tutoring methods. *Direct Instruction News, 3*, 4-7, 23.

Haberman, M. (1987). *Recruiting and selecting teachers for urban schools*. New York: ERIC Clearinghouse on Urban Education, Institute for Urban and Minority Education. Also, Reston, VA: Association of Teacher Education.

Hahn, A., Danzberger, J., & Lefkowitz, B. (1987). *Dropouts in America: Enough is known for action*. Washington, DC: Institute for Educational Leadership.

Halpin, A. W. (1966, Spring). Change and organizational climate. *Ontario Journal of Educational Research, 8* (3), 229-247.

Harp, L. (1990, October 3). Finance reform is struck down by Texas judge. *Education Week, 10* (5), 1, 17.

The Harvard Education Letter. (1988, November-December). Parents and schools. *IV* (6), 1-3.

Herndon, J. (1965). *The way it spozed to be.* New York: Bantam.

Hill, P. T. (1990, January). The federal role in education: A strategy for the 1990s. *Phi Delta Kappan, 71* (5), 398-402.

Hill, P. T., Wise, A. E., & Shapiro, L. (1989, January). *Educational progress: Cities mobilize to improve their schools.* Santa Monica, CA: Center for the Study of the Teaching Profession, RAND Corporation.

Hinds, M., & Eckholm, E. (1990, December 30). 80's leave states and cities in need. *The New York Times,* 1, 16-17.

Hodgkinson, H. L. (1988, February). The right schools for the right kids. *Educational Leadership, 45* (5), 10-14.

Hodgkinson, H. L. (1989). *The same client: The demographics of education and service delivery systems.* Washington, DC: Institute for Educational Leadership, Inc./ Center for Demographic Policy.

Hoffer, T. B., & Coleman, J. S. (1990). Changing families and communities: Implications for schools. In B. Mitchell and L. L. Cunningham (Eds.), *Educational leadership and changing contexts of families, communities, and schools (pp. 118-134).* Eighty-ninth yearbook of the National Society for the Study of Education, Part II. Chicago: University of Chicago Press.

Irwin, D. (1989, August 28). Study: Cities' violent crime up 43% in 10 years; Number of police up 2%. *The Philadelphia Inquirer,* p. 9-A.

Jackson, K. T. (1985). *Crabgrass frontier: The suburbanization* of the United States. New York: Oxford.

Jaffe, M. (1990a, March 6). High lead in 4 million children. *The Philadelphia Inquirer,* 1-A.

Jaffe, M. (1990b, April 15). Lead poisoning's risk far greater than figures show, experts warn. *The Philadelphia Inquirer,* 1-A, 8-A, 9-A.

Justiz, M. J., & Kameen, M. C. (1987, January). Business offers a hand to education. *Phi Delta Kappan, 68* (5), 379-383.

Kagan, D. M. (1990). How schools alienate students at risk: A model for examining proximal classroom variables. *Educational Psychologist, 25* (2), 105-125.

Kasarda, J. D. (1989, January). Urban industrial transition and the underclass. *Annals of the American Academy of Political and Social Science, 501,* 26-47.

Kemp, M. A., & Cheslow, M. D. (1976). Transportation. In W. Gorham and N. Glazer (Eds.), *The urban predicament* (pp. 281-356). Washington, DC: The Urban Institute.

Kirst, M. W., McLaughlin, M., & Massell, D. (1990). Rethinking policy for children: Implications for educational administration. In B. Mitchell & L. L. Cunningham (Eds.), *Educational leadership and changing contexts of families, communities, and schools* (pp. 69-90). Eighty-ninth yearbook of the National Society for the Study of Education, Part II. Chicago: University of Chicago Press.

Kohl, H. (1967). *36 children.* New York: Signet.

Kozol, J. (1967). *Death at an early age: The destruction of the hearts and minds of Negro children in the Boston public schools.* New York: Bantam.

Kozol, J. (1991). *Savage inequalities: Children in America's schools.* New York: Crown.

Lawton, M. (1990a, October 10). 2 schools aimed for black males set in Milwaukee. *Education Week,* 1, 12.

Lawton, M. (1990b, November 21). Ground-breaking voucher program in Wis. rejected. *Education Week, 10* (12), 1, 24.

Lemann, N. (1986, June, July). The origins of the underclass. Part I and Part II. *The Atlantic, 257* (6 June), 31-55, and *257* (7 July), 54-68.

Levin, H. M. (1988). Accelerating elementary education for disadvantaged students. In Council of Chief State School Officers, *School success for students at risk: Analysis and recommendations of the Council of Chief State School Officers* (pp. 209-226). Orlando, FL: Harcourt, Brace, Jovanovich.

Levin, H. M. (1989, Spring). Financing the education of at-risk students. *Educational Evaluation and Policy Analysis, 11* (1), 47-60.

Levine, D., & Havighurst, R. J. (1968). Social systems of a metropolitan area. In R. J. Havighurst (Ed.), *Metropolitanism: Its challenge to education.* Sixty-seventh yearbook of the National Society for the Study of Education (pp. 37-70). Chicago: University of Chicago Press.

Levine, D. U., Levine, R. F., & Eubanks, E. E. (1987). Successful implementation of instruction at inner-city schools. In J. J. Lane and H. J. Walberg (Eds.), *Effective schools leadership: Policy and process* (pp. 65-88). Berkeley, CA: McCutchan.

Lytle, J. H. (1990, September). Reforming urban education: A review of recent reports and legislation. *The Urban Review, 22* (3), 199-220.

Madden, N. A., Slavin, R. E., Karweit, N. L., & Livermon, B. J.(1989, February). Restructuring the urban elementary school. *Educational Leadership, 46* (5), 14-18.

Maeroff, G. I. (1988, May). Withered hopes, stillborn dreams: The dismal panorama of urban schools. *Phi Delta Kappan. 69* (9), 633-638.

Maykuth, A. (1990, January 22). Doctors find a bit of third world in Harlem. *The Philadelphia Inquirer*, 3-A.

McCord, C., & Freeman, H. P. (1990, January 18). Excess mortality in Harlem. *The New England Journal of Medicine, 322* (3), 173-177.

McPartland, J. M., & Slavin, R. E. (1990, July). *Increasing achievement of at-risk students at each grade level.* Policy perspectives series. Washington, DC: U.S. Department of Education, Office of Educational Research and Improvement.

Menacker, J., Weldon, W., & Hurwitz, E. (1989, September). School order and safety as community issues. *Phi Delta Kappan, 71*(1), 39-40, 55-56.

Mitchell, B. (1990). Loss, belonging, and becoming: Social policy themes for children and schools. In B. Mitchell and L. L. Cunningham, (Eds.), *Educational leadership and changing contexts of families, communities, and schools* (pp. 19-51). Eighty-ninth yearbook of the National Society for the Study of Education, Part II. Chicago: University of Chicago Press.

Mitchell, B., & Cunningham, L.L. (Eds.). (1990). *Educational leadership and changing contexts of families, communities, and schools.* Eighty-ninth yearbook of the National Society for the Study of Education, Part II, Chicago: University of Chicago Press.

National Commission on Excellence in Education. (1983). *A Nation at Risk.* Washington, DC: U.S. Department of Education.

Newman, M. (1990, June 13). Finance system for NJ schools is struck down. *Education Week, 9* (38), 1, 18.

Ogbu, J.U. (1981). Origins of human competence: A cultural-ecological perspective. *Child Development, 52,* 413-429.

Olson, L. (1990a, October 3). One year after takeover by state, cautious optimism in Jersey City. *Education Week, 10* (5), 1, 20, 21.

Olson, L. (1990b, December 12). Chicago reeling in wake of ruling rejecting reform. *Education Week, 10* (15), 1, 33.

Ornstein, A. C., & Levine, D. U. (1989, September-October). Social class, race and school achievement: Problems and prospects. *Journal of Teacher Education, 40* (5), 17-23.

Parkay, F. W. (1983). *White teacher, black school.* New York: Praeger.

Phi Delta Kappa (1980). *Why do some urban schools succeed? The Phi Delta Kappa study of exceptional urban elementary schools.* Bloomington, IN: PDK.

Piccigallo, P. R. (1989, January). Renovating urban schools is fundamental to improving them. *Phi Delta Kappan, 70* (5), 402-406.

Purkey, S. C., & Smith, M. S. (1983, March). Effective schools: A review. *The Elementary School Journal, 83* (4), 427-452.

Purkey, S. C., & Smith, M. S. (1985, January) School reform: The district policy implications of the effective schools literature. *The Elementary School Journal, 85* (3), 353-389.

Ravitch, D. (1974). *The great school wars: A history of the New York City public schools.* New York: Basic Books.

Ricketts, E. R., & Sawhill, I. V. (1986). *Defining and measuring the underclass. Discussion paper.* Washington, DC: Urban Institute. As cited in Schorr & Schorr (1988).

Romano, J. (1989, June 18). Schools and asbestos: Law posing problems. *The New York Times,* Section 12, 1, 8.

Rutter, M. (1980). *Changing youth in a changing society: Patterns of adolescent development and disorder.* Cambridge, MA: Harvard University Press.

Sarason, S. B. (1982). *The culture of the school and the problem of change.* Second edition. Boston: Allyn & Bacon.

Schmidt, P. (1990, November 14). Law could bring different mix of immigrant pupils. *Education Week, 10* (11), 1, 32.

Schmidt, W. E. (1990, August 26). Lead paint poisons children despite 1971 law on removal. *The New York Times,* 1, 32.

Schorr, L. B., & Schorr, D. (1988). Within our reach: Breaking the cycle of disadvantage. New York: Anchor.

Scovic, S. P. (1991). Let's stop thinking choice is the answer to restructured schools. *The School Administrator, 1* (48), 19, 21, 26-27.

Shanker, A. (1990, June 17). Deregulating America's schools. Where we stand. *New York Times,* Section 4, E7.

Silver, P. F. (1983). *Professionalism in educational administration.* Victoria, Australia: Deakin University.

Slavin, R. E. (1987, October). Making Chapter 1 make a difference. *Phi Delta Kappan, 69* (2), 110-119.

Slavin, R. E., & Madden, N. A. (1989). What works for students at risk: A research synthesis. *Educational Leadership, 46* (5), 4-13.

Temple University Center for Research in Human Development and Education. (1990, June 15). *Center for education in the inner cities: A technical proposal.* Volume 1. Philadelphia: TUCRHDE.

Terry, D. (1990, August 5). Growing up where violence wants to come play. *The New York Times,* 1, 129.

Testa, M., Astone, N. M., Krogh, M., & Neckerman, K. M. (1989, January). Employment and marriage among inner-city fathers. *Annals of the Academy of Political and Social Science, 501,* 79-91.

U.S. Department of Health, Education, and Welfare and National Institute of Education. (1978, January). *Violent Schools - Safe Schools.* The Safe School Study Report to the Congress. Volumes 1 and 2. Washington, DC: H.E.W. and N.I.E.

Viadero, D. (1989, October 25). Drug-exposed children pose special problems. *Education Week, 9* (8), 1, 10, 11.

Viadero, D. (1990, November 28). Battle over multicultural education rises in intensity. *Education Week, 10* (13), 1, 11-13.

Wacquant, L. J. D., & Wilson, W. J. (1989, January). The cost of racial and class exclusion in the inner city. *Annals of the American Academy of Political and Social Science. 501,* 8-25.

Wagstaff, L. H., & Gallagher, K. S. (1990). Schools, families, and communities: Idealized images and new realities. In B. Mitchell & L. L. Cunningham (Eds.), *Educational leadership and changing contexts of families, communities, and schools.* Eighty-ninth yearbook of the National Society for the Study of Education, Part II (pp. 91-117). Chicago: University of Chicago Press.

Wang, M. C., Haertel, G. D., & Walberg, H. J. (1990, September-October). What influences learning? A content analysis of review literature. *Journal of Educational Research,. 84*(1), 30-43.

Wang, M. C., & Peverly, S. T. (1986). The self-instructive process in classroom learning contexts. *Contemporary Educational Psychology, 11,* 370-404.

Wang, M. C., Reynolds, M. C., & Walberg, H. J. (1988, November). Integrating the children of the second system. *Phi Delta Kappan, 69* (3), 248-251.

Watkins, B. T. (1990, October 10). Boston U. and Chelsea are optimistic, but wary, as they start 2nd year of school-reform project. *The Chronicle of Higher Education*, A14-A17.

Watson, B. C. (1987). *Plain talk about education: Conversations with myself.* Washington, DC: National Urban Coalition.

Wilkerson, I. (1989, September 3). New school term in Chicago puts parents in seat of power. *The New York Times*, 1, 26.

Wilson, J. Q. (1975). *Thinking about crime.* New York: Basic Books.

Wilson, W. J. (1987). *The truly disadvantaged: The inner city, the underclass, and public policy.* Chicago: University of Chicago Press.

Wilson, W. J. (1989, January). The underclass: Issues, perspectives, and public policy. *Annals of the Academy of Political and Social Science, 501,* 182-192.

Wolf, A. (1978, July). The state of urban schools: New data on an old problem. *Urban Education, 13* (2), 179-194.

Wong Fillmore, L. (1983). The language learner as an individual: Implications of research on individual differences for the ESL teacher. In M. A. Clarke & J. Handscombe (Eds.), *On TESOL 82: Pacific perspectives on language learning and teaching* (pp. 157-171). Washington, DC: Teachers of English to Speakers of Other Languages.

Zinsmeister, K. (1990, June). Growing up scared. *The Atlantic, 265* (6), 49-66.

2

Motivating Urban Children
to Learn

PATRICK B. FORSYTH

Many have come to believe that the shadow of wasted human possibility so evident in the worst of our urban schools is the single most important challenge facing our society. Programs have been instituted and specialists have been made available to help solve overwhelming problems, but intermittent and faceless social services housed in bureaucratic structures appear not to be the answer (Borman & Spring, 1984). Professional educators have grown weary of the finger pointing and externally imposed quick-fixes that have followed notoriety. Despite the sometimes overwhelming negative environment that engulfs our urban schools, this chapter advances a belief that energetic and caring adults can create a motivating environment for children that overcomes the residue of poverty and racism. The particular focus of this chapter, as it is for all the chapters, is the principal's role in this task.

Researchers have identified stages that principals go through as they become more effective: administrator, humanitarian, program manager, and systematic problem solver (Leithwood & Montgomery, 1984). The *administrator* is concerned primarily with running a smooth ship; the *humanitarian* directs energies to relationships, especially among the members of the professional staff; the *program manager* uses interpersonal relationships to improve achievement, and the *systematic problem solver* is focused on a "comprehensive set of goals for students," (p. 51) and discovering the best means to reach those goals. For those who find themselves in the principal's office of today's urban schools, it is especially important that they become systematic problem solvers. As problem solvers, principals have immediate and important effects on the school's learning environment, the instructional climate, attitudes of all those who participate in the school community, and consequently on the motivation and achievement of students and teachers (Klug, 1989).

One assumption of the approach used in this book is that the knowledge base for school administration should be constructed and organized inductively, starting from the problems and opportunities facing practicing administrators and ultimately incorporating principles of best practice, research findings, analytical frameworks, and finally, general explanations or theories. As defined in this book, a *problem of practice* is not simply *a* problem, but *a class of related and recurring problems or opportunities* facing public schools. Very importantly, a problem of practice is a way of organizing a set of intervention targets. When the Urban Initiative Project brought together a team of highly successful urban principals to reflect on their work, much of what they said seemed subsumable under a problem of practice that might best be called "motivating urban children to learn." Surprisingly, until recently, very little writing or research focused on the motivational work of principals (Maehr, Midgley & Urdan, 1992). Historically, the motivation of children to learn was considered the domain of teachers alone. What I present here is a set of frameworks to be used by principals for analyzing and intervening to create schools that enhance opportunity and desire to learn. Although much attention is paid here to the conditions of minority children (who make up a majority of many urban school populations), most of the analyses and interventions explored are presumed relevant to the motivation of all urban school children to learn, or indeed to the engagement of all children, regardless of their racial, social, or economic conditions.

In an effort to organize the analysis of the problem, I turn to the work of anthropologist John U. Ogbu who has written extensively about the education of minorities, especially what he calls "involuntary minorities" (Ogbu, 1986b). Ogbu has identified three explanatory focal points for examining learning and motivation among minority youth:

(a) explanations that focus on problems within schools; (b) explanations that focus on parents and family; and (c) explanations that examine cultural conflicts between children, school, and society at large. As Boyd (1991) has pointed out, most researchers would argue that all three focal points should inform a comprehensive approach, but this is seldom the case.

The organizational plan of this chapter might be thought of as three concentric circles with the principal standing at the center. Each circle (representing school, home, and culture) can be analyzed from the principal's perspective to discover how to increase the likelihood that children will be motivated to learn. Distinct frameworks for analyzing these three environmental spheres are appropriate. The formal authority of the principal to act in these spheres decreases as we move from the school itself to the larger society with its constituent cultures, despite the fact that the school's success is contingent on much that happens outside its walls. Consequently, the appropriateness of intervention processes varies as well. This analysis of the principal's role in motivating urban children to learn begins with analytical tools and intervention strategies related to the school itself. It then considers the family and community. Finally, a discussion of aspects of involuntary minority culture is used to provide insight into the urban schools and the challenges facing our society, especially those peoples systematically limited because of poverty and racism.

Motivation: Within the School Itself

First we take up the principal's use of the school itself to enhance motivation of children to learn. Since the principal knows the school and has recognized influence and authority in that environment, it is a good place to start the on-going task of enhancing motivation. In fact, the principal is expected to intervene and change the school, its structures and processes. The problem of practice called "motivation of urban children to learn" helps principals analyze and direct interventions systematically and in ways that consistently increase the probabilities that learners will be motivated.

Two frameworks are helpful in analyzing schools and suggesting comprehensive intervention possibilities for enhancing motivation. The first is a framework directed at reducing student alienation focused mainly on the organizational features of schooling; the second is a framework directed at shaping a task-focused learning environment. These approaches overlap each other and there is nothing to prevent a principal and school from using both frameworks simultaneously. The notion of acting on factors that alienate and factors that enhance involvement at the same time seems quite reasonable.

Reducing Student Alienation

As Comer (1989) has noted, the possibility of school success for urban children will be greatly enhanced if schools can reduce the alienation of children, families, and other groups within the school community. The framework for analyzing and reducing student alienation is based primarily on the work of Newmann (1989). When discussing alienation, Newmann draws on a long history of psychological and sociological literature referring to the fragmentation, estrangement, and separation felt by individuals, as well as objective structural conditions that are political, economic, and social. Newmann (1989) argues that the possibility of reducing alienation creates a moral obligation to do so.

> The fact that schools vary considerably in the extent of student and staff commitment and engagement indicates that the ills of modernization do not fall uniformly on all schools. The evidence that some schools are operated in ways that minimize the alienating features of modern life offers reason enough to continue the quest. (p. 257)

Distilling the literature of organizational theory and social psychology, Newman identifies six general issues related to the reduction of student alienation: the basis of membership, the nature of organizational goals, organizational size, decision-making structure, members' roles, and the nature of the work. In our terminology, these issues can be considered points of analysis and intervention within the school. Each will be considered from the distinctive perspective of the urban school principal.

1. *The Basis of Membership.* Etzioni (1961) argues, organizational participants whose membership is coerced are very likely to be alienated. Referring to some New York City schools of the time, he notes that

coercion plays an especially important role in schools "in which a large number of disciplinary cases are concentrated" (p. 48). It follows from Etzioni's discussions of power and orientation to the use of power, that student alienation "is reduced if students and their parents voluntarily develop and attend schools whose educational purposes they share" (Newmann, 1989, p. 159).

The issue of voluntary choice is an especially troubling issue for many of today's urban schools. They may be the schools that no one would choose, had they any choice; consequently, they are the schools most likely to serve highly alienated students and their families. As an issue of public policy in a democratic society, the choice issue poses a dilemma. On the one side is voluntary choice of school with the derived benefits of student and familial involvement and the probable negative consequences of racial segregation and economic discrimination. On the other side is no choice, student alienation, the likelihood of an increasingly coercive environment, but the benefits of possible racial integration and perceived social justice.

Since the school choice issue has been a state-level policy question, principals operate in a milieu where that decision has already been made. Either parents can send their children to the public school of choice, or they can not. But, it is still important for principals to generate alternatives and offer choices about a variety of school issues to reduce alienation, particularly in schools where students and parents have not freely chosen their school. Being a "problem solver" in Leithwood and Montgomery's (1984) terms, means making aggressive and creative efforts to provide choice for students and parents, regardless of the constraints under which a particular school operates.

Offering choices within the school is important, so that students and parents feel they have, and in fact do exert, some control over their schooling or their child's education. The issues and structures over which choices can be offered are numerous: schedule, teachers, counselors, courses, activities, public service involvement, school subunit membership, unique educational and work related programs, and so on. It is often easier not to offer choices, to treat students as cases being integrated, lockstep, into the existing school program. But generating choices gives students, parents, and teachers reason to come together to discuss the children's best interests. It gives the important adults in each child's life occasions to express visible interest, the importance they attach to education, concern, and affection for the child. It can give the student, parents, and teachers a better understanding of each other's needs, hopes, and limitations, especially if the advice of Noddings (1992) is heeded: "Teachers, whether singly or in teams, should stay with students (by mutual consent) for three or more years" (p. 73).

2. *The Nature of Organizational Goals.* Citing Rutter's study, Newmann (1989) says that the symptoms of engagement or non-alienation, such as "achievement, attendance, students' participation in school beyond the required time, and low levels of delinquency" (p. 161), are found in schools where expectations are clear.

> The call for greater clarity and consistency in school goals is not an endorsement of dogmatic, socially homogeneous schools that violate individuality. Rather, the challenge is to build clear, internally consistent goals which are compatible with the values of the school's clientele but which also respond to individual diversity. (p. 161)

Again, the processes of engagement can seem at odds with the other important goals, such as the embrace of diversity. "Sharper goal definition is also required for communal identity, for if all students pursue different educational missions, nothing binds them to one another except temporary use of a common facility" (Newmann, p. 160).

The challenge for the principal is working with teachers and parents to create an integrated set of clear expectations for all students. As Foster (1986) points out, "Overt or subconscious lowering of behavioral or academic standards for any students or group of students would, in itself, constitute the most insidious form of racism" (p. xii). The motivation literature has examined the notion of teacher expectation in some detail, especially as it affects achievement. But, as Brophy (1985) notes, "there is reason to believe that teacher expectations affect a broad range of student outcomes in addition to achievement, and that expectations about what is appropriate for the class as a whole may be even more important than expectations about individual differences within the class" (p. 210). The writing of the last 20 years is replete with findings supporting the notion that high expectations by adults have a positive effect on student achievement. This is true for children regardless of their economic or ethnic characteristics.

Reducing ambiguity and seeking clear and consistent goals is not something that is likely to happen overnight. It is a long-term activity, a bridge-building exercise that requires trust and self-revelation, listening, and a willingness to gently pursue and articulate an emerging set of community beliefs and the expectations that flow from those beliefs. For the forging of communal identity and a consequent reduction of student alienation, it would seem that bold clarity about a few goals is a more likely route to success than obscure generalizations about a multitude of educational and developmental goals.

3. Organizational Size. Newmann's (1989) assertion about size and its relationship to alienation is quite clear: "The larger the school, the more difficult it is to achieve clear, consensual goals, to promote student participation in school management, and to create positive personal relations among students and staff" (p. 161). The number of students assigned to a particular public school is not determined by the principal. However, there are at least two strategies principals can use to reduce alienation due to the negative effects of large size . One strategy is to develop mechanisms that directly encourage the benefits of small size, for example, consensus on instructional goals. Such consensus might be easily achieved (or already exist) in a small homogeneous school community. To achieve the same level of consensus in an urban school would take more time, and require specific efforts to shape goals by meeting with parents and teachers and by providing opportunities for parents to learn about the existing goals of the school. In the urban environment, principals must use every opportunity to speak with parents, neighborhood groups, church groups, and social gatherings about the goals of the school. They must listen carefully to the ideas and feelings of the community and, where possible, incorporate these into the stated mission of the school.

Much can be done to enhance the participation of students in school management and interpersonal relationships among students and staff, even in very large schools. Schools can be structured to permit and encourage less formal interactions among students and the adults of the school community. Formal and informal opportunities for students to be heard on matters that concern them can be arranged. There is nothing mystical about talking to students about impending school decisions that need to be made, asking for their views, listening to their needs. Principals can help create traditions and expectations of teacher eagerness and availability to listen to the students, even after the school day is over.

A second strategy related to size involves reorganizing the schools so that the units of student identification are in fact small. Schools within schools, a house system, and homerooms are all strategies that have potential for contributing to student identification. The more time children spend in these units and the greater substantive role they play, the more they are likely to reproduce the desirable effects of small schools.

4. *Decision-Making Structure.* Although Newmann (1989) believes schools should maximize student participation (p. 162), he is not suggesting that professional authority of teachers be relinquished, nor that of administrators, nor that of the lay board. He is also not arguing that students should participate formally in all school decisions. He says: "Increasing the amount of sustained time that students spend with individual teachers and broadening the ways in which they relate, for example, is likely to offer greater student input and to increase faculty responsiveness" (p. 162).

So, Newmann would increase the sense students have that their views are listened to and sought out. Most often this would be an informal exchange between students and teachers and students and administrators. The school staff should be seen as inviting an open expression of student views about the school and how it works.

It is not difficult to see links in this line of reasoning to the locus-of-control construct used by Rotter (1966) and other social-learning theorists. Using a locus-of-control analysis, Lefcourt (1976) suggests that "urban dwellers confronted with incidents of violence and crime, and minority groups systematically excluded from opportunity, tend to hold fatalistic, external control beliefs" (p. 25). These are "externals." "Internals," in contrast, believe they can control the events of their lives (p. 21). There is evidence that children can change their locus of control (deCharms, 1972). This seems to be true if they experience connections between their acts and perceived results (Lefcourt, 1976, p. 126). Providing students with increased opportunity to affect their school environment and other aspects of school life gives them a sense of agency, increases the belief in their ability to control events in their lives, and not incidentally, engages them.

5. Members' Roles. Two characteristics of modern schools, specialization and emphasis on individual achievement, militate against the formation of personal and trusting relationships among members of the school community—students, teachers, and administrators. Specialization tends to limit the scope of interactions between teachers (and other school specialists) and students, defining the relationships as professional/technical rather than human, personal, and holistic. Emphasis on individual achievement establishes the relationships among students as competitive rather than cooperative, at least with respect to academic achievement. Many of the structures and traditions of the school encourage competition. Bossert (1979), for example, found that lecture-style classes undermine cooperation by setting up students to compete publicly for teacher approval. In contrast, group-work and individual-seat-work instructional approaches were more likely to encourage student cooperation (Bossert, 1979).

> Trusting relationships are more likely to develop if students spend sustained time with teachers on an individual basis or in small groups, and if they engage together in a range of activities such as recreation, counseling, dining, housekeeping, or even the study of more than one subject. Extension of the student-teacher relationship beyond the typical meeting in a large group for fifty minutes a day to learn a single subject will give students and teachers a more complete understanding of one another. Extended contact generates a greater sense of communality, mutual caring and responsibility, than conventional transient and fragmented roles. (Newmann, 1989, p. 163)

There is a great deal that principals and teachers can do to reverse negative consequences of professional specialization and competition due to emphasis on individual achievement. The principal, working with all members of the school community, can plan immediate and long-term changes in school goals and structures that are directed toward these contributors to alienation.

Newmann suggests that student-to-student relationships could be more constructive if there were expectations that they "counsel, and lend support to one another, and if they were to function in groups to accomplish academic goals, provide recreation, offer community service, and care for the school" (p. 164).

6. The Nature of the Work. In discussing the need for integrated work, Newmann (1989) refers to Oliver's (1976) claim that work should be responsive to the primal and modern dimensions of human nature. "Primal tendencies include the need to experience a direct relationship between work and physical survival, to work with simple tools, cared for and controlled by the worker, and to integrate work itself with human personality" (Newmann, p. 165). Modern tendencies deal with what is more abstract or technological and less with physical work. Newmann sees traditional schoolwork as excessively responsive to modern tendencies and nonresponsive to primal needs. "Schoolwork that incorporates more activities directly related to human survival, involving concrete signs of success and failure, and that highlights unique contributions of individual students, would help to increase students' sense of integration" (p. 165).

Although it is easy to see how integrating school activity with primal aspects of childrens' lives would make school more immediately relevant, this goal seems to be one of the more difficult ones to achieve. The nature and quantity of contemporary knowledge seems increasingly modern, not primal. Yet, especially for children who face the daily challenges of deteriorating urban life, the primal issues are ever present. Principals and teachers will have to struggle with the charge to give more emphasis to the primal issues. Community-based learning, challenge education (programs emphasizing dramatic transition to adulthood by self-testing and risk taking in such things as community service, physical adventure, and artistic creation [Newmann, 1989, p. 168]), and career-vocational education are some directions these efforts can explore.

In sum, an understanding of how school structure and organization can contribute to student alienation provides a useful framework for analyzing the school environment and searching for intervention points likely to improve student motivation. Although not a traditional way to consider the work of the principal, insights gained from investigating alienating characteristics can provide keys to building involvement among all members of the school community.

Shaping a Task-Focused Learning Environment

A second approach to the principal's role in motivating children to learn, focused on the school itself, is directed at the learning environment. The framework presented here for shaping a task-focused learning environment is based on the work of Maehr, Midgley, and Urdan (1992). They underscore the importance of the principal's role in motivating children.

> Our research leads to the proposal that school leaders affect student motivation. They do so as they inaugurate, support, maintain, allow, or permit certain policies, practices, and procedures. Their action or inaction frames the learning environment of the school, that facet of the culture that is especially associated with the purposes of teaching and learning. As leadership and staff deal with fundamental questions of school management, they inevitably reflect a rationale for teaching and learning. They define the meaning of school for students and thereby affect the nature and quality of student investment. (p. 114)

Maehr et al. (1992) cite recent studies of achievement and motivation, especially investigations of the relationship between goals and student investment in learning (p. 411). Two kinds of goals are identified: task focused and ability focused. In a system emphasizing ability-focused goals, children are concerned with comparative judgments made about their abilities. When the system emphasizes task-focused goals, children are concerned with gaining understanding, skill, or meeting a challenge (p. 411).

Maehr and his colleagues believe that goal orientation significantly influences both motivation and learning.

> Children with a task orientation tend to use deep-processing strategies, including discriminating important from unimportant information, trying to figure out how new information fits with what one already knows, and monitoring comprehension. Children with an ability focus tend to use surface-level strategies, including rereading text, memorizing, and rehearsing. (pp. 411-412)

Furthermore, it is argued that goals affect motivation, and that the learning environment affects the goals that students adopt, whether ability focused or task focused. Classrooms differ as to how learning is defined, and these definitions influence which goals students will adopt, ultimately affecting motivation and learning (p. 412). Their argument continues and extends to the school level, which they say also reflects variability in goal emphasis.

In their article titled "School Leader as Motivator," Maehr and colleagues describe a collaborative intervention project in several metropolitan Detroit schools (pp. 410-429). The intervention was directed at aspects of school context that contribute to goal orientation, whether toward ability goals or task goals. Using a body of substantive research as a basis for their plan, the authors "identified seven areas that school leaders could examine in attempting to affect the learning environment of the school" (pp. 415-423), specifically enhancing its task focused orientation.

1. The Nature of Academic Tasks. This notion closely parallels Newmann's (1989) Nature of the Work category described above, but it is discussed from the perspective of increasing motivation rather than limiting alienation. The tasks students undertake in the classroom determine the kinds of goals they will pursue (Maehr et al., 1992, p. 416). If primarily given workbook drills and other kinds of work materials minimally related to their lives, children are more likely to develop ability-focused goals. Given life-relevant and problem-solving tasks, they are more likely to develop task-focused goals. Principals have a great deal to do with what children will do in the classroom. They can encourage teachers to be risk takers and creative, or they can create slavish adherence to textbooks and narrow curricula (p. 416).

The nature of academic tasks is particularly important for developing motivation among urban children, especially those whose daily lives are affected by poverty. Their interests may be quite alien to the traditional curriculum content. Ingenuity and creativity are required to tap their interests and find ways to include what is important to them in the curriculum, as well as to include learning approaches that meet their needs.

2. Opportunities for Student Initiative and Responsibility. This subject also resembles one of Newmann's focal points for examining alienation, namely, Decision-Making Structure. Maehr et al. (1992, p. 417) cite motivation research supporting the notion that the school's provision of opportunities for initiative, responsibility, and choice will likely affect student school goals (Ames, 1990; Deci, 1975; Deci & Ryan, 1985). By increasing the opportunities for student initiative and responsibility, school principals are also likely to increase the task focus of students (Maehr et al., 1992, p. 417).

3. *Recognition.* In the Detroit project, Maehr and colleagues worked with teachers to recognize students on the basis of progress, improvement, and effort, thus fostering a task focus (p. 417). There are recognition programs in schools, usually sponsored by the principal, that for example, reward students for getting the best grades. This approach often communicates to the school community the notion that relative ability is more important than task mastery (p. 418). In many schools, the honor roll is an example of this approach, and often it is the only means for giving academic recognition to students.

Although recognition can play a role in creating a task orientation, deCharms (1983) has warned about the dangers of the uncritical use of reinforcers in schools. "If an action is freely initiated through choice and then it is discovered that someone else desires the actor to do the action so much that the other will reward him or her for doing it, then the actor may lose the feeling of freedom, ownership, and choice" (p. 279). Principals, teachers, and parents need to work carefully to reward effort, the personal best, and deemphasize competitions that simply reward ability.

4. *Grouping.* Ability grouping in American schools is common practice. Children know which ability tracks they have been placed in, and, as Maehr et al. (1992) indicate, this situation "encourages the emergence of a learning environment that stresses the demonstration of ability and minimizes the focus on learning" (p. 419). For those children who have repeatedly experienced the curtailment of opportunity because of race or poverty, placement in the "go nowhere group" reinforces one more time the fact that society, including the school, has already decided their future. Ability grouping is a practice that clearly militates against a task focus, and consequently undermines efforts to motivate children to learn.

Principals can do a great deal to minimize or eliminate ability grouping. The decision to group, at the school level, usually belongs to the principal. But the principal also needs to persuade the faculty, after careful examination of the research, that the benefits of heterogeneous grouping far outweigh any benefits on the other side. Cohen's book, *Designing Groupwork*, describes ways to succeed with multi-ability groups of learners and ways to inhibit the formation of destructive status orders among children (1986).

5. Evaluation Practices.

A large body of literature is available on the effects of evaluation practices on student motivation and learning (Covington
& Omelich, 1987a, 1987b; Hill, 1980; Hill & Wigfield, 1984;
MacIver, 1991). Briefly summarized, the findings indicate that
these practices are fraught with possibilities for encouraging
students to approach academic tasks as competitive contests to
see who is the smartest and the best. Focusing as they do on
outcome and performance, regardless of the place at which the
learner starts, many evaluation practices are likely to suggest
that the purpose of learning is to define relative ability rather
than to assess the individual's progress in mastering a particular skill or acquiring certain knowledge. Investing in the task
for learning's sake, to understand, to gain new knowledge and
skill is probably undermined by typical evaluation practices.
Evaluation practices can and often do define the name of the
game as one in which some win and others lose. Too often, they
define some students as perpetual and inevitable losers. (Maehr
et al., 1992, p. 420)

The elimination of evaluation practices is not being argued here—
on the contrary. Evaluation is an important part of learning. However,
the principal and the school community can create evaluation procedures
and an evaluation environment that stress effort, learning, skill acquisition, and creativity. Generally, evaluations should not be public, since
any evaluation can be turned into a competition. Evaluations should
help children, teachers, and parents to make course corrections, acknowledge learning and effort, and design interventions when they are
appropriate.

6. Resources. Regardless of district policies, principals have some
choices about resource acquisition and distribution. These choices
affect the goal orientation of the school both symbolically and substan-

tially. For example, some schools deny access to certain activities and specialized equipment such as computers to low-achieving students (DeVillar & Faltis, 1991, p. 104; Maehr et al., 1992, p. 421). These policies proclaim the importance of relative ability, excluding those who fail to meet the ability standard or goal (Maehr et al.,1992, p. 421).

The principal's resource choices can emphasize professional development of teachers, instructional innovation, and the purchase of equipment and supplies that are accessible to all children. Although the choices may be far fewer than most principals would like, the choices made convey an important message about what the principal values and the strength of commitment to establishing a task focus within the school.

7. Organization of the School Day. "The schedule should be the servant of instruction, not the boss. It is a significant purpose of leadership to make it that" (Maehr et al., 1992, p. 423). Flexible scheduling is an extremely important facilitating feature of the school. In itself, it does not guarantee a task focus, but it is more suited to a task focus than traditional scheduling, which accommodates lecturing. Flexible schedules can promote heterogeneous grouping, student choices, independent student work, variety in instructional styles, instructional innovation, learning task variety, field trips, project work, variety in evaluation technique, and other possibilities related to a task focus and improved motivation. Traditional schedules are unnecessarily restrictive for students and teachers. The organization of the school day can be a powerful tool to create variety and excitement, while carefully giving students more responsibility and control over their learning.

This completes the discussion of the two frameworks for analyzing and intervening in problems within the school itself. The first framework concentrated on six school characteristics that affect student alienation. The framework can be used by the principal and the school community to help design schools that engage students. The second framework presented seven antecedents to shaping a task-focused learning environment. The ways the principal can affect the learning environment were discussed, with an emphasis on shaping task focus and reducing an ability focus.

Motivation: The Family and the School

A second place principals can focus efforts on enhancing motivation to learn is the family. Obviously the approaches a principal and school can use with families will be quite different than those used within school structures, but there is no question about their importance. "The concurrent influences on children by families and schools may be similar or different, positive or negative, and more or less effective—but the influence is inescapably synchronous from preschool through high school" (Epstein, 1989, p. 259).

This section on parents and family will present a single framework for analysis and intervention. The framework includes six major home structures that affect motivation and that should help principals and teachers collaborate with families to increase motivation to learn.

Home Structures Affecting Motivation

Despite clear and consistent reports on the importance of family environments for student success, there have been few efforts to identify the specific, alterable structures of home environments that create conditions that support children's learning and development. There has been even less attention to the mechanisms by which family organizations and practices motivate children to develop behaviors and attitudes that characterize successful students. (Epstein, 1989, p. 260)

Epstein has identified six variables to help teachers organize instruction. She argues that these structures have analogs in the family and these "should be the target of attention to improve family influence on children's motivation to learn" (p. 261). The structures form the acronym TARGET, referring to Task, Authority, Reward, Grouping, Evaluation, and Time. Each structure will be considered in turn.

1. *Task Structure.* By task structure at home, Epstein refers to

. . . the range of children's activities, including household chores delegated by parents; learning opportunities designed by parents; homework assigned by teachers; and play and hobby activities selected by children. It includes all activities

directly or indirectly related to school learning that are conducted at home by children alone, with parent, siblings, or
others. (p. 261)

The home environment can be a source for organizing a great
variety of tasks. Research demonstrates that the learning opportunities
parents provide have a great many social, academic, and life-skill
related benefits (p. 262). Home-initiated activities are nearly limitless
in terms of location and time flexibility. They can involve a great variety
of people, including parents, siblings, and other children, as well as
social, community, and religious groups. They can involve a variety of
agencies and institutions: museums, public television programming,
libraries, universities, park and recreation departments, and the like.
They can involve the use of technology and games to learn and acquire
skills (p. 261).

As children get older, their tasks need to be adjusted to provide the
appropriate, necessary challenge. In many cases, parents know how to
structure and provide task opportunities for young children, but as
children grow older, parents seem less secure and knowledgeable
about providing challenging tasks. Schools should play a more visible
role in helping families adjust the home task structure appropriately (p.
273). Principals, teachers, children and their parents, need to communicate more completely about the importance of a home task structure.
Schools can use a variety of means to provide examples and specific
activities for home learning (p. 271).

Epstein argues that challenging home tasks result in positive attitudes about all kinds of tasks, including homework. Home tasks that
are not overly predictable can increase natural curiosity, self-confi-
dence, a sense of achievement, knowledge, and other competencies and
can accustom the child to taking on tasks without unwarranted anxiety
(p. 284).

2. *Authority Structure* . "The authority structure at home concerns
the types and frequency of children's responsibilities, self-directed
activities, and participation in family decisions" (p. 263). Patterns of
familial shared decision making may extend to school where children
exposed to participation in the home will be more vocal and participative. Children should increasingly become participants in decisions;
not to increase decision-making opportunities for older children may

have serious consequences for learning and motivation (Epstein, 1983, 1984).

Epstein links authority structure with the locus-of-control concept discussed earlier. She found that in families where children's decision-making opportunities were increased gradually as they mature, children increased feelings of internal locus of control (Epstein, 1983). School programs for parents, close ties between school professionals and parents, and other approaches can be used to encourage developmentally sound authority structures in families.

3. Reward Structure. "The reward structure at home concerns the procedures and practices that recognize children's efforts and accomplishments" (Epstein, 1989, p. 264). Parents develop patterns of paying attention to a variety of their children's behaviors, achievements, or talents. The rewards they offer may be subtle or dramatic; they may be directed at ability, effort, or gains in skill (p. 264). All of these variations have consequences for childrens' motivation to learn.

Most important are the attitudes of parents, other adults, and siblings about the importance of school and schoolwork, which are embedded in the home reward structure. Making school an important and frequent topic of conversation in the home sends a clear message to children. It provides the opportunity and setting for them to talk about their efforts and accomplishments at school. Enthusiastic attention to these expressions is an important reward for children. Placing value on schoolwork and activities associated with the school by families is critical to the motivation to learn.

> Schools need to help parents understand, monitor, and reward students' attitudes and achievements. With each new grade level, parents need more assistance from teachers, administrators, guidance personnel, and others to understand where their children are starting from, what they are working toward, and how to recognize and reward progress in order to maintain or boost children's motivation to learn. (p. 265)

Developmentally, older children probably have different reward needs than younger children. Unable to handle delayed gratification, frequent small rewards and attentions seem generally appropriate for younger children. The reward structure needs of older children may be different. Rewards may be less frequent, take greater variety, be suggested by the child, and be tied to the effort or some special interest. "But, whether frequent or intermittent, attention and recognition from the family continues to be important for children at all grade levels. The goal is to create conditions at home so that, over time, children feel intrinsically rewarded by learning" (p. 275).

There are important consequences of the home reward structure. "High self-esteem is likely to be produced, maintained, and increased for more children if the reward structure at home emphasizes improvement rather than top grades" (p. 284).

4. Grouping Structure. Grouping at home is like school grouping "that determines whether, how, and why students who are similar or different on particular characteristics (for example gender, race, SES [socioeconomic status], ability, goals, or interests) are brought together or kept apart for instruction, play, or other activities" (p. 265).

Families prepare children for their roles in social groups by "training in prosocial behaviors such as comforting, sharing, defending, helping, and cooperating" (p. 266). The fortuitous and planned groups in which children participate in the home, in the extended family, and in the neighborhood provide the training ground for all future social interactions. These efforts affect children's learning, especially when success depends on cooperation with others (p. 266). Social skill development has very important consequences for peer acceptance and the formation of friendships. "Learning problems may develop if children lack the social skills that help them work together and make friends in school with other students" (Epstein, 1989, p. 285).

Schools can help parents recognize the importance of the peer group and siblings in establishing attitudes about school and schoolwork. For example, families can create expectations that homework will be done before other activities. When families that live in close proximity have similar expectations, they are even more effective. Schools can encourage neighborhood, school-related interaction, providing opportunities to demonstrate the community value placed on school and promoting common practices about peer group activities and schoolwork (Epstein, 1989, p. 267).

As children grow into the upper grades, parents should not abandon their interest in their children's peer group. They should know their children's friends and families and they should work to create a warm and open home environment that encourages children to spend time in the home with their friends. When parents fail to show interest in their children's peers, "they may overemphasize the importance of conformity to peer standards and values, and repudiate family and personal values including the importance of learning at school" (Epstein, 1989, p. 277).

5. Evaluation Structure.

The evaluation structure at home concerns (1) the standards that are set by parents and children for learning and behavior, (2) the procedures for monitoring and judging the attainment of those standards, and (3) the methods for providing information about performance or needed improvements. (Epstein, 1989, p. 267)

Many kinds of evaluations of children may go on in the home. Some are more conducive to motivation than others. Positive evaluations by parents, siblings, and peers often motivate, especially when given in front of a group. The frequency of evaluations should be moderate, too many or too few tend to send the wrong message (Epstein, 1989, pp. 267-268). Often evaluations suggesting improvement should be done without an audience. As suggested earlier, evaluations might focus on effort and improvement rather than ability to encourage a task orientation.

Schools need to provide families with information about the school's evaluation goals and practices so that the two structures can be integrated, and so that parents can help children respond appropriately to school evaluations.

If the parents and children set clear, sequential, and attainable standards, the evaluation structure at home will challenge and support the success and satisfaction of most children and will encourage their continued motivation to learn. If the messages are immediate, corrective, constructive, and offered with affection (as opposed to delayed, uninformative, destructuve, and uncaring), children's efforts are more likely to be directed toward learning and improvement. Parents' frequent, informative, and individual evaluations that focus on the child's

improvements are important supplements to schools' heavily
summative evaluations. (Epstein, 1989, pp. 268-269)

Older children can and should participate more in the evaluation
process, helping to set the standards and participating in detailed
discussions about the intensity and quality of their work. Over the
years of their school career, there should be a gradual transfer from
parental to self-evaluation, the former never disappearing entirely
(Epstein, 1989, p. 277).

6. *Time Structure.* "The time structure at home concerns the schedules families set for children's activities and assignments" (Espstein,
1989, p. 269). Family time structures vary a great deal. Some approaches are so relaxed that they result in lateness and incomplete
schoolwork; other families are so tightly scheduled that it is difficult to
find time for school-related work. Neither of these extremes is ideal.

Schools can help families understand their children's time needs
for school-related work. Family schedules need to be adjusted to
accommodate these important needs, sometimes including the need for
quiet. Creating an environment of respect for the time at home
dedicated to homework can be a genuine motivator. Epstein's research
has demonstrated that, regardless of ability and familiy background,
parental time spent helping or monitoring homework improves both
children's attitudes and achievements (Epstein, 1989, p. 270).

Time structures at home that reflect the time needed for learning
increase children's sense of purpose, persistence, and performance on assigned tasks (Maehr, 1984, as cited in Epstein, 1989,
p. 285). These motivating forces lead to better homework
completion, greater accumulated knowledge, and improved
time management. These skills may contribute to the development and maintenance of children's abilities to plan, control,
and complete their work, and they help students see how
school and learning are important investments in their lives.
(Epstein, 1989, pp. 285-286)

The challenge for urban principals and teachers is to find ways to
connect the family and the school, the family's structures and the
school's structures. The difficulties inherent in urban schools, espe-

cially those serving families living in poverty or suffering the cumulative effects of diminished opportunity, require extraordinary effort on the part of the school staff and parents. Parents need to know that the school staff wants to form a partnership to insure the success and happiness of their children. Families in the conditions just described have a special need for respect, support, and the school staff's confidence that parental effort will have positive effects on the motivation and achievement of children. These parents, just because they face the daily hardships of urban life, need to be invited to participate in the construction of a vital school community.

"A common bond between parents and teachers seldom develops naturally or spontaneously. Hence, one priority in the years ahead will be leadership that can bring these adults together as a constructive force for helping all students learn, particularly those who are marginal" (Sinclair & Ghory, 1987, p. 156).

Motivation: Cultural Conflicts and the School

The third focus of the principal's efforts to improve motivation to learn in the city school should be the larger cultural environment. Because of the particular challenge represented by the significant presence of minority peoples in urban communities, long the victims of restricted opportunity, prejudice, and racism, this discussion is based on the cogent and important analyses of Ogbu and Fordham. If schools can give hope to these peoples and engage their children sufficiently to succeed in school, the likelihood is that all children, including those who come from advantaged families, will benefit.

In genteel Sweden, where Finnish people are considered inferior, Finnish children fail in school far more often than Swedish children. In Australia, however, where they are perceived as positively as other Scandinavian immigrants, Finnish children do as well as anyone else. By now it is fairly well known that Japanese American children do as well as or better than most white students in California high schools. What is not so well known is that some of these fine Japanese American students are descendants of the Burakumin, a group whose members are considered genetically inferior by other Japanese and often fail in school in Japan. Similarly, Koreans who live in Japan do poorly in school, but Korean immigrants to the United States do quite well. Finally, blacks who immigrate to St. Croix in the Virgin Islands from nearby non-American islands do better in school than blacks who are natives of St. Croix, and blacks from Jamaica do better in one Washington, D. C., high school under study than do the blacks who grew up in the ghettos of the nation's capital. (Zweigenhaft & Domhoff, 1991, p. 145)

These findings helped Ogbu formulate an explanation for a perplexing question: Why are American-born black children not as successful in school as white children who come from comparable socioeconomic and social class conditions? (1988a, p. 169-170). Clearly, these studies rule out genetic or racial explanations, as well as cultural deficiency explanations (Zweigenhaft & Domhoff, 1991, p. 146). Ogbu's explanation is an intriguing and convincing one that has important implications for urban schools.

Ogbu identifies two distinct types of minorities: immigrants and involuntary minorities. Immigrants voluntarily come to the host country with a hope of improving their lives. They also compare their present situation favorably with the situation in their native country, and very significantly, they retain an identity with a primary culture, usually with its own language. For these reasons, immigrant children tend to do well in the schools of their newly adopted country (Ogbu, 1978). Their voluntary status results in a culture that enhances attitudes and behaviors that are associated with success in school (Ogbu, 1989).

Mark Mathabane both exemplifies and reflects this phenomenon. As a South African attending college in the United States, he was unsuccessful in persuading American blacks to join him on the school newspaper staff. However, two black immigrants from the West Indies did join him and he reflected on this fact.

They confirmed a phenomenon I had encountered before. I had discovered that most black students from immigrant families were less inclined to allow white racism to prevent them from realizing their dreams. They were hardworking, and came from stable families which adhered to strict values of respect, discipline, pride, and success. They knew that racism existed in America; they everywhere confronted obstacles and setbacks; yet they kept fighting, and eventually succeeded in spite of bigotry. (Mathabane, 1989, p. 105)

Ogbu contrasts immigrants to this country with involuntary minorities, peoples enslaved or conquered. In addition to blacks brought here as slaves, he includes as involuntary minorities Native Americans and Mexican Americans of the Southwest, the former who were often placed on reservations against their will, and the latter who "were subjugated and stripped of their land as recently as 1848" (Zweigenhaft & Domhoff, 1991, p. 147). Using these distinctive categories of minorities, Ogbu concludes that the "gaps in school performance appear and persist only when racial groups are stratified in a castelike form" (1988a, p. 169).

Subordinate minorities tend to respond to their exploitation by developing oppositional identities and oppositional cultural frames of reference (Ogbu, 1988a, p. 176). The oppositional identity forms in response to perceived patterns of discrimination and exclusion. For blacks, it is a social identity system "which they perceive and experience not merely as different but more particularly as in opposition to the social identity system of their dominators" (p. 176). Behaviors and attitudes associated with the dominant culture are deemed inappropriate for the dominated culture.

An oppositional cultural frame of reference emerges "which includes devices for protecting their identity and for maintaining boundaries between them [blacks] and white Americans" (Fordham & Ogbu, 1986, p. 181).

> The closely related concept of oppositional cultural frame of reference refers to those beliefs and practices that protect black people's sense of personal identity against the insults and humiliations of the dominant white group. Since these beliefs and practices provide a defense against racism, they necessarily exclude certain white cultural traits as inappropriate, and some of these oppositional practices help to keep whites at a distance when need be. Thus, this oppositional cultural frame of reference creates unconventional ways of moving, gesturing, talking, and thinking that are viewed as irrational and frightening by whites. (Zweigenhaft & Domhoff, 1991, p. 152)

For involuntary minorities, there exist two conflicting cultural frames of reference, one for the dominant culture, and one for theirs. Theirs is an oppositional culture, defining attitudes and behavior appropriate for the minority and inappropriate for the dominant culture. "The oppositional cultural frame of reference becomes particularly important in the school context because black Americans (like similar minorities) generally equate school learning with the learning of the culture of the dominant group, or white culture" (Ogbu, 1988a, p. 177). Thus, for members of involuntary minorities to succeed in school, they must turn their backs on their own cultural frame of reference, their own identities, and act white (p. 177). As Signithia Fordham notes in her fascinating ethnography of a Washington, D.C. high school, "Black adolescents consciously and unconsciously sense that they have to give up aspects of their identities and of their indigenous cultural system in order to achieve success as defined in the dominant-group terms; their resulting social selves are embodied in the notion of racelessness" (1988, pp. 81-82).

Especially within the peer group, acting white can be viewed as cultural betrayal. However, defining behaviors and attitudes as white (such as working hard for grades, punctuality, speaking standard English, and the like) creates serious problems for minorities, since many of these are behaviors and attitudes necessary for success in school (Ogbu, 1988b, pp. 177-178). Minority students who want to succeed in school must adopt some strategy to cope with the conflict between their oppositional culture and the dominant culture of which the school is a part. Ogbu identifies eight coping strategies based on ethnographic research on the black experience (1989, pp. 198-199).

1. Assimilators are those who adopt a white cultural frame of reference. They have come to believe that they cannot be successful in both cultural frames and they have chosen to be successful in school. They are generally successful, but often suffer isolation and criticism.

2. Emissaries play down black identity and cultural frame of reference to succeed, but they do not reject them. They follow the rules and remain marginal members of the black peer group. Their motto is "Do your Black Thing but know the Whiteman's Thing."

3. Alternators adopt the immigrant approach, accommodation without assimilation. They do not reject their black identity or cultural frame of reference, but they also play by the rules. They

tend to adopt secondary coping strategies such as being involved in "black activities" or playing the clown.

4. The Reaffiliated are students who may have rejected the black cultural frame of reference until they encountered powerful examples of racism. They may become more involved with their black peers, but they may also continue to do well in school.

5. The Ivy-leaguers are black youths who exhibit middle-class behaviors. They belong to middle-class social organizations, are well-liked, and appear to be good students.

6. The Regulars are members of the street culture but do not go along with it entirely. They are good students, have close family ties, follow the rules and know how to stay out of trouble.

7. The Ambivalents need to be with their black peer group and they also need to succeed in school. They do not resolve this conflict and so their school performance tends to be erratic.

8. The Encapsulated equate success in school with "acting white," which they refuse to do. They do not try to learn or follow the rules. Generally they do not succeed in school.

These coping strategies underscore the critical importance of the oppositional identity and culture for involuntary minorities who happen to be school children. It is interesting to note that the oppositional identity for American blacks did not always include an ambivalence toward success in school. "The earlier, Southern-based oppositional identity adopted by American blacks held a positive attitude toward education. This attitude toward education persisted among blacks who moved to the North in the years after World War II but seems to have been transformed in the 1960s by the experience of new forms of racism in the inner city" (Zweigenhaft & Domhoff, 1991, p. 156).

Fordham and Ogbu suggest three changes related to alleviating the burden of acting white (1986, pp. 202-203). The first change they argue is a prerequisite for the others, namely, that the job ceiling and related barriers for American blacks must be removed. Obviously this is a change that cannot be enacted by the school principal, yet its importance is clear. The school community can remove these barriers in its own environment first, by working to achieve a cultural and racial balance within the adult school staff, a balance approximating that of the student population.

Second, they urge that "educational barriers, both the gross and subtle mechanisms by which schools differentiate the academic careers of black and white children, should be eliminated" (p. 203). Many of these barriers, along with strategies for eliminating or reducing them, have been discussed in this chapter under the frameworks for reducing alienation and building a task-focused learning environment.

Third, they argue that the learning and performance difficulties resulting from the burden of acting white should be made the focus of educational policies and remediation effort (p. 203).

The black community has an important part to play in changing the situation. The community should develop programs to teach black children that academic pursuit is not synonymous with one-way acculturation into a white cultural frame of reference or acting white. To do this effectively, however, the black community must reexamine its own perceptions and interpretations of school learning. Apparently, black children's general perception that academic pursuit is "acting white" is learned in the black community. The ideology of the community in regard to the cultural meaning of schooling is, therefore, implicated and needs to be reexamined. (p. 203)

About Motivation Theory

Anyone who is familiar with the scholarly literature devoted to the subject of motivation knows that it is extraordinarily complex and non-convergent. In the last 10 years, however, several important research series have contributed immensely to the simultaneous distillation and expansion of this area of inquiry. The *Advances in Motivation and Achievement* research annuals, having published volume 7 in 1991 (Maehr & Pintrich, 1991), is one of these sources. Another extraordinary contributor to this field has been the *Research on Motivation in Education* series, which published volume 3 in 1989 (Ames & Ames). Finally, the Minnesota Symposia on Child Psychology is another rich source, having published its volume 23 in 1991 (Gunnar & Sroufe).

An especially useful and recent theoretical model is that of Connell and Wellborn (1991, pp. 43-77). The approach is useful to school practitioners and researchers partly because much of the early empirical work used to refine the model was based on schools. Connell and

Wellborn's is a model of self-system processes that begins with the assertion that people have fundamental psychological needs to feel *competent*, to feel *autonomous*, and to feel *related*.

For school children, competence includes knowing what it takes to do well in school and believing they have the skills to succeed. Autonomy has to do with why they act to succeed (operationalized as self-regulatory style): because they enjoy school activities and schoolwork, because they will get in trouble if they don't do it, because they will feel bad if they don't do it, or because they believe it will enable them to meet future goals. Relatedness describes their feelings of emotional security with social partners.

According to Connell and Wellborn, these three psychological needs interact with three important social context aspects (structure, autonomy support, and involvement) in the home, school, and classroom. *Structure* is defined as the amount, clarity, and quality of information regarding expectations and consequences. *Autonomy support* is defined as the provision of choice and promotion of connectedness between actions and individual goals. Finally, *involvement* is defined as the degree of knowledge about, interest in, and emotional support for the individual (See Connell and Wellborn, 1991, Figure 2.3, p. 55).

Thus, feelings of competence, autonomy, and relatedness are shaped in the social context of structure, autonomy support, and involvement. These, in turn, affect patterns of action that range from engagement to disaffection. "When psychological needs are being met within particular cultural enterprises such as family, school or work, engagement will occur and be manifested in affect, behavior, and cognition" (1991, p. 52). For example, *engaged cognitive patterns* of action for school children would include flexible problem solving, active coping with failure, attentiveness, preference for hard work, independent work styles, and independent judgment. Contrast the engaged cognitive pattern with the *disaffected cognitive pattern*: rigid problem solving, passive coping with failure, bored, preference for easy work, dependent work styles, and dependent judgment.

This theoretical model, although presented here in dangerously skeletal form, connects quite directly with earlier discussions of alienation, task structure, and family structures, as well as the formation of an oppositional cultural frame of reference.

For example, the social context of Connell and Wellborn's model is considered from the perspective of school environment in Newmann's alienation discussion when he argues the need for choice (related to Connell and Wellborn's autonomy support) and the importance of clear expectations (related to Connell and Wellborn's structure). Likewise, Maehr and colleagues, in their discussion of shaping a task focused learning environment, argue the importance of opportunities for student initiative and responsibility, and the significance of school day organization, which correspond to Connell and Wellborn's autonomy support and structure, respectively. Epstein's home structures are equally relevant to Connell and Wellborn's notion of social context as it affects children's psychological needs. Clearly this is only one of many theoretical perspectives on motivation that might have been referenced in this chapter. This one was included because it is illustrative of some particularly heuristic explanations, it is very relevant to the motivation of children to learn, and it informs the discussion of motivating urban learners as organized in this chapter.

Conclusion

I have relied on Ogbu's original focal points for examining learning and motivation among minority children: the school, the home, and the culture. My approach has been to consider "motivating urban children to learn" as a problem of practice for the principal. By problem of practice, is meant an aggregation of related problems and opportunities organized in such a way as to constitute a substantial chunk of the principal's work. This way of organizing helps to integrate research, knowledge gleaned from practice, reflection, and intervention strategies for enacting change.

To help analyze the motivation problem while focusing on the school itself, two frameworks were introduced, one for examining organizational structures of the school for possible alienating effects on urban children. The other framework concentrated the principal's attention on shaping a task-focused learning environment. Both of these approaches, it was argued, require a principal who can enlist the energies and enthusiasm of a competent staff and whole school community.

To explore the motivation problem while focusing on the home, Joyce Epstein's framework for examining home structures that affect motivation was discussed. Epstein's framework was attractive because its elements have counterparts in the school's structures and the argument can be made that these home and school structures can be made to complement one another. Because the principal's role in this arena of motivating children to learn is rather new, necessity must stimulate invention. The evidence appears to be mounting that the schools cannot improve without creating integral relationships with families.

Finally, to organize the examination of the relationship between motivation to learn and culture conflict, I relied primarily on the research and theoretical perspectives of John Ogbu and Signithia Fordham. They emphasize the formation of an oppositional cultural frame of reference, in response to repeated patterns of exclusion and discrimination, by those termed involuntary minorities such as American-born blacks, Mexican Americans, and Native Americans. In the last 30 years, the oppositional culture has defined success in school as "acting white," producing conflict and stress for non-immigrant minority students who seemingly must choose between their own cultural identity and success in the schools of the dominant culture. Although minority children have developed some coping mechanisms to mediate the conflict, a more satisfactory solution would involve the modification of the oppositional cultural frame of reference in such a way that success in school is not identified as abandoning one's culture or acting white. Principals, especially principals who are members of minority groups, can help precipitate discussions and actions that make it OK for children to succeed in school, regardless of their identity and culture.

References

Ames, C.., & Ames, R. (Eds.) (1989). *Research on motivation in education: Goals and cognitions,* Vol. 3. San Diego, CA: Academic Press.

Ames C. (1990). Motivation: What teachers need to know. *Teachers College Record, 91,* 409-421.

Borman, K. M. , & Spring, J. H. (1984). *Schools in central cities: Structure and process.* New York: Longman.

Bossert, S. T. (1979). Tasks and social relationships in classrooms: A study of instructional organization and its consequences. Cambridge, UK: Cambridge University Press.

Boyd, W. L. (1991). What makes ghetto schools succeed or fail? *Teachers College Record, 92,* 331-362.

Brophy, J. (1985). Teachers' expectations, motives, and goals for working with problem students. In C. Ames & R. Ames (Eds.), *Research on motivation in education*, Vol. 2, *The Classroom Milieu*. San Diego, CA: Academic Press, Inc.

Cohen, E. G. (1986). *Designing Groupwork: Strategies for the heterogeneous classroom*. New York: Teachers College Press.

Comer, J. P. (1989). Poverty, family, and the Black experience. In G. Miller (Ed.), *Giving children a chance: The case for more effective national policies* (pp. 109-130). Washington, DC: Center for National Policy Press.

Connell, J. P., & Wellborn, J. G. (1991) Competence, autonomy, and relatedness: A motivational analysis of self-system processes. In M. R. Gunnar & L. A. Sroufe (Eds.), *Self processes and development*, The Minnesota Symposia on Child Psychology, Volume 23. Hillsdale, NJ: Lawrence Erlbaum.

Covington, M. V., & Omelich, C. L. (1987a). "I knew it cold before the exam": A test of the anxiety-blockage hypothesis. *Journal of Educational Psychology, 4*, 393-400.

Covington, M. V., & Omelich, C. L. (1987b). Item difficulty and test performance among high-anxious and low-anxious students. In R. Schwarzer, H. M. van der Ploeg & C. D. Spielberger (Eds.), *Advances in test anxiety*. Vol. 5. Hillsdale, NJ: Lawrence Erlbaum.

deCharms, R. (1972). Personal causation training in the schools. *Journal of Applied Social Psychology, 2*, 95-113.

deCharms, R. (1983). Intrinsic motivation, peer tutoring and cooperative learning. In J. M. Levine & M. C. Wang (Eds.), *Teacher and student perception: Implications for learning*. Hillsdale, NJ: Lawrence Erlbaum.

Deci, E. L. (1975). *Intrinsic motivation*. New York: Plenum.

Deci, E. L., & Ryan, R. M. (1985). *Intrinsic motivation and self-determination*. New York: Plenum.

DeVillar, R. A., & Faltis, C. J. (1991). *Computers and cultural diversity: Restructuring for school success*. Albany, NY: State University of New York Press.

Epstein, J. L. (1983). Longitudinal effects of person-family-school interations on student outcomes. In A. Kerckhoff (Ed.), *Research in sociology of education and socialization*. Vol. 4. Greenwich, CT: JAI Press.

Epstein, J. L. (1989). Family structures and student motivation: A developmental perspective. In C. Ames & R. Ames (Eds.), *Research on motivation in education, 3, Goals and cognitions.* San Diego, CA: AcademicPress, Inc.

Etzioni, A. (1961). A comparative analysis of complex organizations. New York: The Free Press.

Fordham, S. (1988). Racelessness as a factor in black students' school success: Pragmatic strategy or pyrrhic victory? *Harvard Educational Review, 58,* 54-84.

Fordham, S., & Ogbu, J. U. (1986). Black students' school success: Coping with the "burden of 'acting white.'" *The Urban Review, 18,* 176-206.

Foster, H. L. (1986). Ribbin', jivin', and playin' the dozens: The persistent dilemma in our schools, 2nd ed. Cambridge, MA: Ballinger, 1986.

Gunnar, M. R., & Sroufe, L. A. (Eds.) (1991). *Self processes and development: The Minnesota symposia on child psychology,* Vol. 23. Hillsdale, NJ: Lawrence Erlbaum.

Hill, K. T., & Wigfield, A. (1984). Test anxiety: A major educational problem and what can be done about it. *Elementary School Journal, 84,* 105-126.

Klug, S. (1989). Leadership and learning: A measurement-based approach for analyzing school effectiveness and developing effective school leaders. In M. L. Maehr & C. Ames (Eds.), *Advances in motivation and achievement,* Vol. 6; *Motivation enhancing environments.* Greenwich, CN: JAI Press.

Lefcourt, H. M. (1976). *Locus of control: Current trends in theory and research.* Hillsdale, NJ: Lawrence Erlbaum.

Leithwood, K. A., & Montgomery, D. J. (1984). *Patterns of growth in principal effectiveness.* Paper presented at the American Educational Research Association Annual Conference, New Orleans, LA, 71 pages.

MacIver, D. (1991, April). *Enhancing students' motivation to learn by altering assessment, reward, and recognition structures: An evaluation of the incentives for improvement program.* Paper presented at the annual meeting of the American Educational Research Association, Chicago.

Maehr, M. L. (1984). Meaning and motivation: Toward a theory of personal investment. In C. Ames & R. Ames (Eds.), *Research on motivation in education*, Vol. 1, *Student motivation*. San Diego, CA: Academic Press.

Maehr, M. L., & Pintrich, P. R. (Eds.) (1991). *Advances in motivation and achievement*, Vol. 7. Greenwich, CT: JAI Press.

Maehr, M. L., Midgley, C., & Urdan, T. (1992). School leader as motivator. *Educational Administration Quarterly, 28,* 410-429.

Mathabane, M. (1989). *Kaffir boy in America*. New York: Scribners.

Newmann, F. M. (1989). Reducing student alienation in high schools: Implications of theory. In L. Weis, E. Farrar & H. G. Petrie (Eds.), *Dropouts from school: Issues, dilemmas, and solutions*. Albany, NY: State University of New York Press.

Noddings, N. (1992). *The challenge to care in schools: An alternative approach to education*. New York: Teachers College Press.

Ogbu, J. U. (1978). *Minority education and caste: The American system in cross-cultural perspective*. New York: Academic Press.

Ogbu, J. U. (1988a). Class stratification, racial stratification, and schooling. In L. Weis (Ed.), *Class, race, & gender in American education*. Albany, NY: State University of New York Press.

Ogbu, J. U. (1988b). Diversity and equity in public education. In R. Haskins & D. MacRae (Eds.), *Policies for America's public schools*. Norwood, NJ: Ablex.

Ogbu, J. U. (1989). The individual in collective adaptation: A framework for focusing on academic underperformance and dropping out among involuntary minorities. In L. Weis, E. Farrar & H. G. Petrie (Eds.), *Dropouts from school: Issues, dilemmas, and solutions*. Albany, NY: State University of New York Press.

Oliver, D. W. (1976). *Education and community: A radical critique of innovative schooling*. Berkeley, CA: McCutchan.

Rotter, J. (1966). Generalized expectancies for internal versus external control of reinforcement. *Psychological Monographs, 1.*

Sinclair, R. L., & Ghory, W. J. (1987). *Reaching marginal students: A primary concern for school renewal*. Berkeley, CA: McCutchan Publishing.

Zweigenhaft, R. L., & Domhoff, G. W. (1991). *Blacks in the white establishment: A study of race and class in America*. New Haven, CT: Yale University Press.

3

Managing Instructional Diversity

LINDA F. WINFIELD
RUTH JOHNSON
JOANNE B. MANNING

The issue of *diversity* as a problem of practice faced by urban school administrators emerged as a pervasive theme during the opening discussions at the UCEA-Danforth Select Conference in 1989. However, participants found little agreement on what this concept meant. Principals articulated disparate ideas, such as "problems dealing with heterogeneity," "refugee/immigrant populations," "lack of cultural awareness," "achievement discrepancies among subgroups," "curriculum that does not encompass students at risk," "average/underachievers," and "closing the gap in achievement between minority and nonminority youngsters." Of 101 responses, principals rated "achievement discrepancies among minority and nonminority youngsters," "curriculum for diverse students," and "equity and access to quality teaching" among the top five problems facing urban school administrators. Participants at the conference recognized that these issues were not isolated problems but were related to systemic and structural

---

AUTHORS' NOTE: I would like to thank Joyce Epstein, at The Johns Hopkins University, for providing substantive critiques to an earlier draft of this chapter.

issues, such as recruiting qualified teachers and financing urban schools. Of the 99 items generated in response to the question of imaginable administrative tools for creating successful urban schools, "timely development of curriculum materials for diverse populations," "increased coordination and collaboration between instructional programs," "a strong tutorial program," "fluid across-grade ability grouping," "elimination of tracking by grade level," and "restructuring student assignment based on need" emerged as favored tools. Unfortunately, principals at the conference indicated that strategies for handling these problems were typically learned on the job rather than in administrative preparation programs. In response to a question regarding the most useful things learned about urban school leadership before coming to the job, principals indicated "components of effective schools research relevant in urban schools," "strategies for dealing with student diversity," "development and implementation of plans for school improvement," "working with diverse cultures," "equity of instructional resources," and "sensitivity towards diverse individuals and family structures." These topics indicate that a critical problem of practice in the administration of urban elementary schools is: how principals manage instructional resources.

The core issue is that to provide an effective schooling experience for students from diverse populations, principals must understand how their management decisions regarding resource allocation impact student learning. Administrative decisions concerning time allocation, curriculum/textbook selection, grouping, and student placement influence teaching and learning in all schools (Dreeben & Barr, 1983). What makes the urban school context unique is the interaction of these administrative decisions with the kinds and amount of diversity represented in urban student populations. The differential impact on student learning outcomes is evidenced by the achievement gap between racial/ethnic groups (Lee, Winfield & Wilson, 1991).

The goal of this chapter is to synthesize and present information that may help current and aspiring urban school principals understand the relationships that exist between management/organizational practices, instructional resources, and learning outcomes of diverse student groups. Although the primary focus of the chapter is on elementary schools, the content is also appropriate for secondary-school principals.

In dealing with diversity, two strategies typically used in schools to allocate and manage instructional resources are the assignment of students to various programs and groupings and the assignment of personnel to various classes. These strategies result in particular teacher beliefs about student learning and inequities in students' access to knowledge. The following review of the extant knowledge base is organized around three interrelated components: (a) conceptions of student diversity in urban schools, (b) assignment of students, including a historical perspective, and (c) access to knowledge. The final section presents implications for urban school administrators as well as for institutions of higher education.

What We Understand

Student Diversity

The issue of diversity in urban schools developed initially out of a concern for students from various racial/ethnic groups and lower socioeconomic backgrounds. Gordon (1982) notes:

> In earlier work, great attention was given to the characteristics of these populations and the ways in which they differed from the so-called majority population. As that work progressed, we have come to realize that it was in error. . . . by implying they represented a relatively homogeneous group. They do not. . . . They have poverty and low status and certain kinds of neglect and maltreatment as common characteristics, but in terms of their other characteristics they vary as much within this group as they do between the lower- and higher-status groups. . . . Ethnic and class status is important for political purposes but relatively unimportant for pedagogical purposes. (p. 1975)

Epstein (1988) has discussed a similar concept of student diversity that refers not only to social and ethnic backgrounds but also intra-group differences in learning rates, motivation, and other factors that result in varied achievement outcomes. Thus, student diversity within the urban context includes differences in native language groups as well as diversity in developmental stages, home academic support, "giftedness," religion, and handicapping conditions. Within each particular student grouping, individual differences in learning rate, student attitude, interests, and motivation also increase the differences that schools and teachers must accommodate.

Managing instructional resources to accommodate student diversity in learning outcomes begins with questions regarding whether differences in learning outcomes should be reduced, maintained, or increased (Epstein, 1988). Differences between groups can be reduced or eliminated by restricting the advancement of capable students or by increasing the advancement of slower students. Instructional methods such as whole class instruction, mastery learning, remedial instruction, and emphasis on minimum competency testing are designed to minimize diversity, whereas individualized instruction, homogeneous grouping, gifted and talented programs, and advanced placement courses are designed to increase diversity among students (Epstein, 1988). In general, whether to promote or reduce diversity of outcomes is not a cut-and-dried management decision. School community values as well as philosophy of the district may be considered. Schools may choose to minimize differences in achievement in some subjects (for example, basic skills in reading), and increase diversity in others (for example, advanced level mathematics). With the advent of many district, state-level, and proposed national assessment programs, the decision regarding which subject areas are considered important for all students to master has been partially predetermined. The proponents of national testing and examination systems would set universal standards for students; in general, these systems fail to take into account the diversity of learners (Winfield & Woodard, 1992). At the same time, the movement toward site-based management provides schools with greater discretion to determine the "how" of arriving at these outcomes. In urban schools, any consideration of the process must take into account the issue of managing instructional resources to meet diverse student groups.

Cultural Mismatch

The high proportions of students from diverse racial/ethnic and SES backgrounds who experience failure in America's urban schools suggest a systemic problem. Educators acknowledge the ideals of cultural pluralism but, traditionally, schools have not been effective for large numbers of students from diverse cultures, socioeconomic backgrounds, and racial/ethnic groups (Barton & Wilder, 1964; Winfield, 1991b). Over a decade ago, Arciniega (1977) noted that public education had successfully focused blame for the failure of schools to meet the needs of minority students onto those students:

> They have pulled off the perfect crime, for they can never be truly held accountable, since the reasons for failure in school are said to be the fault of poor homes, cultural handicaps, linguistic deficiencies, and deprived neighborhoods. The fact that schools are geared primarily to serve monolingual, white, middle-class, and Anglo clients is never questioned. (p. 54)

Despite many reforms in the last decade, few schools have made progress incorporating information into the curriculum concerning the achievements of traditionally underrepresented groups. A Euro-centric bias continues to dominate the American educational system (Hare, 1989; Pine & Hilliard, 1990; Trachtenberg, 1990). A pluralistic environment requires a fundamental change in a school's self-image, philosophy, curriculum, and approach to a multi-ethnic student population (Hare, 1989; Banks & Banks, 1989). Some researchers suggest that the curriculum must be completely restructured rather than simply expanded (Banks & Banks, 1989). This modification is achieved when underlying assumptions of the curriculum are changed and students are enabled to view concepts, themes, and problems from several ethnic perspectives. Throughout the curriculum, frames of reference, history, culture, and perspectives of various ethnic groups are infused. This fundamental change in the school's curriculum acknowledges the extent to which Western culture has been intertwined with other cultures, and emphasizes appropriateness, legitimacy, and acceptance of African-American and Hispanic cultures as subjects of study equal to Euro-American culture (Trachtenberg, 1990). Recent reforms based on a cultural infusion model have focused on changing curricular content to be more appropriate for diverse student populations (Shujaa, 1991). This emphasis is needed and necessary but not sufficient to eradicate the overrepresentation of African-American and Hispanic students as "school failures." The problems of inequity of access to knowledge and opportunity to learn require total restructuring of the system in order to optimize the fit and connections between schools' instructional resources and diversity of student needs.

One of the challenges facing urban school administrators is managing available instructional resources to maximize the fit between programs and students' learning regardless of racial/ethnic group or socioeconomic background. Identifying and recognizing patterns of diversity among students means that management decisions must be made regarding time allocation, assignment of personnel to classrooms, and assignment of students to instructional groups. Such decisions regarding resources will impact students' access to knowledge and opportunity to learn. Traditional solutions that "blame the victim" and attempt to change the student have generally failed. For example, we continue to see a rise in the use of Ritalin in school-age populations, a solution that appears to be an easy and quick fix. The alternative-to change the schools-is much slower, more difficult, and based on the premise that all children, except those who have obvious biological or physical problems, have the capacity to learn school-related subjects. The difficult but effective solution is that school and classroom organization must adapt to student needs (Epstein, 1988).

What We Know

Remnants of Past Attempts at Dealing With Diversity

Educators and policymakers, nearly 25 years ago, recognized the issue of diverse student needs based on inequitable learning outcomes. The Elementary and Secondary Education Act, Title 1, of 1965 (reauthorized as Chapter 1 of the Educational Consolidation and Improvement Act of 1981) and Public Law 94-142 (Education for All Handicapped Children Act, passed in 1975) were designed to target resources to schools based on student needs. In the case of ESEA Title 1, criteria were based on educational and economic need, whereas for PL 94-142, criteria focused on exceptionalities or special needs. These two federal programs provided substantial fiscal and legal incentives for school districts to offer additional instructional services for their children, many of whom were from diverse backgrounds and experienced difficulties in the regular curriculum (Allington & McGill-Franzen, 1989). In general, all American public schools now provide both remedial and special education services. Title 1, now known as Chapter 1, became the largest of the compensatory programs and set a precedent for federal aid to education.

Implementation of Programs

With the increased funding to schools and districts, government regulations for compliance were expanded. At the school and district level, separate administrative structures were established to oversee federal categorical programs. At the district level, typically, a director of federal programs was in charge of hiring staff and overseeing curriculum and instruction for Chapter 1 eligible students. This person often had little or no interaction with other directors or curriculum supervisors in the district who may have been in charge of instructional services for other students. Most districts had separate administrative structures for Chapter 1 and Special Education (Allington & McGill-Franzen, 1989). In most districts, the process for identifying students was separate from instructional planning. Group-administered standardized achievement tests were used to determine eligibility, no identified curriculum for reading instruction was provided in support programs, and there was little overlap in participants in the two programs (Allington & McGill-Franzen, 1989).

At the school level, federal regulations required that the allocation of resources be restricted to poor or low-scoring students.[1] Chapter 1 supported teachers could provide additional instructional services to eligible students only. Because Chapter 1 is a supplemental program, students are also to receive instruction in the regular school program. One of the regulations ("supplement not supplant") indicated that the eligible Chapter 1 student should receive instruction in addition to classroom instruction and not in lieu of it. This rule has often been misinterpreted to mean that instruction in Chapter 1 has to be totally different from the regular classroom and, as a result, a lack of curricular congruence or consistency can occur (Allington & Johnston,1989; Johnston, Allington & Afflerbach, 1985). The implementation of these regulations results in a *profession-oriented* delivery of instructional services (Venezky & Winfield, 1979). This type of service delivery occurs when each program retains its own independence, emphasizes its own special instruction and materials, and establishes territorial claims to certain groups of students. The typical instructional mode for Chapter 1 services continues to be the pull out model, in which students are physically removed from their regular classroom to receive their supplemental instruction.

Thus, past attempts at managing instructional diversity in urban areas have resulted in a proliferation of separate categorical and special programs, labeling, and dramatic increases in the number of students placed in special education.   The translation of direct services for students became mediated by a self-protective and self-perpetuating bureaucracy. The rigidity that developed in operating the system made it virtually impossible to serve students adequately (Carter,1984; Winfield,1986a). Consequences of these past attempts in urban settings were that the regular teaching staff, and often the principal, did not assume responsibility for ensuring that the lowest-achieving students (many of whom were Chapter 1 or Special Education students) would succeed (Winfield, 1986b). Also, the school experience of students enrolled in these programs was typically fragmented and of a lower quantity and quality of instruction (Allington, 1984; 1987; Allington & Broikou, 1988; Allington & Johnston, 1989; Johnston, Allington & Afflerbach, 1985).

In urban schools, problems of coordination are compounded by other programs based on a profession-oriented delivery system (for example, English to Speakers of Other Languages, Gifted, Speech and Hearing, Resource Room).   Urban principals have many resources available, yet there are difficulties managing them in order to adapt instructional programs to students' needs. The major problem with past attempts to meet the diversity of student needs is an underlying assumption that schools themselves did not have to change (Kaestle & Smith, 1982). Rather, federal regulations required separate administrative structures that coexisted within the school organization and, once established, these structures became immutable at the district and school level. Moreover, many schools serving disadvantaged students failed to show a measurable impact on facilitating achievement outcomes. Those few exemplary school programs in urban areas that were successful in improving student outcomes had derived systems for coordinating service delivery based on students needs (Venezky & Winfield, 1979). In several schools, principals were key in facilitating the collaborative, coordinated environment; in others, district officials were critical (Allington & McGill-Franzen, 1989; Venezky & Winfield, 1979). Where this effort did not occur, students' access to knowledge and opportunity to learn were severely limited (Winfield, 1986b).

Because of training, experience, and other factors, most school building principals are quite comfortable in managing school facilities, budgets, and personnel matters, but experience some difficulties in managing instructional resources. Many urban school principals, when asked to list or name the number and types of supplemental instructional programs or personnel within their school building, cannot do so without considerable difficulty (Winfield, 1982).

Problems of Access to Knowledge

As implemented, categorical programs produced conditions that limited access to knowledge for students. Although the original intent of federal funding (such as Title I) was to promote educational equity, separate administrative structures and profession-oriented services tended to reduce students' access. These conditions produced inequities in the quality of teaching and the curriculum. The quality of the teaching force in urban areas can be considered in terms of personal characteristics of teachers and structural characteristics (working conditions, how personnel are assigned, contractual obligations). It is beyond the scope of this chapter to provide a comprehensive review of all factors that influence quality. The following discussion, therefore, is limited to two issues of teacher quality that affect students' access to knowledge. The first, teacher beliefs, is related to the notion of personal responsibility for students' learning. The second, assignment of personnel, reflects a management decision regarding the allocation of resources.

Teacher Beliefs

Knowledge of the content of teacher beliefs in urban settings is an initial step toward identifying variables within the school that mediate the thinking and practice of teachers (Bunting, 1984). Beliefs about teaching and learning influence expectations and judgments made about student abilities, effort, and progress within a particular classroom. In case studies of urban schools, teacher beliefs about low-achieving students could be categorized on two dimensions. One dimension, labeled *improvement-maintenance,* indicated whether teachers believed some type of instructional assistance was needed to improve the achievement of low-achieving students or whether they ignored the students' low levels of performance. A second dimension of teacher beliefs reflected specific behaviors and practices in dealing

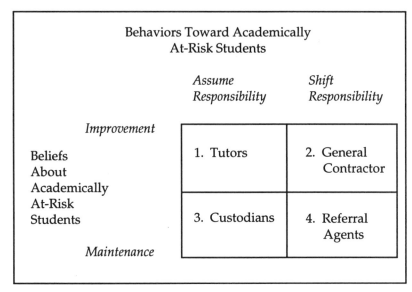

Figure 3.1. Cross-Classification Matrix of Teachers' Beliefs. SOURCE: *The Urban Review,* Vol. 18, No. 4. 1986, Teacher beliefs toward academically at risk students in inner urban schools, p. 257.

with these students. These behaviors were categorized by whether teachers assumed the responsibility for improving instruction or shifted the responsibility to others. A cross-classification analysis revealed four possible types of belief/behavior patterns within this framework. These patterns are depicted in Figure 3.1.

An example of teachers' responses identified in the first cell was, "I work with the low group about 20 minutes a day to reinforce skills." Teachers in this cell were labeled tutors since they indicated it was their responsibility to provide instruction necessary to improve the reading achievement of the bottom reading group. Teachers' responses in the second cell indicated that remedial instruction was needed, but that it wasn't necessarily their responsibility. A frequent response from teachers listed in this category was, "I send my bottom group to the Title I (now Chapter 1) aide." Another response was, "We have a district-funded supplementary remedial program for the low achievers." These teachers were called general contractors, since students were distributed to other individuals who were responsible for improving achievement.

Teachers' responses identified in the third cell reflected the belief that there was little or nothing that could be done to improve the performance of academically at-risk students. An example of a response in this category was, "A few will be on grade level, the other students will just get passed on." Another frequent claim was, "These kids need some high-interest/low-level reading materials." Teachers in this cell were labeled custodians because their primary concern was maintenance of low levels of achievement. Teachers in the fourth cell, referral agents, reflected an attitude similar to the custodians, however the responsibility for maintenance was shifted to others. Unlike "general contractors," teachers in this fourth cell felt that at-risk students were generally incapable of learning in a classroom situation or in supplementary programs. These teachers commonly referred students for psychological testing or special education.

Teachers' beliefs derive from their perceptions or sense of control over classroom learning, or their knowledge (or lack thereof) of appropriate strategies and interventions in urban settings. The larger school context also influences teachers' beliefs. The proportion of teachers' responses categorized as maintenance-oriented (cells 3 and 4) were substantially higher in those urban schools with multiple instructional programs utilizing a profession-oriented service delivery model. Within the context of these models, the responsibility for diverse student groups who are having difficulty becomes diffused. Teachers must use information from a variety of sources in making pedagogical decisions and behave rationally according to simplified models of reality that they construct (Shavelson & Stern, 1981). In a model of teacher decision making, Shavelson and Stern (1981) suggested that institutional constraints influence teacher judgments and decisions.

In many inner-urban schools, the absolute number of federal- and district-funded supplementary instructional programs may function as institutional constraints that influence teachers' judgments and discretionary behavior. Some teachers become "general contractors" in response to the management of a particular supplementary program within their school buildings. Alternatively, supplementary programs might be considered an institutional license that allows some regular classroom teachers to avoid teaching the less academically able students. These students are more easily dismissed as being the responsibility of special programs, remedial reading teachers, or federal programs.

Assignment of Personnel

In addition to teacher belief systems, the assignment of teachers to classrooms affects the quality of teaching for diverse student groups. Maeroff (1988) noted that "urban schools have no monopoly on uninspired teaching, but it takes a terrible toll on students who are already unmotivated" (p. 638). Similarly, Oakes and Keating (1988) suggest: "Those who need good teaching and who have the least resources for remedying the effects of social and economic isolation draw the least prepared and temporary teachers" (p. 32). Underqualified teachers are disproportionately found in predominantly black, Hispanic, and Native American schools and classrooms (Oakes, 1985; 1986). Teacher shortages are greater and higher numbers of underqualified entrants to teaching are generally found in central-city schools where most poor and racial/ethnic minority students reside (Darling-Hammond, 1990, Watson & Traylor, 1988). Darling-Hammond (1990) suggests that teacher shortages diminish educational quality by making it difficult for districts to be selective in the quality of teachers they hire and by forcing them to hire short- and long-term substitutes and assign teachers out of their fields.

In general, urban school administrators have little discretion over teachers assigned to their schools. District personnel policies and union contractual agreements impose limits. However, two factors contribute to the inequality in personnel assignments. First is an incentive structure that makes less difficult assignments the only reward for seniority and skill. As a result, beginning teachers typically teach the most challenging students in tougher schools, then transfer out to schools where there are better working conditions and students who are easier to teach (Darling-Hammond, 1990). Second, and related to the first concern, is the tracking of teachers within a school building. Teacher assignment to classes reflects a decision regarding the allocation of instructional resources. Several studies have found that lower-level classes are often taught by poorer teachers (Coleman et al., 1966; Spady, 1973). This may be due in part to the preference of more able teachers to work with higher-level classes, to seniority, or to a school level assignment policy that favors the brighter students (Finley, 1984; Hargreaves, 1967; National Education Association, 1968; Rosenbaum, 1976).

In one urban elementary school, the principal acknowledged that the group of second-grade teachers in his school was "weak" (that is, inexperienced, or lacking skills in teaching reading). All of the class-rooms were organized hetereogeneously. Managing such a classroom requires training that few teachers receive and skills that relatively few of them acquire (Darling-Hammond, 1990). For the previous two or three years, students' performance at this particular school in second grade had been far below the standardized test performance of the other grades. The principal's solution was to assign all of the "weak" second-grade teachers to teach third grade, rather than to mobilize available resources to assist and strengthen teachers' skills in teaching reading or assigning well-prepared, highly skilled teachers to that group of second-graders (Winfield, 1982). In his view, the immediate problem at second grade was solved; however, for that cohort of students who would have the "weak" teachers again at third grade, the problem was exacerbated. In other urban elementary schools, what is known as an "X roster" is established, which consists of all of the students with academic and behavior problems identified by teachers; the new, inexperienced teacher, or long-term substitute, is usually assigned to this class. At the other extreme, the most skilled teachers offer rich, challenging curricula to select groups of students identified as "gifted" (Darling-Hammond, 1990).

At the secondary level, teacher assignment reflects compromises and tacit agreements regarding the allocation of desirable and undesir-able classes. Finley (1984) noted that teachers use a variety of strategies to avoid teaching the remedial classes. Although teachers indicate their formal preferences, an informal process occurs among department members. Electives and advanced courses are considered the property of teachers who currently teach them. However, creation of a selective course in the elective program or a new course targeted toward higher-ability students would reduce the number of allotted classes and minimize the likelihood of teaching remedial students. Another means that teachers have of improving their job rewards is by decreasing the numbers of the worst students in the classes they teach. Teachers influence class composition by encouraging certain students who may be having problems to transfer out in the first weeks of school. Other teachers may gain a reputation of being tough for failing many remedial students so that the least motivated students select other teachers of the same course. The lower social status attributed to lower tracks (for example, academic versus vocational tracks) is also attributed to teach-ers. This situation results in negative self-perceptions as well as institutional selection of teachers for the lower curricular tracks. The various activities of teachers used to increase their individual rewards actually helped to shape the tracking system by creating above-average, below-average, middle-track classes, and the advanced track for gifted students. Added to the institutionalized tracking that occurs in secondary schools, this situation results in curricular inequities for many students from diverse backgrounds.

Inequity in Curriculum

Numerous studies have found minimal effects for most forms of ability grouping (Slavin,1987;1988) and tracking (Gamoran & Berends, 1987); however, the rationale typically provided by schools and teachers is to increase the fit between school programs and students of different abilities (See Oakes & Lipton, 1990, for a review of this area). Schools are limited in their effort to accommodate instructional programs and classes to fit student capabilities by the distribution of student ability, class size, physical arrangement of classrooms, availability of teachers and other instructional resources, imposed curricular requirements, and the norms governing access of students to educational resources (Hallinan & Sorenson, 1983). Despite these structural and organizational constraints on the formation of homogeneous groups, this has been the primary method of managing instruction for diverse groups.

The major issue is whether those in the lower groups/tracks have equal access to knowledge and opportunity to learn.[2] More often than not, racial/ethnic minorities and students from lower SES backgrounds are overrepresented in the lower or non-college bound groups, and are underrepresented in programs for the gifted (Braddock, 1989; Darling-Hammond, 1985). Oakes (1985) suggests that assumptions are made about what different kinds of students are able to learn. This extends not only to what teachers believe they are able to master in the way of skills, but also ideas and concepts teachers believe appropriate for them to be exposed to. Several studies have found that, in lower tracks at the secondary level, instruction is conceptually simplified and proceeds more slowly than in higher-tracked classes (Gamoran & Berends, 1987). In lower-tracked classrooms, teachers lower academic standards, tend to emphasize basic skills and factual knowledge, and resort more frequently to structured activities and drill (Evertson, 1982; Hargreaves,

1967; Heathers, 1969; Keddie, 1971; Leacock, 1969; Metz, 1978; Oakes, 1985; Rosenbaum, 1976; 1980; Schwartz, 1981). Teachers may omit topics from their lessons altogether (Oakes, 1985). Oakes (1985) found that much of the content of lower-tracked classes was such that it would lock students into that track level not so much as a result of the topics that were included for instruction but because of what was omitted.

At the elementary level, inequality in the curriculum is reflected in opportunity to learn and varies substantially for those students in lower-ability groups. Barr and Dreeben (1983) have shown that the average aptitude of instructional groups exerts greater influence on learning pace than individual aptitude. Similarly, Rowan and Miracle (1983) found that students in fourth-grade lower-ability classrooms were paced more slowly (controlling for their individual ability) than students in higher-ability classrooms and that differential pacing reinforced initial achievement differentials. A study of grouping for reading instruction in a first-grade classroom indicated a sequence of lower attentiveness leading to greater teacher management, to more disruptions of reading turns, and to less time on learning in lower-ability groups. Members of the lower groups paid attention only about 60% of the listening time, while their counterparts in the higher group were attending nearly 80% of the time. There were twice as many management acts and reading-turn disruptions in lower as in higher groups (Eder, 1981). For students in remedial reading, such as Chapter I, both the quantity and quality of instruction was less (Allington, 1987; Allington & Johnston, 1989). Most children in remedial or LD classes for learning disabled students were found to spend the majority of scheduled pull-out instructional time engaged in non-academic activities. Counting time for traveling to site, social greetings, wait and off-task time, there was little time left for instruction. The instruction that did occur was focused on short, low-level tasks and typically not coordinated with the regular classroom instruction.

The problems of teacher quality and inequities in the curriculum in urban schools affect access to knowledge critical for the success of diverse student groups. The challenge for urban school principals in managing instruction requires a working knowledge of how management decisions and administrative policies (concerning such factors as the formation of classroom groups, teacher assignment and rewards, curricula differentiation, allocation of time, and coordination of special programs) impact on instructional conditions that influence student learning for diverse groups. This knowledge must be translated into change-oriented strategies to solve many of these problems. Special programs for at-risk students are unlikely to succeed if they do not consider the structural conditions of schools that place these children at risk (Darling-Hammond, 1990).

Implications for Urban School Administrators

Finding ways to effectively provide for the needs of diverse student groups in urban schools has become a major focus of current school restructuring efforts. Restructuring requires taking a critical look at all aspects of schooling, including mission and goals, organization and management, curriculum and instruction, and family and community involvement. Thus, principals, teachers, researchers, policymakers, parents, and community members must all reconceptualize how schools should function and be managed. For significant change, schools involved in restructuring must reexamine the restrictive policies and procedures developed at district and state levels.

The most effective schools provide learning environments that are responsive to a wide range of student needs and focus on achieving specific academic outcomes, social skills, attitudes, and behaviors. The particular configuration of programs in schools that are effective vary and are developed at the building level, since each school differs considerably in human and material resources and in school improvement and implementation needs. Many schools perceive their role as presenting education to students and perceive the students' role as adapting to the school's method of presentation. However, the most effective schools provide learning environments that are responsive to a wide range of student needs. These schools incorporate a social organization of remediation that addresses not only instruction in academic skills but also the social support systems needed for students who require different methods for achieving schooling success (Epstein, 1988). Accommodating student diversity requires that schools focus more on individual students and do so differently than in the past. Significant improvement of urban schools serving diverse school populations will occur only when current notions of grouping, teaching, core curricula, teacher development, and parent involvement are reexamined.

Based on the extant knowledge base of how instructional resources are managed and allocated within schools to meet these needs, there are several implications for urban school administrators. These implications are organized around four functional categories: (1) coordinated instructional programming and related service delivery, (2) adaptation of curriculum, (3) social service and community support, and (4) renewal and development of staff.

Coordinated Instructional Programming and Related Services

The goal of every school should be to establish and maintain educational environments that ensure optimal opportunities for learning success for all students. Site-based management is being used to establish coordinated programming and instructional "teams" that make decisions in accordance with the needs and resources of a particular school. The inclusion of stakeholders in school leadership, decision making, and problem solving directly engages their expertise and provides an incentive to use their initiative (Guthrie, 1986; Guthrie & Reed, 1986).

In urban schools where dealing with diversity, academic skills, social skills, and personal characteristics are organizational goals, school teaming among teachers and related resource personnel is critical (Winfield, 1992, Winfield, Hawkins, & Stringfield, 1992). Implementation of school teaming requires the delegation and distribution of formal decision-making authority among school participants who share resources and responsibilities for all the students in the school. Since decision making on the part of administrators, teachers, students, parents, and others in the school community is an alterable feature of the authority structure, it can be changed to reflect a team approach. Team approaches allow for a wide range of instructional styles, use of specialist support, flexibility in student grouping and scheduling, and time to come together to share successes and analyze additional needed changes. Coordinated programming promotes closer relationships among teachers and increases the number of learning alternatives. Outcomes such as increased decision quality, satisfaction, commitment, productivity, and student learning result from allowing participants to believe that their involvement has a real influence on student success (Darling-Hammond, 1988; Guthrie, 1986).

The building principal can impact the structure of a school by becoming a team leader. The effective-schools literature clearly suggests that the principal is a key to implementing an integrated, cohesive instructional plan that serves children. The principal must provide leadership that incorporates clear statements of where the school is going and an understanding of how to build commitment to that vision. In partnership, the principal and staff in each school should have the authority to make decisions related to curriculum; to the technology of teaching and learning; to the acquisition of materials and the use of facilities and equipment; to the allocation of personnel in matters associated with teaching and learning; to those aspects of administration, scheduling, teaching, and staff professional development that deal with time; and to the allocation of money (Manz & Sims, 1987). Such leadership assures an effective process by forging the disparate members of the school staff into a working team, motivated by a desire to help all students learn more effectively (Blum, Butler & Olsen, 1987; Manning, 1987).

Adaptation Curriculum and Instruction

Although there is usually a core curriculum used in urban schools, refinement of the curriculum is necessary to meet the instructional and related service needs of individual students. A central idea in the current view of learning is that students do not simply receive and store information but that they transform it, link it to knowledge already held, and use it to build a coherent interpretation of the world and its events. Therefore, students need the opportunity not only to acquire knowledge but also to use what they know to cope with the intellectual and social demands of schooling.

The adaptation of programs is guided by the beliefs that most, if not all, students will require support and that curriculum and instruction should be realigned when necessary to meet the individual needs of students. In addition, administrators and teachers must recognize and accept the fact that some students require additional instructional support and longer periods of time to learn, while others require very little instruction from teachers. A primary task is to find the most efficient and effective ways to alter conventional instructional arrangements to meet the unique learning needs of individual students. (For a review of programs effective with diverse student populations, see Slavin, Karweit & Madden, 1989.) Schools that adapt curriculum and instruction produce students who perform better academically, and have more positive attitudes toward school, increased self-esteem, higher task completion, and improved peer and adult relationships (Glatthorn, 1987).

Restructuring schools to reflect such beliefs requires instructional approaches that stress active learning and student self-responsibility and at the same time recognize the school's responsibility to define what is to be learned and to structure lines of study that are most likely to foster learning. Students are expected not to just sit and listen to a teacher lecture but to participate with teachers in decisions, such as selecting topics for study and discussion, deciding how long to work before being evaluated, and determining when to ask for help. The content, sequence of curriculum, design of classwork and homework, level of difficulty of the work, materials required to complete assignments, and amount of time for learning are altered when necessary.

In urban schools, curriculum and instruction-development work must also reflect and accommodate the vast changes that have occurred in society, including technological developments, advances in modern sciences, and shifting economic and employment patterns. School curriculum and instruction are changed by incorporating a new definition of human intelligence, more sophisticated methods of assessment, increased emphasis on collaborative learning, greater use of innovative instructional strategies, curricular shifts from presenting data to evaluating and synthesizing ideas, and a focus on solving real-world problems using concepts and skills from multiple subject areas.

Community Support/Social Services

The level of community that includes families', businesses', churches', and social service agencies' involvement in schools is integral to meeting the needs of diverse student groups. Existing research suggests that school-community partnerships are more likely to be successful when they are designed with high expectations for community involvement, when they recognize that communities are changing, when they provide a variety of ways for community members to be involved, and when they accommodate the needs of the communities to be involved. Schools that encourage frequent and meaningful interaction and networking of families and neighborhood organizations and agencies find that school effectiveness, student attendance, and student achievement are improved (Coleman & Hoffer, 1987; Comer, 1986; Eastman, 1988; Epstein, 1988).

In urban schools, involving communities suggests coming to terms with the discrepancy between the attitudes of communities and of educators (See Nettles, 1991, for a review of research on communities). Communities, especially parents, are interested in being involved in schools at all levels, from tutoring to decision making. Educators, however, continue to consider traditional limited roles of community involvement.

The design and implementation of family, community, and school partnership programs should include a wide range of options designed to meet diverse interests, expertise, and service needs of families and communities. Urban school administrators have to address access to information about school programs and services, instruction and training in how to work with children at home, assistance with classroom activities, and participation in school-based management committees. Increased participation means that authority does not reside with the principal and teachers alone. The greatest possible distribution of authority at the school is required. School-based management requires that the school community should have the authority to make and implement decisions that enable it to adapt to the needs of the school's students, to have the flexibility to change when needed, to establish a wide leadership base, and to initiate and implement school improvement efforts that can have significant results. Such decisions might involve the development of school mission and goals.

An approach initiated to develop school-based teams in which school staff, parents, organizations, and community agencies work collaboratively to deliver school, social services, and community support has been particularly effective in urban settings. In this approach, the school serves to facilitate the communication of information both in and out of the school (Manning, 1987). The Comprehensive Social Service Support (CSSS) model uses a school-based team to join the school, parents, and community resources in order to address attendance, counseling, special education, parent involvement, public service resources, and staff development needs. The school is considered to be the most stable institution in the community and it creates an important social network that children and families can benefit from.

Development and Renewal of Staff

Teachers in urban schools may be more likely than teachers in other settings to be in less favorable work environments and to suffer higher rates of stress and burnout. In addition, urban schools may be more likely to have higher numbers of first-year teachers with little or no experience. Thus, the urban school administrator must be able to tap available district, state, and community resources to provide opportunities for developing professional expertise and renewing existing staff. Using faculty meeting time to initiate and sustain staff development in specific areas and over a school year is likely to be more beneficial for developing a sense of community among staff than using this time for administrative tasks or one-time speakers on a variety of subjects.

Two important developments documented in the literature include the increased amount of educational research that can be applied to practice and the improved design of staff development programs that pay off in higher student and teacher outcomes (Joyce & Showers, 1987). To maximize staff development gains, training should be adapted to the needs and interests of individual staff members by scheduling meetings and training sessions on a regular basis, including content that relates to the day-to-day needs of staff and by encouraging active participation by school staff and resource personnel in decisions regarding staff development goals and procedures (Huberman, 1983; Melle & Pratt, 1981; Mertens & Yarger, 1981). Ultimately, staff development should increase teachers' ability to select and use appropriate practices from a repertoire of program options. Carefully implemented staff development can be expected to help students improve achievement, higher-order thinking, problem solving, social skills, and attitudes. Teacher outcomes include increased self-esteem and increased knowledge (Joyce & Showers , 1988).

The four functional categories briefly described above are areas in which instructional resources are managed and allocated to meet diverse instructional needs. There are many descriptions of programs that attempt to accommodate diversity (see Slavin, Braddock, Hall & Petza, 1989; Winfield & Manning, 1992); urban school administrators should be knowledgeable of such programs. However, meaningful solutions to accommodate student diversity require a *problem-solving* as opposed to *program-oriented* response on the part of school administrators (See Johnson, in press).

Summary

Urban administrators generally seem to be unaware of the powerful effects their resource management decisions have on the learning outcomes of students. Further, when they do become aware, they are often at a loss as to how to go about making changes that would enhance those outcomes. Administrators face major challenges in producing high-quality learning outcomes for all students. Issues of concern include low student achievement outcomes, appropriate curricula for diverse populations, and equity in access to quality instruction. These concerns must be dealt with simultaneously with budget constraints and staffing vacancies. In order for meaningful change to occur, these issues must be examined in the context of practices, policies, and structural features of urban schools.

Urban schools are innundated with a myriad of categorical and other special programs. Each of these programs typically has a separate administrative structure coexisting in the same school. Over time, formal regulations and informal practices have built invisible walls around each program. These perceived walls inhibit collaboration at all the program, school, and district levels. The absence of communication, coordination, and a common instructional philosophy have resulted in fragmentation and a lower-quality instructional program. Because students in low-track or lower-ability groups are seen as incapable of mastering the regular curriculum, instructional outcomes for these students are often seen as the responsibility of the special program staff. In addition, teacher allocations are connected to the program status. Newer and less experienced teachers are most often allocated to remedial programs and lower-level tracks and the reward structure for seniority and skill is assignment to higher-level classes. Since there is very little incentive to teach the students with the highest need, these students receive the least experienced teachers, and, at times, long-term substitutes. Under these conditions, it is not surprising that patterns of persistent underachievement continue to exist. In schools where there is a coordinated delivery system that results in higher student achievement, the principal plays a pivotal role.

Feedback from principals in the field suggests that administrative preparation programs fail to address how to change real-world urban school conditions, such as low teacher and student expectations, fragmented instructional programs, unresponsive instructional programs for diverse student populations, and structural features such as tracking that adversely affect student achievement. Unfortunately, strategies for handling these changes are typically learned on the job. Systemic changes in practices, policies, and structural features of urban schools can reverse poor achievement patterns. To reverse these practices fundamental changes in the schools' organization must occur, especially with regard to the provisions of quality learning outcomes for all children regardless of ethnicity or economic background.

Conclusion

Administrators of urban schools and districts are being called on to change radically the learning outcomes for schools with diverse populations. They are being asked to make changes that they are unprepared to tackle. Changing what appears to be an intractable bureaucracy will require administrators who are not only knowledgeable about what and why things need to change to improve student outcomes, but who also have skills in implementing the needed changes. A reconceptualization of school organization will require new ways of thinking about schooling for all children. Resource allocation decisions must move away from those that are focused on professionally oriented delivery systems to those that are student-centered. The allocation of resources must derive from a shared mission related to the learning needs of all children. The goal of the school must reflect a belief system that includes the premise that all children have the opportunity to learn a high-quality instructional program.

The coordination and collaboration of the human and material resources to achieve this goal will require ongoing and continuous professional development. Enhancing the skills of the entire school community, inside and outside the walls of the school, must be considered. School professionals will need to work collegially and engage in ongoing learning and discussions. Administrators play a key role in allocating time and opportunities for professional sharing to occur. Professional development focused on learning is required in order to (1) transform thinking about the capacity of all children to learn high-order thinking, (2) build the capacity of adults to learn new skills, and (3) develop new ways to organize schools that are instructionally effective.

In order to respond to the needs of diverse populations, the adults in the organization must challenge and change many of their underlying assumptions about the students, their parents, and the communities in which the students live. A reconceptualization of purpose and priorities may require collaboration, integration, and/or the possible elimination of some programs. Administrators may have to ask hard questions of themselves and of the staff. Are the way that these programs currently structured of benefit to students? Whether the answer is yes or no, decisions must be justified by outcomes over time. If programs do not benefit students, whom do they benefit? A closer examination may reveal that current resource allocations are rooted in past practices that focus on allocating positions in the organization and maintaining the adult status quo. As management decisions become tied to a clear mission that is focused on achievement outcomes for students and that involves the family and community in the learning experience, students will reap the rewards. The leaders of urban schools with diverse student populations must have a strong sense of purpose, a vision for what can be, and skills to lead an often recalcitrant staff to achieving high-level results for diverse populations.   This is the challenge for those leading schools into the 21st century.

Implications for Higher Education

Information from principals in the field suggests that their administrative preparation programs have fallen short of giving them experiences needed to lead today's urban schools with diverse populations (UCEA-Danforth Select Conference, 1988). Although much attention has been focused on teacher preservice preparation and ongoing professional development, little attention has been paid to the educational preparation of administrators, particularly in urban schools. Even less attention has been given to the ongoing professional needs of principals in these schools.   Most of the literature focuses on the identification of characteristics of successful principals rather than on their development. This emphasis on characteristics calls for some rethinking about the mission and delivery systems of current administrator preparation programs. Institutions that prepare administrators should prepare them not only for certification but also for the ongoing professional development needs of administrators in the field.

A multidimensional paradigm for the selection and preparation of educational administrators (Sander & Wiggins, 1985) suggests four areas of competence in educational administration: economic, pedagogical, political, and cultural. *Economic competence* is based on efficiency and use of resources to attain goals. *Pedagogical competence* reflects a capacity to formulate educational objectives and prepare effective pedagogical scenarios and means to attain such objectives. *Political competence* defines the abilities to perceive the external environment and its influence on the educational system and its participants. It requires a capacity to adopt strategies of concrete action for the responsive satisfaction of the social and political necessities and demands of the community and its educational system. *Cultural competence* includes a demonstrated capacity to conceive of solutions and exercise leadership in the implementation of these solutions under the criterion of relevance.

Since the urban school context is unique, administrative training programs need to incorporate these four areas into the real-world issues that these schools are facing and make both competence and relevance a part of its mission. This may call for the same types of rethinking in which K-12 public schools are being asked to engage. The university must critically examine its current administrator preparation programs to determine if they are educating individuals who can effectively lead urban schools with diverse populations. Are preparation programs more oriented toward the development of technocrats who efficiently manage bureaucratic institutions for student populations and a society of yesterday? Is the knowledge base current and does it reflect information and research about the conditions and complexities of those schools? What are the orientations and philosophy of the faculty? Are they rooted in a narrow framework about school administration?

Although it is important to consider course competencies, it is also important to look at new approaches. The research agenda for accommodating student diversity should be collaborative and designed in partnership with those building-level administrators in the field with a proven track record for improving student outcomes. This process would call for the university to examine how it allocates its resources of time, money, and people to achieve desired outcomes. Consideration might be given to partnerships designed to inform and improve current practice. Some suggested approaches that might be implemented are:

1. Professors of educational administration could be assigned to schools to work together and collaborate with selected mentor school principals at a school site for a semester. Combining information in the literature and the everyday knowledge of the

practitioner would result in substantially improving the instructional quality and the knowledge of those who work in both higher education settings and K-12 schools.

2. Mentor principals, who are currently effective in managing instructional diversity and improving student achievement outcomes, might become principals in residence at the university. These individuals would teach for a semester or a year and bring the real-world experiences of the field to the classroom. They would also develop the capacity to integrate theory with practice and engage in critical reflective thought about the complex problems in their schools.

3. Fieldwork assignments for all in administrative preparation programs should be of high quality. Too often aspiring administrators are involved in fieldwork that offers only routine experiences. Schools with mentor principals who will provide high-quality experiences should be identified. These schools would be desirable fieldwork sites, even though there may not be a big enough pool of such sites. Students could be assigned to fieldwork sites where the participating administrator would agree to participate in joint professional development with the aspiring administrator. The two would be brought together in a seminar experience to identify and resolve problems. A major theme of these seminars would include an understanding of the culture of the organization and how mangement decisions impact the learning experiences of diverse students.

4. Professional seminars should provide practicing urban administrators (both at the school site and central office) information on systemic change and how to better allocate resources to improve academic outcomes for diverse populations.

An analysis of mission, course content, and delivery needs to accompany any structural changes. With the rapid rate of change in the society and schools, administrators will need a strong conceptual framework as a basis for their decision making. Suggestions for some of the knowledge components that should be included in course content are described below.

1. Courses need to provide a firm understanding of how social and political forces affect schools, how the schools need to respond to benefit students, and how to go about systematically leading changes in institutions that may seem impervious to fundamental change. Future administrators will likely be dealing with conditions that cannot be predicted.

2. Universities also operate with separate administrative structures that limit collegial opportunities. Opportunities are needed for team teaching across disciplines, with sociologists and anthropologists as well as with professors in foundations and curriculum and instruction to help administrators develop a broader and more in-depth perspective about what is occurring in schools. These opportunities could help aspiring administrators better analyze and deepen their knowledge base about the possible implications of their decisions.

3. All courses should include problem solving and simulation activities to help aspiring practitioners experience the types of management decisions they will need to make in the field, particularly as they relate to resource allocations for instructional programs. Problem solving should include issues of how to allocate time, people, and money to optimize instructional effectiveness.

4. Creating learning environments that foster high learning outcomes for all students is rooted in changing the behaviors of individuals in the organization. Aspiring administrators must know how to implement professional development programs that are comprehensive and that will institutionalize the desired behaviors.

5. Aspiring administrators will need to be grounded in how structural features of a school can inhibit or enhance achievement. They will need to learn how to carefully analyze and evaluate programs in their school and determine whether or not they contribute to the school's mission. This suggests that they must be critical, reflective thinkers who in turn help other adults in the school setting become reflective. These administrators will have to know how to use data at the organizational and instructional level in order to understand the context for changing behaviors, policies, and practices that fail to accommodate

student diversity. They will also need to know how to identify practices that negatively affect students who are not monolingual and middle class and guide the implementation of alternatives to tracking. And, they will need to understand how teachers respond to students in the classroom.

Aspiring administrators should leave preparation programs with the knowledge that they have some control over student outcomes and have some confidence that they have learned how to tackle tough issues. They also should leave with some strategies for acquiring assistance and knowledge of resources available to assist them in the field. They should leave knowing that they don't have all of the answers, but that they do have some approaches to getting answers. In sum, future administrators should leave preparation programs with the knowledge that they need to be life-long learners.

Notes

1. With the passage of the Hawkins-Stafford amendments in 1988, schools and districts are now able to service all students in a school if 75% of the students are eligible according to economic criteria. This change allows more flexibility in delivering instructional services and funding of personnel than was previously allowed. Schools not meeting the 75% criterion continue to serve pupils on an individual basis.

2. Although these two terms, groups and tracks, are used interchangeably, they have different meanings. *Ability grouping*, which is usually confined to elementary schools, is a method of organizing students according to ability or achievement for instruction, in order to reduce heterogeneity. *Tracking* is the practice of dividing students into separate classes for high, average, and low achievers and entails different curriculum paths for students aspiring to college and for those who plan to enter the work force. The point, however, is that students in the lower groups and/or tracks do not have the same opportunity to learn and access to knowledge.

References

Allington, R. L. (1984). Policy constraints and effective compensatory reading instruction: A review. In J. Hoffman (Ed.), *Effective teaching of reading: Research and practice*. Newark, DE: International Reading Association.

Allington, R. L. (1987). Shattered hopes: Why two federal reading programs have failed to correct reading failure. *Learning, 16(1),* 60-62.

Allington, R. L., & Broikou , K. A. (1988, April). The development of shared knowledge: A new role for classroom and specialist teachers. *The Reading Teacher, 41* (8), 806-811.

Allington, R. L., & Johnston, P. (1989). Coordination, collaboration and consistency: The redesign of compensatory and special education interventions. In R. Slavin, N. Madden, & N. Karweit (Eds.), *Preventing school failure: Effective programs for students at risk* (pp. 320-354), Boston: Allyn-Bacon.

Allington, R. L. & McGill-Franzen, A. (1989). School response to reading failure: Instruction for Chapter 1 and special education students in grades 2, 4, and 8. *Elementary School Journal, 89* (5), 529-542.

Arciniega, T. A. (1977). The challenge of multicultural education for teacher educators. *Journal of Research and Development in Education, 11* (1), 52-69.

Banks, J. A., & C. Banks. (1989). *Multicultural education: Issues and perspectives*. Boston: Allyn & Bacon.

Barr, R. & Dreeben, R. with Wiratchai, N. (1983). *How schools work*. Chicago: University of Chicago Press.

Barton, A. H., & Wilder, P. E. (1964). Research and practice in the teaching of reading: A progress report. In M. B. Miles (Ed.), *Innovations in Education*, New York: Teachers College Press.

Blum, R. E., Butler, J. A., & Olsen, N. L. (1987). Leadership for excellence: Research-based training for principals. *Educational Leadership, 45*(2), 25-29.

Braddock, J. H., II. (1989). *Tracking of Black, Hispanic, Asian, Native Americans and White Students: National Patterns and Trends*. Baltimore, MD: The Johns Hopkins University, Center for Research on Effective Schooling for Disadvantaged Students.

Bunting, C. E. (1984). Dimensionality of teacher education beliefs: An exploratory study. *Journal of Experimental Education, 52* (4), 195-198.

Carter, L. F. (1984). The sustaining effects study of compensatory and elementary education. *Educational Researcher, 13,* 4-13..

Coleman, J. S., Campbell, E. Q., Hobson, C. J. McPartland, J., Mood, A., Weinfield, F. D., & York, R. L. (1966). *Equality of Educational Opportunity.* Washington, DC: U. S. Government Printing Office.

Coleman, J. S., & Hoffer, T. (1987). *Public and private high schools: The impact of communities.* New York: Basic Books.

Comer, J. P., (1986). Academic and affective gains from the school development program: A model for school improvement. Eric Document # ED 274750.

Darling-Hammond, L. (1985). *Equality and excellence: The educational status of Black Americans.* New York: The College Board.

Darling-Hammond, L. (1988). Accountability and teacher professionalism. *American Educator, 12* (4), 8-13, 38-43.

Darling-Hammond, L. (1990). Teacher quality and educational equality. In J. L. Goodlad & P. Keating (Eds.), *Access to knowledge* (pp. 237-358). New York: College Entrance Examination Board.

Dreeben, R. L., & Barr, R. (1983). Educational policy and the working of schools. In L. S. Shulman & G. Sykes (Eds.), *Handbook of teaching and policy* (pp. 81-96). New York: Longman.

Eastman, G. (1988). *Family involvement in education.* Madison, WI: Wisconsin Department of Public Instruction. ERIC Document # 316802.

Eder, D. (1981). Ability grouping as a self-fulfilling prophecy: A micro-analysis of teacher-student interaction. *Sociology of Education, 54* (3), 151-162.

Epstein, J. L. (1988). *Effective schools or effective students: Dealing with diversity* . In R. Haskins & D. MacRae (Eds.), *Policies for America's Public Schools* (pp. 89-126). Norwood NJ: Ablex.

Evertson, C. M. (1982). Differences in instructional activities in higher- and lower-achieving junior high English and Math classes. *The Elementary School Journal,* (82) 329-350.

Finley, M. K. (1984). Teachers and tracking in comprehensive high school. *Sociology of Education, 57,* 233-243.

Gamoran, A., & Berends, M. (1987). The effects of stratification in secondary schools: Synthesis of survey and ethnographic research. *Review of Educational Research, 57,* 415-435.

Glatthorn, A. A. (1987). *Curriculum renewal..* Alexandria, VA: Association for Supervision and Curriculum Development.

Gordon, E. (1982). Urban education. In H. E. Mitzel (Ed.) *Encyclopedia of Educational Research,* 5th Ed., Vol. 4, (pp. 1973-1980). New York: Macmillan.

Guthrie, J. W. (1986). School-based management: The next needed education reform. *Phi Delta Kappan, 68* (4), 305-309.

Guthrie, J. W., & Reed, R. J. (1986). *Educational administration and policy: Effective leadership for American Education.* Englewood Cliffs, NJ: Prentice-Hall.

Hallinan, M. T., & Sorenson, A. B. (1983). The formation and stability of instructional groups. *American Sociological Review, 48,* 838-851.

Hare, B. S. (1989). State University of New York SUNY-wide, Task force for the cultivation of pluralism. Stony Brook, NY: SUNY. (Unpublished manuscript)

Hargreaves, D. H.. (1967). *Social relations in a secondary school.* London: Routledge and Kegan Paul.

Heathers, G. (1969). Grouping. In R. L. Ebel (Ed.), *Encyclopedia of Educational Research,* 4th Ed. (pp. 559-570). New York: Macmillan.

Huberman, A. M. (1983). School improvement strategies that work. *Educational Leadership, 41* (3), 21-25.

Johnson, R., & Wong, L. (in press). Restructuring schools: The debate. In L. Rendon (Ed.), *Educating the New Majority.*

Johnston, P. H., Allington, R. L., & Afflerbach, P. (1985). The congruence of classroom and remedial instruction. *Elementary School Journal,* (85), 465-478.

Joyce, B., & Showers, B. (1987). Staff development and student learning: A synthesis of research on models of teaching. *Educational Leadership, 45* (2), 11-23.

Joyce, B., & Showers, B. (1988). *Student achievement through staff development.* Longman: New York.

Kaestle, C. F., & Smith, M. S. (1982). The federal role in elementary and secondary education 1940-1980. *Harvard Educational Review, 52* (4), 384-408.

Keddie, N. (1971). Classroom knowledge. In M. F. D. Young (Ed.), *Knowledge and control* (pp. 133-160). London: Collier-Macmillan.

Leacock, E. (1969). *Teaching and learning in city schools.* New York: Basic Books.

Lee, V. E., Dedrick, R. B., & Smith, J. B. (1991). The effect of the social organization of schools on teacher satisfaction. *Sociology of Education, 64,* 190-208.

Lee, V. E., Winfield, L. F., & Wilson, T. (1991). Academic behaviors among high achieving African American students. In L. F. Winfield (Ed.), Resilience, Schooling and Development in African American Youth. *Education and Urban Society, 24* (1), 65-86.

Maeroff, G. I. (1988, May). Withered hopes, stillborn dreams: The dismal panorama of urban schools, *Phi Delta Kappan, 69* (9), 633-638.

Manning, J. B. (1987). Roles and activities of special education elementary support team members; Perceptions of Philadelphia school principals. Unpublished doctoral dissertation, Temple University.

Manz, C. C., & Sims, H. P. (1987). Leading workers to lead themselves: The external leadership of self-managing work teams. *Administrative Science Quarterly, 32* (1), 106-128.

Melle, M., & Pratt, H. (1981). Documenting program adoption in a district-wide implementation effort: The three year evolution from evaluation to an instructional improvement plan. Paper presented at the annual meeting of the American Educational Research Association, Los Angeles.

Mertens, S. K., & Yarger, S. L. (1981). *Teacher centers in action.* Syracuse, NY: Syracuse University, Syracuse Area Teacher Center.

Metz, M. H. (1978). *Classrooms and corridors: The crisis of authority in desegregated secondary schools.* Berkeley, CA: University of California Press.

National Education Association. (1968). Ability grouping: Research summary. Washington, DC: National Educational Association, Research Division.

Nettles, S. M. (1991). Community involvement and disadvantaged students: A review. *Review of Educational Research, 61* (3), 379-406.

Oakes, J. (1985). *Keeping track: How schools structure inequality.* New Haven, CT: Yale University Press.

Oakes, J. (1986a, September). Keeping track, part 1: The policy and practice of curriculum inequality. *Phi Delta Kappan,* 15-20.

Oakes, J. (1986b, October). Keeping track, part 2: Curriculum inequality and school reform. *Phi Delta Kappan,* 21-26.

Oakes, J., & Keating, P. (1988) *Access to knowledge: Breaking down school barriers to learning.* Paper supported by the Education Commission of the States, Denver, CO, and the College Board, New York, NY.

Oakes, J., & Lipton, M (1990). Tracking and ability grouping: A structural barrier to access and achievement. In J. I. Goodlad & P. Keating (Eds.), *Access to knowledge* (pp. 87-204). New York: College Entrance Examination Board.

Pine, G. J., & Hilliard, A. G. (1990). Rx for racism: Imperatives for America's schools. *Phi Delta Kappan, 71* (8), 593-600.

Rosenbaum, J. E. (1976). *Making inequality: The hidden curriculum of high school tracking.* New York: Wiley.

Rosenbaum, J. E. (1980). Social implications of educational grouping. In D. C. Berliner (Ed.), *Review of Research in Education* (pp. 361-401). Itasca, IL: Peacock.

Rowan, B., & Miracle, A. W. Jr. (1983). Systems of ability grouping and the stratification of achievement in elementary schools. *Sociology of Education , 56,* 133-144.

Sander, B., & Wiggins, T. (1985). Cultural context of administrative theory: In consideration of a multidimensional paradigm. *Educational Administration Quarterly, 21* (1), 95-117.

Schwartz, F. (1981). Supporting or subverting learning: Peer group patterns in four tracked schools. *Anthropology and Education Quarterly, 12,* 99-121.

Shavelson, R. J., & Stern, P. (1981). Research on teachers' pedagogical thoughts, judgments, decisions and behaviors. *Review of Educational Research, 51* (4), 455-498.

Shujaa, M. J. (1991, April). Does it matter what teachers think?: Teachers' perceptions of a new policy to infuse African and African American content into the school curriculum. Paper presented at the Annual Meeting of the American Educational Research Association, Chicago.

Slavin, R. E. (1987). Ability grouping and student achievement in elementary schools: A best evidence synthesis. *Review of Educational Research, 57,* 293-336.

Slavin, R. E. (1988). Synthesis of research on grouping in elementary and secondary schools. *Educational Leadership,* September, 67-77.

Slavin, R. E., Braddock, J. H., Hall, C., & Petza, R. J. (1989). *Alternatives to ability grouping.* Baltimore, MD: The Johns Hopkins University, Center for Research on Effective Schooling for Disadvantaged Students, Center for Research on Elementary and Middle Schools.

Slavin, R. E., Karweit, N. L., & Madden, N. A. (1989). *Effective programs for students at risk.* Boston: Allyn & Bacon.

Spady, W. G. (1973). The impact of school resources on students. In F. N. Kerlinger (Ed.), *Review of Research in Education* (pp. 135-177). Itasca, IL: Peacock.

Trachtenberg, S. J. (1990). Multiculturalism can be taught only by multicultural people. *Phi Delta Kappan, 71* (8), 610-611.

Watson, B. C., & Traylor, F. M. (1988). Tomorrow's teachers: Who will they be, what will they know? In J. Dewart (Ed.), *The State of Black America*. New York: Urban League.

Winfield, L. F. (1982). Principals' *instructional behavior in inner urban schools*. Paper presented at the Annual Meeting of American Educational Research Association, Boston.

Winfield, L. F. (1991a). Case studies of evolving schoolwide projects. Educational Evaluation and Policy *Analysis, 13* (4), 353-362.

Winfield, L. F. (1991b). Resilience, schooling and development among African American youth: A conceptual framework (5-14). In L. F. Winfield Special Issue, Resilience, schooling and development in African American youth. *Education and Urban Society, 24*(1), 5-14.

Winfield, L. F., Hawkins, R., & Stringfield, S. (1992). A description of *Chapter 1 schoolwide projects and effects on student achievement in six case study schools*. Baltimore, MD: The Johns Hopkins University Center for Research on Effective Schooling for Disadvantaged Students. CDS Report #37.

Winfield, L. F., & Manning, J. (1992). Changing school culture to accommodate diversity. In M. E. Dilworth (Ed.), *Diversity in Teacher Education: New Expectations*. Jossey-Bass: San Francisco.

Winfield, L. F., & Stringfield, S. (1991). *A description of schoolwide projects*. Baltimore, MD: The Johns Hopkins University, Center for Research on Effective Schooling for Disadvantaged Students: CDS Report # 16.

Winfield, L. F., & Woodard, M. D. (1992). Where are equity and diversity in Bush's Proposal 2000? *Education Week,* Jan. 29, p. 31.

4

Building Open Climates in Urban Schools

JAMES R. BLISS

From 1978 to 1989, the percentages of African Americans under 18 years of age living in poverty grew from 41.2% to 43.7% (Current Population Reports, 1991). Comparable figures for Latinos were 28.0% and 36.2%. Comparable figures for whites were 11.8% and 14.8%. A family below the poverty line was a family of four with income of less than $12,675. African Americans and Latinos together constituted 68% of urban disadvantaged students compared to non-Latino whites. Nearly one-third of poor urban students live only with their mothers (Hispanic Policy Development Project, 1991). Only about 57% of the parents of poor urban students have completed high school. Ninety percent of poor urban students attend public schools, and 80% of poor urban students score in the bottom half of standardized tests for reading and mathematics. Inner-city school leaving rates have been estimated at approximately 40% (Krasnow, 1991). In one major city, most gang-related shooting and stabbing occur within a six-block radius of a school. Relationships among students, teachers, administrators, and parents of the inner cities often seem fractured beyond repair. What can be done to improve the relationships among these major groups of stakeholders involved in urban schools?

A complex network of perceived relationships comprises the climate of any school. Perceptions of these relationships are central to issues of motivation and effort put into teaching, learning, curriculum development, and overall governance. Aside from the lack of monetary resources, school climate is a central problem of urban schools today. As a problem of practice, the key question can be stated as: What can be done in schools with poor African American and Latino students to improve the interpersonal relationships (and perceptions of same) among students, teachers, parents, and administrators? Partly because of these imperfect relationships, it has been said that African American children, and by extension other minority-group students of the inner city, sit in classrooms "un-centered" (Focus, 1992).

The urban school principal's commitment to the education of African-American and Latino students is what motivates his or her continuing efforts to understand more about key problems of practice and to remind colleagues that students, school personnel, and parents must work together to resolve them. The urban principal reflects credit on colleagues and self by working diligently to remove barriers that prevent students, teachers, and parents from taking advantage of opportunities to improve their relationships with one another. In preparing this chapter, a commonsense perspective emerged on building open urban school climates, based on the image of a four-sided closed figure whose corners represent students, teachers, administrators, and parents.

Mainstream School Climate Concept

The concept of *organizational climate* has a long history in social psychology and educational administration (Anderson, 1982; Campbell et al., 1970; Ekvall, 1987; Forehand & Gilmer, 1964; Halpin & Croft, 1963; Hellreigel & Slocum, 1974; Hoy, Tarter et al., 1991; James & Jones, 1974; McDill et al., 1969; Miskel & Ogawa, 1988; Victor & Cullen, 1987; Woodman & King, 1978). The study of organizational climate has offered modest hope that urban schools can become more effective through improved relationships among persons under the stress of organizational life.

School climate as a concept (or metaphor) appeals to common sense. Atmosphere and environment matter to many things, and research shows that school learning and other educational outcomes may depend strongly on school climate. Although progress has been made in delineating the functions and effects of principal-teacher and teacher-student relationships in suburban schools, little attention has been devoted to the structure of climate in *urban* schools. A part of the difficulty, perhaps, has been that mainstream discussions of school climate have been methodologically driven or shaped by the availability of existing climate surveys. The time has come to revisit school climate as a concept and apply what we know about it to urban schools. How can urban principals begin to grasp what school climate means in relation to poor inner-city urban schools, in order to sort out their priorities and filter out some of the "noise" that interferes with constructive action?

A Definition of School Climate

School climate is the relatively enduring quality of the school environment that is experienced by participants, affects their behavior, and is based on their collective perception of behavior in schools (Hoy & Miskel, 1987; Hoy et al., 1991; Tagiuri, 1968).

Climate as a Problem of Urban School Practice

The urban principal sets the tone and creates the conditions for a broad range of perceptions (Bliss, 1991). With respect to climate, perceptions *are* the reality. There are two general methods by which a principal can evaluate or gain balance and sense of direction on school climate issues. First, think deeply about ideal relationships among key stakeholders (students, teachers, parents, and administrators) and compare these ideals to current realities. Second, locate and review theoretical work related to issues of improving the full spectrum of human relationships in schools. The urban principal should not look on building school climate as his or her sole responsibility. According to Lomotey (1989), some successful African-American principals do not provide direct leadership in the areas of goal development, energy harnessing, communications facilitation, and instructional management. These issues represent organizational challenges that require collaborative efforts. The principal, however, must effectively create the conditions that students, teachers, and parents need to complete their work. Improved conditions subject to local influence are necessary, even though not sufficient, for improved perceptions of relationships among students, teachers, administrators, and parents in urban schools.

Relationships Within Schools

Relationships within schools are essentially relationships among the major groups of people who are required to be there. Things we measure or try to evaluate in schools are things that matter to us. But oddly, despite all of the testing that occurs in urban schools, the human factor has been largely ignored. To communicate that interrelationships among students, teachers, parents, and administrators *matter*, urban principals must discover better ways of speaking about five kinds of relationships within schools. The student who may be on the receiving end of a racist remark does not simply react as a representative of a group; he or she experiences the pain or humiliation personally (Brittan & Maynard, 1984).

1. *Between Students and Students.* Recent applied work in psychology has emphasized the notion that people have multiple intelligences (Gardner, 1991; Sternberg, 1988). How might the concept of multiple intelligences apply to improved perceptions of relationships between students and students? A well-rounded education for urban students should give continuous attention to interpersonal skills development. Too often, urban schools are centers of violence among youth. There seems little point to emphasizing the development of academic intelligence or formal school learning while school-age urban children so often exhibit such dysfunctional interpersonal skills. The quality of relationships among boys and girls requires direct attention.

Rarely do mainstream discussions of school climate address the issue of relationships among students. But this is not because student-student relationships are not important to school climate. Urban practitioners lead the way in delineating what needs to be considered and evaluated in this domain. Forthcoming reports of work by Shirley Brice Heath and Milbrey W. McLaughlin at Stanford University regarding the socialization of inner-city youth are promising: Inner-city youth outside of schools are showing remarkable sophistication in interpersonal skills.

Studies of neighborhood-based organizations (many of which compete with street gangs for affiliation of the young) reveal a number of features that contribute to their success, including viewing their members in a positive light and creating environments that provide physical and emotional security for members (Seawell, 1992). Urban school principals must work to discover new strategies to promote the expression of positive student-student relationships in schools, if schools are to be relevant to the lives of inner-city youth.

2. *Between Students and Teachers.* In this domain, principals should ask: What conditions are needed to maximize quality day-to-day interactions in school between students and their teachers? Obstacles to improved perceptions of interactions are complex. For example, withdrawal and loss of motivation may be characteristic of castelike minorities (Ogbu, 1978). Very often, there is a mismatch in race and class between students and teachers (Jones, 1991). Restructuring efforts in major cities such as Chicago, where site-based management experiments are in progress, have possibly heightened the perceptions of this mismatch. The particular location of subject in terms of race, class, and gender can generate virulent and self-destructive strategies of resistance (Brittan & Maynard, 1984). Not surprisingly, the discourse between urban students and teachers is too often discipline-centered rather than skill-centered, student-centered, or subject-centered. Inner-city youth, however, need the best mix of teachers available, and patronage systems should have no place in the staffing of urban schools.

Urban schools generally fail to provide high-quality teachers, sufficient instructional time, challenging curricula, and strong incentives for success (see chapter 7 by Winfield in this volume). Adept personnel practices, including professional development programs, are essential to improved discourse between students and teachers. In some cities, urban schools are plagued by the consequences of low-quality personnel decisions and inadequate supervision. In other cities, personnel selection decisions are treated as critically related to educational improvement and, therefore, are given the prominent attention they deserve. With or without high-quality personnel selection, student-results-oriented staff development for teachers can make a difference in student-teacher relationships.

Why do patterns of low concern and little caring develop between teachers and students? Sixty years ago, Willard Waller found that teaching often causes rigidity of personality, excessive concern with one's own status or place in the field, authoritarianism, and lack of creativity (see Roberts, 1968, p. 310 for discussion). According to Waller, these unattractive qualities have considerable utility in helping teachers to cope with the demanding nature of their work. Moreover, urban schools are generally understaffed, especially in relation to students' academic and socio-emotional needs. One urban teacher I know refers to his school as a virtual "black hole" of need, and says, "the [school] drains everything you've got, every day."

In a more positive vein, however, there are relevant technical—rational solutions that should be considered. Relationships between students and teachers can be improved through better classroom management routines, provision of consistent and motivating feedback, reduction of arbitrary discipline, adjustments in the pacing of instruction, emphasis on fair grading, instructional clarity, and thoughtful organization of content. There is growing evidence that students and teachers have a common problem when it comes to how they feel about their work in schools (Ashton & Webb, 1982; Bandura, 1977). The self-efficacy beliefs of both students and teachers in urban areas contribute to school failure by African-American and Latino students who are remarkably quick and confident outside of school. Urban principals can improve the quality of discourse between students and teachers by hiring the best personnel available and permitting them to help identify structural barriers that can be addressed collaboratively.

However, rational—technical solutions to student-teacher relationship issues will not suffice alone. Urban teachers and students require new frames of reference yet to be developed that allow each to "leap-jump" to a different (higher) interpretive level when thinking about their work. This leap-jump may be thought of as a cross between the notion of double-loop learning and transformational leadership (Argyris, 1980; Bass, 1990). How can students and teachers get there? A rich theory of education will work for some people. The arts will work for others; band drama, sculpture, or Afro-centric curricula for others. The Boys Choir of Harlem shines brightly because of its leap-jump to a different level of interpretation and effort.

3. *Between Students and Administrators.* The urban principal's relationships with students are mostly indirect. The principal creates the architecture that fosters school climate, whether it be dysfunctional, adequate, orderly-restrictive, or orderly-enabling (Knapp, 1991). But

since the architecture of the organization will tend in the long run to more or less resemble the architecture of the principal's own thoughts regarding the education of African-American and Latino children, urban principals must continually reassess their own thinking on the problems of practice discussed in this volume. Between students and administrators, one of the central issues in building a more open school climate will continue to be how to implement incentives for pleasant, healthy, and productive human encounters. Again, the potential for improved encounters between students and adults may depend greatly on a combination of structural and leap-jump improvements.

One example of the kinds of structures (within the purview of principals) that inhibit the quality of contact between teachers and students is *"hard" tracking.* Tracking schemes based on standardized testing (Ascher, 1990) that relegate students to the lowest groups year after year often lead to school leaving. They also may promote strained relationships between teachers and students. Pernicious tracking continues in urban schools, despite the contraindications of many related studies in recent years. Early testing for track placement rather than diagnosis, for example, has been a long-standing practice in urban schools. Tracking has implications for climate because it represents the indirect relationships between students and administrators. Urban principals must create different internal architectures, without stigmatizing their students. There is a lot to be learned about how to improve multicultural sensitivity, gender disequity, English proficiency, and school safety in urban educational environments.

Other kinds of urban workers across the country have discovered the power of *core teams*, for example, to assist primary providers of service in meeting the needs of those to be served. Core school support teams consisting of administrators, teachers, community members, and representatives from outside social agencies can be assembled on a voluntary basis by the principal to redesign an urban school's internal architecture and operating systems. In addition, core teams could initiate parent support groups and a wide variety of drug-free activities by assisting the development of an effective human infrastructure for these activities (Madden, 1991). Urban principals may be surprised to find so many voluntary advisors and intermediaries who care.

4. *Between Teachers and Administrators.* The urban principal's relationships with teachers are often turbulent and conflictful. Subject

to opposing forces of centralization (top-down management and strong unions/associations) and decentralization (teacher empowerment and school-based decision making), the urban principal faces much personal and professional conflict. But other nascent professional occupations in urban life are stressful, too. Edmonds and his colleagues in the effective schools movement suggested that leadership is a key, perhaps the most important key, to effective schools. There is evidence that principal behavior can help alleviate teacher stress and may boost student achievement (Bliss & Pavignano, 1990; Finneran, 1990). In various ways, effective leadership helps to make the workplace better for people-safe, orderly, and otherwise pleasant. Urban principals demonstrate effective leadership when they proactively create forums, spaces, opportunities, and time in which teachers can work.

Teachers depend somewhat on administrators for a sense of self-efficacy. We know that constructive adult-to-adult contact can be encouraged or suppressed by the principal. The urban principal sets the tone and creates the structures that allow or discourage teacher collegiality in urban schools. In addition, structures that provide teachers with feedback as to their positive contributions can improve perceptions of professional self-worth and self-efficacy. Traditional supervision as oversight, however, can be counterproductive (Swap, 1990). Urban teachers find certain supervisory practices demeaning, including close surveillance, checklisting, unannounced visitations, and incentives for teaching to standardized tests.

The effective urban principal recognizes the importance of teacher self-efficacy (Ogbu, 1974), thinks about the differential impact of resource constraints on the self-efficacy of inexperienced versus veteran teachers, looks for opportunities to broker mini-grants for professional development, and organizes open-house activities to show off teachers' accomplishments. Here, again, the notion of core teams (like those in urban drug-prevention work) can help the urban principal to improve his or her relationships with teachers by providing a source of alternative strategies and by serving as an intermediary agency should the school climate become overly politicized.

5. *Between Teachers and Teachers.* In general, teachers have been poorly trained and socialized for collegial problem solving. More important, typical school schedules make it difficult for teachers to get together for problem solving work during the school day. With respect

to teacher-teacher relationships, there is evidence that adult collegiality promotes teacher self-efficacy, reduces stress, and enhances trust in some schools. Many teachers have grown cynical about the seemingly endless procession of fads, wherein pat phrases such as "teacher collegiality" and "teacher collaboration" seem old, even at first hearing. I have suspected for a long time that teachers are embarrassed by the foolishness of committee work that goes nowhere in terms of substantive changes in schools.

In urban schools, destructive teacher cliques can develop when formal relationships fail to meet people's needs. Cliques are a substantial barrier to teacher collegiality, even though perhaps functional, according to Waller (Roberts, 1968). Urban schools also experience relatively high turnover rates among both students and teachers. Transiency among teachers makes it difficult to develop teacher collegiality. Mintzberg (1991) has recently argued that organizational politics will often succeed where other strategies fail in breaking up centers of resistance to change. Urban principals should work to reduce destructive cliques, using help from a thoughtful core team when required.

Home-School Relationships

Between Parents and Teachers. Lightfoot (1978) offered a sensitive analysis of the gap that often separates parents from school. Not unlike other teachers, urban teachers have trouble coping with differing perceptions of home versus school responsibilities. Urban teachers, generally closer to mainstream backgrounds than students, may object to the notion that schools should accommodate parental demands. They may believe that certain parents are not good enough to raise the children they have. Some people, including many teachers, relate inadequate resources to inadequate parental participation (Etheridge, 1990). However, most teachers readily acknowledge the power and potential of parents to mediate their efforts in the classroom and to contribute to positive academic outcomes for children (Bempechat, 1990).

There is evidence that low-income parents *do* want to help (Clark, 1983). Yet, regular parent-teacher conferences have been dropped in many areas, because of low parental participation. Nonetheless, urban teachers need forums and structures wherein parents and teachers can communicate. Some urban schools have made promising efforts in this regard. The importance of open parent-teacher relationships should not be underestimated. Not every teacher needs to become involved with initiating expanded frameworks in each climate domain mentioned in this chapter. Teacher routines should not be unduly disrupted. But the goal of capitalizing on parent expertise, interest, and influence in schools provides reasonable grounds for expanded parental involvement. Strong parent involvement programs are grounded in a literature, contain a model of action, and include directions for activating the model (Brooks & Sussman, 1990).

Between Students and Parents. Mainstream parents model certain skills and attitudes without which students appear slow, incompetent, or even deserving of punishment (Comer, 1986). In addition, mainstream families are more likely to have both mothers and fathers at home to assist and encourage their children. Some African-American and Latino parents feel helpless to assist their children in school. Urban school practitioners must show restraint in making judgmental interpretations of parental behavior. Parental distancing from schoolwork helps to account for racial and social-class differences in academic and interpersonal skills.

Urban principals, with help from their core teams, can initiate parenting classes to improve relationships between students and parents. Again, it may be necessary to seek outside support from community and social-services agencies.

Between Administrators and Parents. Urban principals who wish to improve perceived relationships between administrators and parents may begin by reviewing some of the more popular books on home-school relationships. Epstein (1987), for example, delineates six home-school functions: school support for families, communications between home and school, family support for schools, family involvement in learning at home, family involvement in school governance, and school-community joint projects. Urban educators sometimes speak wistfully of strong parental involvement in the suburbs, but their efforts to work for improved parental involvement are often limited. Home-school relationships require a combination of compassion, persistence, and risk taking. A principal sets the tone in these regards.

A number of strategies have been documented for structuring parental involvement opportunities in urban schools. Activities such as award assemblies for parents, providing babysitting for conferences, open meetings, workshops, and newsletters are among the fairly standard practices. In addition, people have offered buffets, dinners, insistent phoning, schedules of relevant events, not to mention referrals and interventions on behalf of parents in a whole range of health and human services issues. Where successful, individual parent-involvement strategies may be part of wider school climate improvement efforts and involve a socio-psychological leap-jump of a sort on the part of paid school personnel.

Conclusion

The concept of school climate found in the literature on mainstream schools has no clear location in theory. But operationally, school climate simply amounts to the perceptions of relationships among students, teachers, administrators, and parents in schools. In this chapter, application of the concept of climate to urban schools was accomplished by setting up a framework that consisted of paired relationships among these four groups. Each of these relationships was discussed as part of the overall problem of practice that served as the focus of this chapter; that is: "What can be done to improve the relationships among major groups of stakeholders involved in urban schools?"

To improve the quality of human relationships in urban schools, principals should consider and continually rethink the four-sided image that has been suggested here. The whole image can be held in mind at once. And urban educators can undertake the process of locating additional relevant scholarship by using combinations of this model's keywords to launch electronic searches of other pertinent educational data bases. Principals may wish to initiate any number of suggestions for change, including the use of voluntary core teams, to work towards resolution of this critical problem of practice.

Urban principals occupy an exciting position in society today. Although barriers to positive human relationships may sometimes seem insurmountable, we know that educational climate has been dramatically improved through concerted efforts in certain urban schools. Many small victories of imagination and commitment are needed. It is my hope that some of the ideas presented in this chapter may serve as tools for launching additional victories.

References

Anderson, C. S. (1982). The search for school climate: A review of research. *Review of Educational Research, 52* (3), 386-420.

Argyris, C. (1980). Educating administrators and professionals. In Chris Argyris and Richard M. Cyert (Eds.), *Leadership in the '80s: Essays on higher education* (pp. 1-38). Cambridge, MA: Institute for Educational Management.

Ascher, C. (1990). *Testing students in urban schools.* Urban Diversity Series No. 100. Clearinghouse on Urban Education. Institute for Urban and Minority Education. Teachers College, Columbia University, New York. (ERIC Document Reproduction Service No. 322283.)

Ashton, P., & Webb, R. (1982). *Teachers' sense of efficacy: Toward an ecological model.* Paper presented at the annual meeting of the American Educational Research Association, New York. Teachers College, Columbia University, New York. (ERIC Document Reproduction Service No. 322283.)

Bandura, A. (1977). Self-efficacy: Toward a unifying theory of behavioral change. *Psychological Review, 84,* 191-215.

Bass, B. (1990). *Bass & Stogdill's handbook of leadership: Theory research, and managerial applications.* New York: Free Press.

Bempechat, J. (1990). *The role of parent involvement in children's academic achievement: A review of the literature.* Trends and Issues No. 14. ERIC Clearinghouse on Urban Education. Institute for Urban and Minority Education. Teachers College, Columbia University, New York. (ERIC Document Reproduction Service No. ED322285.)

Bliss, J. R. (1991). Strategic and holistic images of effective schools. In J. R. Bliss, W. A. Firestone, & C. E. Richards (Eds.), *Rethinking effective schools: Research and practice.* Englewood Cliffs, NJ: Prentice-Hall.

Bliss, J. R., & Pavignano, D. (1990). Notes on authenticity and climate. Unpublished paper, Rutgers, The State University of New Jersey, New Brunswick.

Brittan, A., & Maynard, M. (1984). Sexism, racism and oppression. New York: Basil Blackwell.

Brooks, M., & Sussman, R. (1990). *Involving parents in the schools: How can third-party interventions make a difference?* Boston, MA: Institute for Responsive Education. (ERIC Document Reproduction Service No. ED330465.)

Campbell, J., Dunnett, M., Lawler, E., & Weick, K. (1970). *Managerial behavior, performance, and effectiveness.* New York: McGraw-Hill.

Clark, R. (1983). *Family life and school achievement: Why poor black children succeed or fail.* Chicago: The University of Chicago Press.

Comer, J. (Feb., 1986). Parent participation in the schools. *Phi Delta Kappan, 67* (6), 442-446.

Current Population Reports. (1991). *Poverty in the United States: 1988 and 1989.* (ERIC Document Reproduction Service No. ED336485.)

Ekvall, G. (1987). The climate metaphor in organizational theory. In B. M. Bass & P. Drenth (Eds.), *Advances in organizational psychology: An international review.* Newbury Park, CA: Sage Publications.

Epstein, J. L. (1987). Parent involvement: What research says to administrators. *Education and Urban Society, 19* (2), 119-136.

Etheridge, C. P. (1990). Leadership, control, communication, and comprehension: Key factors in successful implementation of SBDM. (ERIC Document Reproduction Service No. ED328655.)

Finneran, R. (1990). The effects of school climate, minimal competency testing (HSPT), and teacher efficacy on teacher stress. Unpublished doctoral dissertation, Rutgers, The State University of New Jersey, New Brunswick.

Focus [Summary]. (1992). Proceedings of the Nineteenth Annual Conference of the National Association of Black School Educators, *13* (1).

Forehand, G. A., & Gilmer, B. (1964). Environmental variations in studies of organizational behavior. *Psychological Bulletin, 62* (6), 361-382

Gardner, H. (1991). *The unschooled mind: How children think and how schools should teach.* New York: Basic Books.

Halpin, A. W., & Croft, D. (1963). *The organizational climate of schools.* Chicago: Midwest Administration Center of the University of Chicago.

Hellreigel, D., & Slocum, J. W., Jr. (1974). Organizational climate: Measures, research, and criticism. *Academy of Management Journal, 17* (2), 255-280.

Hispanic Policy Development Project, Inc. (1991). Disadvantaged urban eighth-graders: Where they are and how they do? (ERIC Document Reproduction Service No. ED335431.)

Hoy, W. K., & Miskel, C. G. (1987). *Educational administration: Theory, research, and practice (3rd ed.).* New York: Random House.

Hoy, W. K., Tarter, C. J., & Kottkamp, R. B. (1991). *Open schools/healthy schools: Measuring organizational climate*. Newbury Park, CA: Corwin Press.

James, L. R., & Jones, A. P. (1974). Organizational climate: A review of theory and research. *Psychological Bulletin, 81* (2), 1096-1112.

Jones, T. G. (1991). The connection between urban school reform and urban student populations: The composition of action in two case studies of school reform. Paper presented at the annual meeting of the American Educational Research Association. (ERIC Document Reproduction Service No. ED336453.)

Knapp, M. S. (1991). What is taught and how, to the children of poverty: Study of academic instruction for disadvantaged students. Washington, DC: SRI International. (ERIC Document Reproduction Service No. ED331181.)

Krasnow, J. H. (1991). Teacher action research teams, building collaborative structures for schools: A report from the schools Reaching Out Project. Paper presented at the annual meeting of the America Educational Research Association, Chicago. (ERIC Document Reproduction Service No. ED331181.)

Lightfoot, S. L. (1978). *Worlds apart: Relationships between families and schools*. New York: Basic Books.

Lomotey, K. L. (1989). *African-American principals: School leadership and success*. New York: Greenwood Press.

Madden, N. A. (1991). Success for all: Multi-year effects of school-wide elementary restructuring programs, Report No. 18. Baltimore, MD: Center for Research on Effective Schooling for Disadvantaged Students. (ERIC Document Reproduction Service No. ED336492.)

McDill, E. L., Rigsby, L. C., & Meyers, E., Jr. (1969). Educational climates of high schools: Their effects and sources. *American Journal of Sociology, 74* (6), 54-67.

Mintzberg, H. (1991). The effective organization: Forces and forms. *Sloan Management Review, 32* (2), 54-67.

Miskel, C. G., & Ogawa, R. (1988). Work motivation, job satisfaction, and climate. In N. J. Boyan (Ed.), *Handbook of research of educational administration* (pp. 279-304). New York: Longman.

Ogbu, J. U. (1974). *The next generation: An ethnography of education in an urban high school*. New York: Basic Books.

Ogbu, J. U. (1978). *Minority education and caste: The American system in cross-cultural perspective*. New York: Academic Press.

Roberts, J. I. (1968). *Scene of the battle.* Garden City, NY: Doubleday.

Seawell, M. A. (Jan./Feb., 1992). Can inner-city organizations learn from street gangs? *The Stanford Observer* (Stanford School of Education supplement).

Sternberg, R. (1988). *Metaphors of mind: Conceptions of the nature of intelligence.* New York: Cambridge University Press.

Swap, S. M. (1990). Schools reaching out and success for all children: Two case studies. (ERIC Document Reproduction Service No. ED330466.)

Tagiuri, R. (1968). The concept of organizational climate. In R. Tagiuri & G. W. Litwin (Eds.), *Organizational climate: Explorations of a concepts.* Boston: Division of Research, Graduate School of Business Administration.

Victor, B., & Cullen, J., (1987). A theory and measure of ethical climate in organizations. In W. C. Frederick (Ed.), *Research in corporate social performance and policy* (pp. 51-71). Greenwich, CT: JAI Press.

Woodman, R. W., & King, D. C. (1978). Organizational climate: Science or folklore? *Academy of Management Review, 3* (3), 816-826.

5

Collecting and Using Information for Problem Solving and Decision Making

ROBERT O. SLATER

In the mid-1970s, school administration researchers began to do descriptive studies of school principals (see, for example, Peterson, 1978). Influenced by Henry Mintzberg's work on middle-level corporate managers, these scholars were after a rather detailed picture of the day-to-day life of school principals. What they found, among other things, was that the school principal's work is characterized by very many short interactions with a variety of people about a rather broad range of issues. School principals, it seemed, spent most of their time dealing with problems of all sorts and making rapid-fire decisions about them. Principals, this research tells us, are mainly problem-solvers and decision-makers.

This chapter is partly about the logic of problem solving and decision making. That the job of the school principal is mainly one of solving problems and making decisions seems to be true no matter whether a principal's school is urban or rural, large or small, rich or poor. The particular problems that principals may encounter in these

AUTHOR'S NOTE: I would like to thank Dr. Richard Folea for his helpful comments on earlier drafts of this manuscript.

different types of schools may differ, but they are all alike in being problems and are all subject to a general point of attack.

This chapter is also concerned with the role that information plays in the process. The quality of problem solving and decision making is to a large extent a function of information. Although we know that school principals spend much if not most of their day solving problems and making decisions, we know little of how they get, use, and keep the information needed to do these things well. Information about the nature of a problem is needed before goals can be set and information is required for the discovery and design of alternative courses of action that might be taken to achieve the goals. To the degree that the quality of the principal's activities affects student performance and school's effectiveness, to this degree information affects student performance and school effectiveness. Thus, school principals might be able to improve their schools by improving the ways in which they acquire, use, and manage information.

The main question addressed in this chapter, therefore, is: What can school principals do to improve the quality of the information needed for problem solving and decision making in their schools? To properly address this question, however, it is first necessary to deal briefly with some prior questions. For example, what is information and how does it vary? What role does it play in the problem-solving decision-making process? What does that process look like? More concretely, what kinds of problems and decisions do school principals, particularly urban school principals, typically face? How might the information required for solving their kinds of problems and making their kinds of decisions be effectively and efficiently acquired, used, and managed?

These and related questions are dealt with in this chapter in three major parts. The first deals with the nature of information and its role in the problem-solving decision-making process. The second explores what the research says about the relationship between information and the problem-solving decision-making process, including the kinds of problems and decisions that typically emerge in the school setting. The third presents some practical things principals can do to improve information management in their schools. My overall aim, then, is to answer three questions: 1) What do we understand about the nature of information or how do we think about it in its relation to problem solving and decision making? 2) What do we know or what does the research say about information, problem solving, and decision making, especially the kinds of problems and decisions that face principals today, and how they get, use, and manage information to solve problems and make decisions? and 3) What might principals do to improve the acquisition, use, and management of information for problem solving and decision making in their schools?

In addressing these three questions, the aim is not to do an exhaustive literature review but to use the research selectively to illustrate the dynamics of information in the problem-solving decision-making process. The research on decision making is usually broken down into two categories: studies that deal with the structure of decision making and those that deal with the process of decision making. The first type, heavily mathematical and theoretical, is not covered here. The main focus of this effort is the process (Abelson & Levi, 1985). The aim of this chapter, as a whole, is practical.

General Model of the Problem-Solving Decision-Making Process

Problem solving and decision making are here assumed to be two phases of a single process. Some scholars view problem solving and decision making as if they were separate processes. Others take the two terms to be synonyms that refer to the same process. Still others maintain that the two terms refer to related but distinct stages or phases of one continuous process. For present purposes, I will adopt the third position and consider problem solving and decision making to be two stages in a single process (National Academy of Sciences, 1986).

In adopting this position, we assume that decisions and decision making presuppose problems and problem solving. As Arnold puts it, "The need for a decision presupposes the existence of a problem" (Arnold, 1978). We assume, in other words, a temporal ordering of the two activities—problems are presumed to precede decisions.

In taking this approach, I am of course aware that in real life things can get messy and that situations arise when several problems and choices present themselves all at once. In these cases, it sometimes happens that decisions for one problem spill over into or attach themselves to other problems. Problems and decisions usually come mixed together simultaneously. More will be said on this point in due course. At this juncture, our aims are two: 1) To describe the main components of the problem-solving decision-making process in their logical or rational sequence, and 2) to describe the role that information plays at each stage.

What Is a Problem?

A problem is a gap between expectation and perceived reality. A problem may be viewed, at least for present purposes, as a difference or gap between what is and what ought to be, between peoples' perception of reality and what they expect reality to be. Problems, in other words, arise when the facts do not measure up to expectations.

In general, the larger the gap between perceived reality and expectations, the more serious the problem.

What Is Information?

Given this view of the nature of problems, we define information to be any oral or written communication that reduces a decision-maker's doubts or uncertainty about a particular problem or situation (Levin, 1991). When one student reports to the principal that another student is selling drugs on campus, thus helping to confirm what the principal already believed to be the case, the principal is getting information. When a principal questions a teacher about a discipline problem, wanting to know the facts of the situation, the principal is getting information.

Major Components of the Problem-Solving Decision-Making Process

The problem-solving decision-making process is generally conceptualized in terms of five basic steps:

1. Identify the problem.
2. Set goals.
3. Design alternative courses of action.
4. Evaluate alternative courses of action.
5. Choose from alternatives the course of action to be pursued.

Identify the Problem. From the definition of a problem that was presented above, it should be clear that what becomes or fails to become a
problem depends on peoples' perceptions of reality and their expectations.
Because different people expect different things from their environments,
(that is, hold and judge it by different standards), the same reality can
present a problem to some people but not to others. Probably one of the
best examples of this can be found in studies of effective schools. These
studies have repeatedly shown that teachers and administrators in effective schools tend to have high expectations for learning (Levine & Lezotte,
1990). In such schools a failure rate of, say, 15% is likely to cause deep
concern and concerted action. In contrast, in a school where children are
not expected to learn, this, or even a higher percentage of failure, might be
deemed acceptable. What constitutes a problem depends on what people
expect, on their standards.

To say this, of course, is, to say that problem identification depends
on peoples' values. For what else is a standard if it is not a value? When
a teacher expects children to read at a certain level, that teacher is
operating with a standard against which student reading progress is
measured. The standard, moreover, is not likely to be neutral in the
sense that the teacher can take it or leave it. Standards usually come
with a strong sense of obligation and desirability attached to them, even
when they are informal. Standards, then, operate as values.

Problem identification depends not only on how people judge or
evaluate what they see in the world; it also is a function of their
perceptions. This is important because problem identification depends
on some agreement about what is real; it is difficult to weigh the facts of
a situation against one's own and others' expectations if no one can agree
on what the facts are. For example, when 542 randomly selected
elementary and secondary principals in 11 southern states were asked
whether they felt they had sufficient autonomy over educational reform
activities, 46.2% indicated they did not while 53.8% felt they did (Lucas,
1991, p. 57). Not surprisingly, principals in each group viewed teacher
empowerment differently. Those in the first group, those who felt they
did not have enough power, expressed less willingness to share decision
making with teachers, while those in the second group were more willing
to do so. The rationale put forward by those reluctant to share power was
simply that they could not give what they themselves did not have.

Now, it would not be surprising if many of the principals who felt
they did not have power actually had more say then they thought, that

is, they misread their own situation. But whether or not they in fact have power is beside the point. That they believe they do not is what counts and what influences their reluctance to share power. Their perception of reality influenced what they saw as a problem. Problem identification, therefore, depends on perceptions of reality that often vary from one person to the next.

One implication of the above is that when confronted with a problem a principal has the following logical options: (1) to ignore it; (2) to dissolve it by persuading individuals involved that their perception of reality is incorrect, or that their expectations are unrealistic; or (3) to solve it by making the perceived reality come up to expectations.

Set Goals. In general, goals are statements or images of future states of affairs. From a problem-solving perspective, goals are statements or images of a problem solved, which usually comes down to seeing oneself rid of something that is not wanted or in possession of something that is. For example, in the case of schools that suffer from a drug problem, the goals would presumably involve images of a drug-free campus. In the the case of schools that suffer from too little parental involvement, goals might be images of parents working with children in classrooms and on the playgrounds, after school as well as during.

To the degree that goals are images, it follows that one of the tasks of leadership is seeing to it that the same or at least similar images of the goal are shared by all members of the organization. Otherwise people may be operating with radically different images of what is wanted. The key here is good communication, and good communication often comes down to sending the same message in as many different ways to as many different people in the organization as often as possible.

To say this, however, is to say that one of the school principal's most important tasks is to build organizational culture, for a culture is founded on shared images of what is important in and for the organization (see Deal & Peterson, 1990).

Design Alternative Courses of Action. Once one has in mind some kind of picture of what things would look like if the problem were solved, then one can begin thinking about how to turn imagination into reality. Sometimes this is done by thinking "backward," that is, by imagining the steps that would have to be taken right before the goal was achieved, and then the steps that would be necessary to achieve those steps, and so on until one worked back to the present condition.

In public school administration, most design activities take the form of coming up with alternative programs, a program being a number of people using various resources to do a variety of things in some kind of sequence or order, all of which is supposed to alleviate some particular problem or set of problems.

Evaluate Alternative Courses of Action.   The term evaluation is usually reserved for things said and done by way of determining whether or not some problem-solving decision-making process has been successful or effective. For present purposes, however, the term is employed to refer to the thought processes and behaviors that go into determining what the best course of action is. That is, one evaluates the various alternative courses of action for the purpose of determining which, among those available, is most desirable.

Choose the Course of Action.   The evaluation of alternatives and the selection from among them comprise what is properly called *decision making*. Someone once said that a decision is what is done after there is no more time for gathering information, and the truth in this statement is that a decision ends deliberation.

The Role of Information in the Problem-Solving Decision-Making Process

Given this understanding of the problem-solving decision-making process, what role does information play in it? Where, in other words, does information come into the picture? The short answer to this question is that information can and, in the interest of rationality, should play a role at each step of the process. First, for example, the less information one has about the nature of the problem or situation at issue, the more difficult it is to set goals or define solutions that address the problem. Second, setting goals or defining solutions requires information about what is feasible, which often includes knowledge of current technology. Third, designing alternative courses of action or programs to achieve the goals or solutions requires information about the relevant means-ends relations. Fourth, evaluating the alternative courses of action available demands information about the resource constraints within which one is working. Some programs might solve the problem but prove too expensive or complicated for the resources at hand. Fifth, choosing from among the alternatives available requires information about the degree to which implementation is likely to occur after the decision is made.

Ill-Defined and Well-Defined Problems and Alternative Decision Models

Many practicing urban school principals, confronted daily with a myriad of problems and decisions, may think the discussion above is an interesting academic exercise but hardly a description of the probem-solving decision-making process as they experience it in everyday life. They may feel that things are not so simple or clearcut as our model makes them seem. In real life, problems do not come one at a time but in bunches. Goals are not the result of careful reflection but are often inherited or adopted for "political" reasons. Courses of action may not be suitable for achieving goals but may in fact simply be chosen because they are convenient or because there has already been an investment in a particular program even though it may not address the problem at hand. Then, too, it is not possible to come up with or even evaluate all the possible alternatives simply because there is not enough time to gather all the information that is necessary. Finally, choosing from among the alternatives available is often an outcome of a mix of emotion, time pressures, convenience, the resources at hand, ignorance, and being too tired to deal further with the issue.

Such thinking, it should be pointed out, is fully consistent with that of problem-solving and decision-making theorists who distinguish between well-defined and ill-defined problems (Abelson & Levi, 1985). It is also consistent with research done on the problem-solving capacity of school principals. Leithwood and Stager (1989) interviewed 22 principals and found, among other things, that expert problem-solvers dealt more effectively with messy problems than did principals with less expertise. Expert problem-solvers, for example, tended to place significantly more emphasis on the problem-identification step of the process than did nonexperts.

In well-defined problems, the decision-maker has a clear idea of what objectives should be attained and is aware of the available alternatives and their associated outcome probabilities. In ill-defined decision problems, however, the decision-maker does not have a clear idea of the objectives to be attained or of the alternative available choices. Group and organizational strategic decisions are representative of ill-defined decision problems.

Most scholars consider the five-step process discussed above to be an ideal model or what the process would look like from a strictly logical point of view. They are aware that in real life the assumptions underlying this "rational" model do not always hold. Accordingly, they have developed at least three other alternative models that purport to describe decision making under realistic conditions (Estler, 1988).

The first of these is sometimes called the *administrative model* because it deals with decision making in the organizational context. Perhaps best articulated by Herbert Simon (1957) in *Administrative Behavior*, the major assumption of this model is that the decision-maker does not attempt to get all the information available at any point in the decision process. Instead of "maximizing" information, the decision-maker "satisfices," that is, makes do with the information that can be gotten in the time available with the resources at hand.

Reflection on this model may help the reader understand the purpose of the present chapter. The general aim here is to give school principals a logical picture of the problem-solving decision-making process, some facts about how that process works and gets distorted in real life, and, some practical techniques for improving the acquisition and use of information in that process. In a sense, then, this chapter is an effort to raise the satisficing threshold of school decision-makers and problem-solvers. I assume that administrators and other decision makers in schools will continue to satisfice. But I hope that when they do reach the point at which they no longer seek new or more information, they have more useful information at hand than they would have without having read and reflected on the present work.

A second common alternative conception of decision making is often referred to as the *political model*. Here, decision-makers are presumed to have their self-interest at heart. Their first question when considering alternatives is what each will mean for them. This model also assumes that cooperation between groups is not likely without incentives, and it assumes that parts of an organization are not well coordinated. In the jargon of organization theory, the organization's various departments and functions are said to be "loosely coupled."

Finally, a third interesting alternative to the rational model outlined above is what is known as the *garbage can model* of decision making. According to this perspective, problems do not come singly but all at once. At the same time, there are also present various solutions for different problems. These problems and solutions get mixed together like garbage in a garbage can and get attached to one another in an unpredictable fashion. A good example of this latter model is the case in which a school has in place a program (a solution) but the problem for which it was invented is no longer present. Nonetheless, because the organization is already heavily invested in it, the solution gets attached to another problem for which it is not suited.

In view of these alternative ways of thinking about the problem-solving decision-making process, one may well wonder why it is worth bothering with the rational model at all, let alone devoting so much space and attention to it. If it does not accurately describe reality, why discuss it?

In the first place, without some prior knowledge of the rational model, descriptions of the alternative models would make less sense. For this reason alone the rational model warrants discussion.

More important, however, the rational model of problem solving and decision making is worth detailed treatment mainly because the present aim is practical not theoretical, and in the world of administration, rational action is always the ideal to be sought—even if it is never attained. Administrative rationality is the efficient fitting of means to end. Administratively rational decisions are those that maximize organizational effectiveness as efficiently as possible. Being and acting rationally, in this sense, is one of the primary imperatives of administration. And if administrators are to follow this imperative and act rationally, it is helpful, indeed probably even necessary, for them to have an ideal in mind as they go about the business of solving problems and making decisions. Unlike academics, practitioners are not mainly concerned with describing the problem-solving decision-making process. This is simply because they are not interested in describing anything at all. Their chief purpose is not to describe reality but to act within it, and to make their actions as rational as possible. Administrative rationality serves as their paradigm for action.

Administrative rationality is not the only kind of rationality, of course. There is also the rationality that exists when we obey laws. In governing our behavior by rules, we act rationally in a manner that differs from administrative rationality. Administrative rationality is action that is focused on consequences. We say that administrative action is rational because it is oriented toward some end or purpose and focuses on the consequences of behavior. Rule rationality, however, involves action that is oriented less toward consequences and more toward principles. Much more could be said on this point but for present purposes it is sufficient to note the distinction.

Knowledge of alternative ways of thinking about problem solving and decision making can help practitioners make their action more rational. Purporting to be more accurate descriptions of the real world, the alternative models can alert administrators to potential unintended consequences of their actions and thus help them reduce uncertainty within their organizations. For these reasons, then, the rational model is the central focus of this chapter.

The Information Process

Nested within the problem-solving decision-making process is the information process. There are several models of this process in general and of its occurrence in the context of schooling in particular. McLaughlin and McLaughlin's (1989) view of the general process contains all the major components and has the virtue of being relatively succinct. From their point of view the acquisition, use, and management of information involves five steps or functions:

1. Selection—deciding what to collect information about
2. Capture—collecting and caring for data
3. Manipulation—giving facts meaning
4. Delivery—presenting information to users
5. Influence—enhancing the value of information

What does the research that might be of interest to school principals and their staffs have to say about each of these five functions and their related activities?

Selecting Data

Information for What?

Information selection is dependent on problem identification. To select information one must first have some notion of what kind of information is needed, that is, one must answer the question: Information on or for what? Knowing one's information needs depends on knowing what one's problems are. So, information selection is first and foremost a function of problem identification; useful knowledge is knowledge that can help solve problems. Just as every decision is preceded by a problem so also is information selection.

In the next section of this chapter, a step-by-step process for identifying problems is described. This procedure or technique is useful not only for identifying problems but also for building cohesion among the organization's members. For present purposes, however, it is not necessary to go through that process to know what some of the more common problems of schools are. Common experience and the research can be combined to generate a preliminary, working list of problems that typically face school principals and their staffs, whether in urban, suburban, or rural settings. What are these problems?

Some Problems Typical of Schools and Schooling

Burstein (1984) suggests that schools and school systems need information about three general kinds of problems or areas. They need information for

1. Examining the functioning and impact of existing school programs.
2. Monitoring key school "health" indicators.
3. Planning, guiding, and examining new instructional improvement initiatives.

A more detailed analysis of the problems that typically confront schools and principals is provided by Hanson (1991) who, borrowing from work by Bacharach and Mitchell, suggests that there are five general types or categories of problems that confront schools: (1) allocation, (2) security, (3) boundary problems between the school and the home and community, (4) evaluation problems, and (5) instructional problems.

Each type of problem suggests the kind of data that needs to be collected. To deal effectively with allocation problems and decisions, for example, school personnel need to have data for three major allocation functions: budgeting, scheduling, and staffing. Budgeting information might include data on the costs of resources within each department, on the costs of athletic equipment and resources for other extracurricular activities, and so on. Scheduling might involve data on such things as test scores, previous grades, and student course preferences, which all could be used to decide the placement of students in honors courses. Staffing or personnel decisions might require data on the educational backgrounds and certification of each teacher or employee. Security problems and decisions would require information about the presence of unauthorized individuals on campus, the presence of gangs, drug use, theft, vandalism, campus and classroom discipline problems, attendance, and so on.

Boundary problems and decisions call for information on supportive and obstructionist coalitions and constituencies in both the community and the school, on parent involvement, on state regulations and rules, and, in the case of special programs, on federal guidelines and mandates. Evaluation problems and decisions demand information about teacher and student performance. Instructional problems and decisions require information on student backgrounds and abilities, on curriculum and course content, on special programs, and so on.

To solve these problems, principals need to collect at least seven kinds of data: They need: (1) student data, (2) school climate data, (3) finance data, (4) human resource data, (5) demographic data on the community, (6) community attitude data, (7) data on local, state, and federal governmental laws and regulations.

The preceding discussion deals with research that can be used to address the selection problem via the question of problem identification: Information for what? An alternative approach to selection, however, is to deal with the question: What information? What kind of data, in other words, is likely to be available and needed for problem solving in schools?

Herman (1989) argues that data collection must have a systematic internal and external scanning structure—external scanning focusing on those in the school's environment and internal scanning on variables inside the school building. He says that there are four major sources of internal scanning data:

1. Student-related data

2. School-climate-related data

3. Finance-related data

4. Human-resource-related data

and that there are five major sources or types of external scanning data:

1. Demographic-related data

2. Finance-related data

3. Attitude-related data

4. Governmental laws, rules, and regulations and policy-related data

5. Miscellaneous data that may be unique to the school

Most school systems routinely collect these and related types of data. In most urban districts, however, it is collected and managed at the system level, usually by a data processing department. The chief problem for school principals and their staffs is to find out what data are available and then to get access to them. More will be said on this point in due course.

Capturing Data

The Levin Study

In most cases, the literature is fragmented on how these five functions figure into the problem-solving and decision-making activities of managers in general and school principals in particular. One exception, however, is Levin's recent paper, "The Information-Seeking Behavior of Local Government Officials" (1991).

Levin begins his study with the observation that current trends in decentralization in local government have made local policy-making both more complex and urgent. To respond effectively to these changes local officials must access relevant, timely, and accurate information, which he defines as "any oral or written message that reduces an officials doubts or uncertainties about a given topic" (1991, p. 272).

Levin surveyed 156 high-ranking municipal and county officials in the San Francisco Bay region. In addition to demographic data, the questionnaire sought information on the following:

- Amount of time devoted to information seeking
- Satisfaction with information received
- Difficulties in locating information
- Types of information needed at work
- Sources of information consulted
- Usefulness of computer-generated information

In general, Levin found what has often been found in studies of school principals: The work of city managers and other public officials is hurried, subject to interruption, and interactive. Of more interest, perhaps, were his particular findings.

Twenty-one percent of those surveyed felt that local data bases and records were inadequate. They complained that information was either not available or kept at the wrong level of government; that past employees had not kept proper documentation; and that extant records were difficult to locate. They also reported problems with getting data to solve new problems and with getting colleagues to share data and information.

Levin also found that at least 30% of respondents reported that they needed the following types of information:

- Directories of names, addresses, and phone numbers
- Legal information
- Information on policies of city council or board of supervisors
- Agency rules and regulations
- Departmental budget or financial information
- Information about new developments in respondent's field
- Information on local agencies and organizations.

In general, local officials wanted information about broad policy that would help them understand the underlying causes of urban problems.

Searching for Information

As more and more schools and school systems move toward site-based management and participative decision making and problem solving, local schools and their staffs are themselves likely to become increasingly interested and involved in information processing tasks. Accordingly, it may be useful to summarize the factors that influence how much information is sifted through before searching ends. What, in other words, determines the length or scope of a search?

There is a tendency to think of the role that information plays in decision making in terms of numbers of alternatives; the information most wanted by the decision-maker is information about what alternatives are available. Information on the number of alternatives is not, however, the only knowledge about alternatives that is wanted. To even search for alternatives requires knowledge of their attributes; one has to have some notion of what an alternative looks like. In general, the research indicates that the greater the number of attributes searched for, the narrower the information search. Moreover, it seems that the scope of the research is influenced more by the number of attributes one has to search for than the number of alternatives. For example, "Individuals will tend to use more information when considering five alternatives with three attributes than when considering three alternatives with five attributes (Abelson & Levi, 1985, p. 262).

Stylistic Differences: Perceptive vs. Receptive Style

When managers gather information to make decisions, they tend to concentrate either on the "big picture" or on details. The former strategy is called the *perceptive style*, whereas the latter is known as the *receptive style* (McKenny & Keen, 1979). There is no consistent evidence that one style is better than the other for decision performance, suggesting that the purpose of the data influences which style is most effective.

Search Behavior and Information Overload

The conjunctive rule of decision-making. Descriptive analyses of decision making have resulted in a few generalizations, one of which is the conjunctive rule. This rule states that decision-makers often simplify their search by setting some minimum standard or standards which must be met for alternatives to be considered. The higher the standards, the fewer the alternatives. For example, a principal may only interview candidates with a master's degree.

The compensatory rule of decision-making. The compensatory rule of decision making states that if decision-makers find an alternative lacking in some attribute they may consider it anyway if it has more of another attribute that is also desired. In this manner, an abundance of one attribute compensates for the lack of another. For example, a prospective teacher may lack many of the qualifications but may have grown up in the community. A principal may consider this fact more important than all of the others.

Time, quantity of information, and decision rules. In general, the research suggests that time and the quantity of information have much the same ill-effects on decision-makers. Too little of the former and too much of the latter will cause decision-makers to abandon a compensatory strategy and adopt a conjunctive approach. For example, as time pressures or the amount of information increases, decision-makers tend to weight unfavorable information disproportionately. This seems to be because the more that an individual comes under pressure to make a decision, the more attention he or she pays to reducing the chances of making a mistake. In general, the research indicates that reliance on simple rather than complex rules of decision making lowers the quality of decisions (Abelson & Levi, 1985).

Although the research indicates that decision-makers prefer to make the decision process as simple as possible, it also suggests that the more complex the decision process, the better the decision. The practical problem for principals, therefore, is how to make the process more complex without making it more burdensome (see "A General Strategy for Solving Problems").

Two obvious implications of this research for school principals (and others) have to do with teacher recruitment and innovation. For example, a principal under increasing pressure to make hiring decisions might begin, according to this research, to pay less attention to positive attributes of the candidates and look more for negative things that could be used to eliminate them from further consideration. The result is that teachers are hired more for what they are not than for what they are.

Another implication is that principals under pressure to make decisions will be less likely to take the risks required for innovation and change. Instead of focusing on achieving goals, their attention will be concentrated instead on avoiding mistakes.

Manipulating Data: How Accurate Are Student Records?

Surprisingly little research has been done on the accuracy of public school records and record keeping, but what little research there is paints a dismal picture: School records could well turn out to be more inaccurate than many care to believe.

Data are usually collected in "raw" form and, before they can be used in decision making and problem solving, they need to be transformed into a number of summary statistics. If a survey instrument was used to collect the data, the responses for each item for each respondent have to be tabulated so that the range of responses for each question can be calculated along with other descriptive statistics. These descriptive statistics then have to be put into a form that is accessible to policymakers who are often not familiar with basic statistical procedures. The instruments used to collect data and the process of getting data from the instruments to more usable form constitutes the "manipulation" phase. At this stage, accuracy is a major consideration, for data manipulation can result in errors that can distort the outcomes of statistical analysis.

For example, education programs, school budgets, staffing, and resource planning generally begin with information about students. All planning data is ultimately linked to such things as the number of students, student attendance, performance and achievement, student eligibility to attend school and other similar student characteristics. Much of this information is gotten from individual student records that are routinely maintained by each school. These records contain, among other things, such basic data as birth date, gender, race, citizenship, and an identification number assigned by school officials.

How accurate are these records? In a systematic review of the literature on school recording keeping, Folea (1991) concluded that surprisingly little research has been done in this area. Folea's review was a prelude to his own study in which he assessed the accuracy of student records in seven secondary public schools in a large East Coast school system. He examined 120 student records in each school. He found that student registration forms were missing for 5.8% of the students, forms that are required by law to be collected and maintained by the schools and that must be certified by parents and verified and validated by school officials. In addition, 30% of student registration forms were either not certified by parents, as mandated by law, or did not contain required student information. Of the remaining 64.2 % of the forms, almost three-fourths contained errors made during handling and processing.

Folea also examined affidavits of residence, which are required by state law to be certified by parents and verified and validated by school officials. A review of these prerequisites for admission showed that 44% of the records did not contain an affidavit. Of the remaining 56% of the records, over one-fourth had not been verified or validated by school officials.

Student performance records also contained errors. Folea found that 2.6% of the students had no such record in their files; 4% did not contain required student identification information; 12% had birth dates that were either missing or incorrect; 20% of the genders on student performance records were either missing or miscoded; 8% of the records were incorrectly coded for race; and 4% had misspelled the names of the students.

Finally, when Folea examined the records that contained standardized tests score results, he found that 45.5% of them contained errors of one kind or another. For example, roughly 5% had the student's identification number wrong; 11.7% had the student's birth date recorded incorrectly; 19.5% had the gender either wrong or miscoded; and 5.2% had the student's race misidentified or not coded properly.

More research is needed to determine the extent to which the inaccuracies that Folea found in his seven-school study are typical of public secondary schools in general, and urban schools in particular. But if other schools' records are discovered to contain similar inaccuracies, then not only policymakers have cause to be concerned but also researchers and practitioners who use these data.

Delivering or Presenting Information

There is considerable evidence that the quality of decision making is affected by how information is presented. In general, studies suggest that compatibility plays an important role in judgment (Slovic et al., 1990). Take, for example, the current favorite among Nintendo games, Super Mario. According to this theory, it should be easier to process and react to the visual information coming from the television screen if the control deck involves a left movement to move Mario to the left and a right movement to move him to the right rather than vice versa. Or, to take another example, a bicycle rider should find it easier to give a left turn signal if the gesture for the signal is itself a left-arm movement.

Not much research has been done on the presentation of information in school settings. What little we know, however, suggests that the format in which information is presented is highly important. Sirotnik and Burstein (1984), for example, studied the role of information in the school improvement efforts of a high school, and discovered, among other things, that one of the teachers' greatest concerns was that information fit on 8 1/2 x 11" paper so that it could be put in their notebooks. This format issue alone, it seems, influenced whether or not the information was kept and used.

Enhancing the Value of Data

Having low-quality information does not always mean low-quality decisions. It is still possible to get decisions to go one's way or to make a good decision even if the information at hand is only poor, vague, or of a low quality. One can be persuasive by presenting poor information in a vivid manner. Also, one can make the right decision without the requisite information if one pays close attention to the context of the situation and uses it to "fill in" the missing data.

It will probably come as no surprise to learn that one line of information research suggests that the person who presents a case with the most vivid information is most likely to win the debate or argument (Kahneman et al., 1982; Nisbett & Ross, 1980; Ungson & Braunstein, 1982). Less obvious, however, may be the proposition that vague information need not have a negative impact on decision performance. Although it is natural to suppose that the more precise and accurate the information at one's disposal, the better one's decision making, some research suggests this is not always so. The key factor seems to be the degree to which goals or objectives are shared. Apparently, the more that decision-makers have the same end in view, the less trouble vague information causes. Knowing of each other's ends, the individual decision-makers seem better able to "read between the lines" or piece together the missing parts of the communication. Accordingly, although vivid information may be a powerful advantage, communicating vaguely when the information warrants it may not be the disadvantage intuition suggests it should be (Slovic et al., 1990).

Organizational Barriers to Effective Information Use

McLaughlin and McLaughlin's (1989) conception of information functions has already been discussed. Their most interesting contribution, however, is not simply their perspective on the information process but their idea about what can happen to the process in the context of organizations. In other words, they argue that there are organizational barriers to effective information use. When people in organizations try to select, capture, manipulate, deliver, and influence information, they run up against problems that do not occur when individuals attempt these same functions.

McLaughlin and McLaughlin offer a view of organizations familiar to students of Talcott Parsons who maintained that organizations could be thought of as having three levels: technical, managerial, and institutional. Like Parsons, they also see organizations as having three levels: operational, managerial, and strategic. Each level presents barriers to effective information use. For example, information selection is made problematic at the strategic level by the presence of multiple or shifting goals. Communication gaps threaten selection at the managerial level. Inadequate measures interfere with information selection at the operational level.

A General Strategy for Solving Problems, Making Decisions, and Developing an Information System for a School

Probably one of the most important practical implications of the research on problem solving and decision making is that decision-makers want naturally to simplify the decision process, but their decision making would probably be better if the process were more complex. How can principals maintain a level of sophistication in the decision process but not have it become burdensome?

The short answer to this question is that they can institute a general process of decision making that relies on groups of individuals, the quality of which is not dependent on any one individual. Such a model is described in this section. It is an adaptation and modification of a program suggested by Sirotnik and Burstein (1984). In passing, it can also be pointed out that the type of process described below also fits well with most schools' restructuring/school-site management plans.

Establish a Schoolwide Problem-Solving Committee

Schools involved in site-based decision making or restructuring will probably already have a school-based advisory committee. To maximize its usefulness, this committee ought to be thought of as a Problem-Solving Committee and should be so designated.

The size of the committee should to some extent be determined by the size of the school, though a committee of more than, say, 12 to 15 members quickly becomes unmanageable. If possible, parents and community members should be included among the committee's members.

Identify the Problems

A problem, as we have already seen, usually appears as a gap between how people see reality and what they expect it to be. So long as people accept things as they are or as they perceive them to be, there is no problem. When, however, people see one thing and expect another, a problem exists. When a problem is indicated, the school's problem-solving committee has several alternatives. It can (a) ignore the problem, (b) try to persuade people that their perceptions are incorrect, (c) try to change people's expectations, or (d) solve the problem by bringing reality in line with expectations. All of these alternatives require the committee to go through at least part of the information process. To identify problems the committee can do at least the following things:

A. Establish a committee or subcommittee of three or four teachers, parents, and community members to serve as the Information Committee. If your school is engaged in site-based management, this committee could be a subcommittee of the school's advisory committee. It is highly recommended that the school-library media specialist be one member of the committee.

B. Have the Information Committee design and distribute a simple one- or two-page questionnaire that lists the problem areas articulated by Hanson (1991, pp. 103-104). Ask school personnel to check the kinds of problems or problem areas which they believe to be most important in their school. Include space for brief explanations and for identifying areas not on the list.

C. After identifying what school personnel believe to be the three or four greatest obstacles to learning in their school, have the Information Committee contact the data-processing department in the central office to determine what information or data are available that might be used to address the problems mentioned. For example, if teachers report that they believe poor discipline is the greatest obstacle to learning in the school, then the Information Committee should request data on discipline problems. Such data might include:

1. Number of students referred to office for discipline problems
2. Number of students referred to office by each teacher for discipline problems
3. Most common type of discipline problem reported
4. Number of detentions, in-school suspensions, alternative school placements, expulsions, and so on per month or per year
5. Any other data that could be used to judge the extent and nature of the problem

D. After identifying some problems and gathering information as to their severity, have the Information Committee present these data to the problem solving committee as a whole. The presentation of the data might take the format described below sometimes called the *chart essay* (Smith et al., 1986).

A *chart essay* is simply a single sheet of white cardboard approximately 2' x 3' on which a piece of information is presented in three parts. In the top one-third of the chart the question that is being addressed is stated in interrogative form. For example, "What is the extent of the discipline problem in our school as measured by detentions, suspensions, and expulsions?" The middle one-third of the chart should present the relevant statistics, preferably in the form of a graph. In the case of discipline, it might take the form of a bar chart with a single bar devoted to each indicator. Presenting the data in this form enables the group to easily compare the proportion of detentions to suspensions. The bottom third of the chart should again be text but instead of the question it should contain a summary statement of what the statistics say. For the discipline example, there might be a statement along the following lines: "Our school had 131 detentions, 9 suspensions and 2 expulsions last year," or "Our school had 131 detentions last year and of these 80% were for leaving campus without permission, 15% were for violation of dress codes, and 5% for fighting," and so on.

Set Goals

Having documented the existence and scope of the problems, the Problem-Solving Committee's next task is to develop realistic goals relative to the problems. If, for example, it is felt that students are not learning because of low parental involvement, the goal might be to increase the number of parents attending PTO or PTA meetings.

Develop Alternative Strategies for Achieving Goals

Once some realistic goals for dealing with the school's problems have been defined, the Problem-Solving Committee should hold one or two sessions devoted to brainstorming for alternative strategies for achieving the goals defined in the previous step. The job of the Information Committee at this point is to identify successful programs that are in other school systems and that are described in the literature. Quick phone calls to neighboring systems and state and national agencies is one way to handle the first task. The literature review can be done in short order by having a member of the committee peruse the last several years of ERIC indexes and make copies of the relevant articles for the Problem-Solving Committee.

Evaluate Alternative Strategies

After the Problem-Solving Committee has defined some realistic goals and developed alternative strategies for achieving each goal, the Information Committee should then re-survey the teaching staff and other interested parties to determine whether or not there are goals they failed to consider and the degree to which the goals they identified are felt to be realistic. They also want to get input on the various alternative strategies they have developed for achieving the goals and some assessment on how realistic they appear to be.

The next step is for the Information Committee to present the results of the survey to the members of the Problem-Solving Committee. Again, this should be in a clear, straightforward format in which pieces of 2' x 3' poster board are used. Each chart should contain (1) the problem in interrogative form, (2) a statement of the goal to be achieved, and (3) a listing of the alternative strategies for achieving the goals. *Choose Strategy or Program for Solving the Problem*

School Climate and Culture Problems

The identification of a school's culture or climate problems requires some type of climate or culture diagnostic tool. There are no doubt several of these around but some good ones are:

- The Effective Schools Battery (ESB)

Developed by researchers at The Johns Hopkins University (Gottfriedson & Hollifield, 1988), the ESB involves surveys of students and teachers. It gives a profile of the school's climate, suggests ideas for improvement, and helps keep track of progress. The instrument indicates whether morale is low or high, whether the school is safe or not, whether there is tension between teachers and administrators, and so on.

- A three-phase survey for teachers who do not wish to be identified with their views (Tewel, 1990).

Identify the informal leaders among the teachers and involve them in the development of a simple multiple-choice questionnaire of 25 to 30 items. Do not ask respondents to identify themselves. Design the questionnaire so that questions can be answered by using check marks instead of writing. Do not code blank forms. Provide a ballot box in which completed forms can be placed. Have an outside volunteer group or agency tabulate the results of the poll.

Some Common Practical Techniques for Solving Problems and Making Decisions

Problem Identification: The Nominal-Group Technique

Sometimes individuals in a group situation are reluctant to speak out or voice their opinions. The *nominal-group technique* helps get over this communication barrier. Here are the steps:

1. Distribute to each member of the group a 3" x 5" card.

2. Ask each member to write on the card what they consider to be the school's most important obstacles to learning.

3. Collect the cards.

4. Write all the ideas on the cards on large sheets of paper that can be taped on the wall for all to see. Leave no idea out.

5. Order the ideas in terms of priority (see "Techniques for Evaluating Alternatives")

Technique for Evaluating Alternatives

The Weights and Criteria Technique

Research studies suggest that when it comes to rules for making decisions, the more complex the decision rule the higher the quality of the decision. One decision rule is more complex than another if it takes into account more features or attributes of a thing. For example, the person who decides to buy a car on the basis of one attribute, say, its color, is less apt to make as good a decision as the one who buys a car on the basis of a number of attributes, say, not only color but also safety, economy, interior appointments, and so on. In general, the more attributes one can take into account, the better the decision is likely to be.

The research also says, however, that the greater the number of attributes being considered, the shorter the search. In other words, the person who tries to find a car with a number of attributes is likely to consider fewer alternatives, that is, consider fewer cars.

The *weights and criteria technique* is designed to allow several attributes to be considered on several alternatives. To use this technique, one begins by drawing a figure such as that in Figure 5.1. The alternatives are listed down the side, each alternative forming a single row. The attributes (criteria) are listed across the top where each serves as a heading for a column. Above each attribute a number or weight is assigned according to its importance to the decision-maker. Assume, for present purposes, that the importance of the attributes are indicated by a scale of 1 to 5, a 1 being low priority and a 5 being high priority.

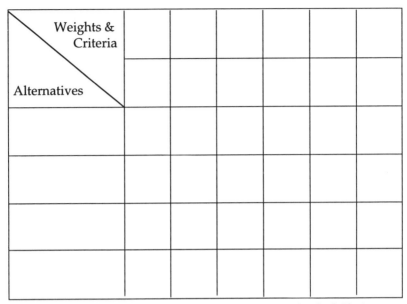

Figure 5.1. Form for the Weights and Criteria Method of Choice.

Suppose, for example, that you want to use the weights and criteria method to help you buy a house. Before you begin looking at houses you should sit down with the form in Figure 5.1 and across the lower portion of the top fill in the various attributes or criteria you want a house to meet. In Figure 5.2, for example, I've listed the following criteria: Price, Location, 3 Bedrooms, 2 Baths, Pool, School. In the space above each of these criteria I have assigned a "weight." So, I have weighted Location with a 5 because it is important. In contrast, although I would like to have a pool, I do not think it as important as the location of the house, so I have weighted Pool with a 2. The other criteria have been given weights according to my feelings about their relative importance.

Having completed this much of the form, and knowing some of the most important things I want in a house, I begin looking at actual houses. Let us suppose that I look at about 20 houses and end up with four that I like very much. Now, under each criterion I put a score for each of the four houses depending upon how I feel each meets that criterion compared to the others. For example, House # 2 is in a great

Weights & Criteria	4	5	3	4	2	5	
Alternatives	Price	Location	3 Bedrooms	2 Bath	Pool	School	
House #1	5	3	5	3	0	4	
House #2	3	5	5	5	0	5	
House #3	5	4	4	5	3	5	
House #4	4	2	5	4	5	4	
House #1 =	4 x 5	5 x 3	3 x 5	4 x 3	2 x 0	5 x 4	
=	20	15	15	12	0	20	= 82
House #2 =	4 x 3	5 x 5	3 x 5	4 x 5	2 x 0	5 x 5	
=	12	25	15	20	0	25	= 97
House #3 =	4 x 5	5 x 4	3 x 4	4 x 5	2 x 3	5 x 5	
=	20	20	12	20	6	25	=103
House#4 =	4 x 4	5 x 2	3 x 5	4 x 4	2 x 5	5 x 4	
=	16	10	15	16	10	20	=87

Figure 5.2. Examples of the Use of the "Weights and Criteria" Method for Choosing Among Alternatives.

location so it gets a 5 under that criterion but it does not happen to have a pool, so under the pool criterion I give it only a 0. By contrast, House # 4 has a terrific pool but is in a bad location, so it gets high marks for the pool but low marks for its location.

After the form is completed, the next step is to calculate the total score for each of the alternatives (houses). This is done by first multiplying each alternatives score under each criterion by the weighting assigned to the criterion (see bottom of Figure 5.2). This results in a total score for that criterion. Then the scores for each of the criteria are added up to give a total score for that particular alternative. In Figure 5.2, House #3 scores highest with 103, and so it would seem to come closest to meeting my criteria and the importance I have attached to them.

Few people would probably rely solely on a technique such as this one for making a decision as important as a house purchase. This is simply because there are always "intangible" elements that figure in to the calculation but cannot themselves be quantified. For example, while House #3 has the highest score, House # 2 may, for various reasons, "feel" right whereas # 3 does not. In such cases, an exercise such as this is helpful if only it causes one to think more carefully about the alternatives available. One may in fact end up buying House # 2 but only after having given it more thought than otherwise might have been the case were the weights and criteria technique not employed.

Techniques for Narrowing Alternatives:

The Spend-A-Buck Method

This is a technique for ranking problems in order of their importance.

1. Have all of the alternatives listed on large sheets of paper and taped to a wall so that all can see and read them easily.

2. Distribute to each member of the group two or three colored dots with adhesive on one side.

3. Ask the group's members to think of each dot as a "buck," which they can spend on one alternative, that is, each member is to place a dot next to an alternative he or she consider to be the most important or among the three or four most important problems.

4. The problems receiving the most dots are kept for further consideration, the others are postponed.

Conclusion

Administrative work in general and the work of school principals in particular is mainly the work of solving problems and making decisions. Theoretically, problem solving and decision making may be viewed as different parts of a continuous process that has five basic steps: (1) problem identification, (2) goal setting, (3) generation of alternative strategies for achieving the goals, (4) evaluation of alternatives, and (5) decision or choice. However, these five steps often get distorted in practice. Sometimes strategies chosen for different problems get attached to the problem at hand. Sometimes goals are determined before problems are identified. Seldom are administrators able to get all the information available about alternative strategies, and so on. Nonetheless, the rational model of problem solving can serve as a handy reference point that decision makers can use to understand the peculiarities and non-rational elements at work in their own situations.

The quality of problem solving and decision making is to no small degree a function of the quality and quantity of information available. In this chapter I have suggested various ways in which information affects problem solving and decision making. My emphasis throughout has been on practice and the practical. Accordingly, the mathematical and more technical aspects of problem solving and decision making have not been discussed.

Finally, I have also suggested some practical strategies school principals can use to improve the quality and quantity of information available to them, and I have described the steps they can take to involve their faculty and community members in an informed problem solving and decision making process.

References

Abelson, R., & Levi, A. (1985). Decision making and decision theory. In G. Lindzey and E. Aronson (Eds.), *Handbook of social psychology*, Vol. 1, New York: Random House.

Adams, C. R. (1977). *Appraising information needs of decision makers*. New Directions for Institutional Research, No. 15. San Francisco, CA: Jossey-Bass.

Arnold, J. (1978). *Make up your mind.* New York: Amacom.

Boyd, W. (1979). *Problem-finding in educational administration : Trends in research and theory.* Lexington, MA: Lexington Books.

Burstein, L.(1984). *Information use in local school improvement : A multi-level perspective.* Los Angeles, CA: University of California at Los Angeles, Center for the Study of Evaluation.

Deal, T., & Peterson, K. (1990). *The principal's role in shaping school culture.* Washington, DC: U.S. Department of Education, Office of Educational Research and Improvement.

Estler, S. (1988). Decision making. In N. Boyan (Ed.), *Handbook of research on educational administration* (pp. 305-319). New York: Longman.

Ewell, P. (1989). *Enhancing information use in decision making.* San Francisco, CA: Jossey-Bass.

Folea, R. (1991). An exploratory study of the effect of handling and processing on student information quality in seven east coast public secondary schools. Ph. D. Dissertation, The University of Maryland, College Park, MD.

Folea, R. (1986). Errors in an instant: How to check the accuracy of computerized records. *The American School Board Journal 173* (8).

Gray, J. L., & Starke, F. A. (1984). *Organizational behavior.* 3rd ed. Columbus, OH: Merrill.

Gottfriedson, G., & Hollifield, J. (1988). How to diagnose school climate: Pinpointing problems, planning change. *NASSP Bulletin 72;* 63-71.

Hanson, E. M. (1991). *Educational administration and organizational behavior.* Boston, MA: Allyn & Bacon.

Herman, J. (1989). External and internal scanning: Identifying variables that affect your school. *NASSP Bulletin, 73,*48-52.

Hogarth, R. (ed.) (1990). *Insights in decision making.* Chicago, IL: University of Chicago Press.

Kahneman, D., Slovic, P., & Tversky, A. (1982). *Judgment under uncertainty: Heuristics and biases.* New York: Cambridge University Press.

Leithwood, K., & Stager, M. (1989). Expertise in principals' problem solving. *Educational Administration Quarterly, 25,* 126-161.

Levin, M. (1991). The information-seeking behavior of local government officials. *American Review of Public Administration 21,* 271-286.

Levine, L. U., & Lezotte, L. L. (1990). *Unusually effective schools: A review and analysis of research and practice.* Madison, WI: National Center for Effective School Research and Development.

Lucas, S. (1991). Principals' perceptions of site-based management and teacher empowerment *NASSP 75*,56-62.

McKenny, J. L., & Keen, P. G. (1979). How manager's minds work. Harvard Business Review, 79-90.

McLaughlin, G. W., & McLaughlin, J. S. (1989). Barriers to information use: The organizational context. In P. T. Ewell (Ed.), *Enhancing information use in decision making*. San Francisco, CA: Jossey-Bass.

National Academy of Sciences. (1986). *Research briefing 1986: Report of the research briefing panel on decision-making and problem-solving*. Washington, D.C.: National Academy of Science.

Nisbett, R., & Ross, L. (1980). *Human inference*. Englewood Cliffs, NJ: Prentice-Hall.

Peterson, K. D. (1978). The principal's tasks. *The Administrator's Notebook, 26*, 1-4.

Ross, K. N., & Postlethwaite, T. N. (1988). Planning the quality of education: Different information for different levels of decision-making. *Prospects 13*, 315-331.

Simon, H. (1957). *Administrative behavior*. New York: Free Press.

Sirotnik, K. (1984). *Using vs. being used by school information systems*. Washington, DC: National Institute of Education.

Sirotnik, K., & L. Burstein. (1984). *Making sense out of comprehensive school-based information systems*. Los Angeles, CA: Center for the study of Evaluation.

Slovic, P., Griffin, D., & Tversky, A. (1990). Compatibility effects in judgment and choice. In R. Hogarth (Ed.), *Insights in decision making*. Chicago, IL: University of Chicago Press.

Smith, R., McNamara, J., & Barona A. (1986) Getting "good results" from survey research: The SISD-TAMU experience. *Public Administration Quarterly 10*, 233-243.

Tewel, K. (1990). Improving in-school communications: A technique for principals. *NASSP Bulletin, 74*, 39-41.

Ungson, G. R. & Braunstein, D. N. (1982). *Decision making: An interdisciplinary inquiry*. Boston, MA: Kent Publishing.

Wallsten, T. (1990). The costs and benefits of vague information. In R. W. Hogarth (Ed.), *Insights in decision making* (pp. 28-43). Chicago, IL: University of Chicago Press.

6

Acquiring and Using Resources

LAURENCE PARKER

"What are the imaginable organizational/structural/administrative tools for creating urban school environments that succeed?" When this question was posed, the response of the Select Conference of practicing school professionals centered on "flexibility of resources, funding, curriculum, calendar, and scheduling." The conference, sponsored by the University Council for Educational Administration and the Danforth Foundation, was intended to gather and exchange information on problems of practice faced by administrators and youth service professionals in urban public school settings. An underlying premise of the conference was that practice could inform theory in the field of urban educational administration.

When analyzing the responses of the Select Conference members to the question of resources, a number of subtopics emerged in the form of "problems of practice." Briefly, these subtopics were related to lack of funds, time as a scarce resource, the acquisition of resources, and the utilization of human resources (staff expertise) to improve schools and services for students. The special needs of urban public schools demanded that these principals and youth service professionals rely on what few resources they could secure for the benefit of staff and students.

Resources, both monetary and human, are crucial elements of any plan to improve the lives of students in urban schools. The purpose of this chapter is to provide an overview of several general and specific aspects of resource acquisition and utilization. A key question in this conceptualization of resources and resource development will be: Given limited means, what can be done by urban school principals, teachers, and youth service professionals to address various resource-related problems of practice at their sites?

It is clear that those who are interested in the survival and improvement of urban schools must continually and forcefully press for increased funding from federal, state, and local governments. It is also clear that urban schools have serious physical plant needs and student problems that require massive assistance. Some say that these schools have been virtually abandoned by government funding sources. But as Seashore Louis and Miles (1990) aver, "It depends on where you throw money and how" (p. 240), in terms of improving the urban public schools. This is because both monetary and human resources have to be arranged and targeted carefully in order to ameliorate impoverished conditions and promote academic learning in urban schools. Scarce resources must be engaged in such a way as to promote meaningful changes in the lives of urban students. Such changes entail a commitment by school principals to re-evaluate the status quo and to raise and address questions such as: (1) How can this school develop educational policies and practices that provide students with needed academic and social skills as well as the knowledge to question and seek remedies for broader problems related to schooling, such as poverty and institutional racism? (2) How can this school inform and mobilize students and staff against sexism and violence in their communities? and (3) How can this school break the cycle of class distinctions and stigmatization, especially for low socioeconomic students?

This chapter addresses several areas of urban school needs, including access to resources and resource utilization. First the chapter will review the conflict over resources from a theoretical and empirical standpoint, placing urban resource issues within a larger context of debate about how much and what kind of resources should be expended on public schooling. The next part explores the issue of resource needs and urban schools, documenting the special needs of schools in large cities. Once these problems are highlighted, they are connected in the third part to lower student achievement and life outcomes in urban contexts. This section of the chapter demonstrates how the lack of resources and the unique problems of city schools combine to produce a deleterious effect on urban students. In addition the monetary and nonmonetary resources needed to improve urban public schools will be highlighted. Key instances of resource utilization by schools and principals are highlighted as examples of resource acquisition and utilization. These include school-business partnerships, community connections, and outside professionals for school improvement. Finally, the chapter offers suggestions to urban school professionals, educational administration programs, political and business leaders, and urban communities as to how to address the resource needs of urban students in public schools.

To Spend or Not to Spend: Framework for Urban School Resource Needs

An article in Forbes by Brimelow (1990) bluntly illustrates the argument that has been made by advocates for less spending on public education:

> If increased spending on education offered a way out of the problems, everyone would no doubt favor the spending: There are few items on the national agenda more important. But the problems of the U.S. education industry, like those of the Soviet economy, are structural. In both cases, the problems cannot be resolved by mere tinkering reforms—or more spending. You don't fix a car that isn't running properly by pumping more gasoline into the tank. (p. 82)

Human capital arguments have historically undergirded the question of how much the United States should spend on public schooling (DeYoung, 1989). Some have argued in favor of Brimelow's position: Increased spending on public school students really won't help them or the U.S. economy, because the public schools are in such a terrible state of affairs. These critics of increased spending contend that public schools have never been models of efficiency. Therefore, the argument goes, why should we increase spending on a hopeless operation? As evidence, these critics have cited: (1) the decline of U.S. students on standardized test measures; (2) the lack of necessary technical and basic job skills to enter and excel in the work force; and (3) the moral value decline of students, particularly as manifested in urban areas by the high dropout rates, teen pregnancy, and student discipline problems. These critics have argued that increased spending on public schooling will not cure the aforementioned ills. Instead, they propose that schools should be forced to compete for students through school choice plans. Through a school choice or voucher plan, families could use their own judgment as to what would be the best education for their child (or children) and could spend their voucher(s) accordingly. Proposals such as this have been advocated by numerous groups and agencies, perhaps most notably the Bush Administration. In essence, this position asserts that public schooling has not delivered much "bang for the buck" in terms of improving student performance, particularly in urban areas.

The proponents of this position have utilized various measures of effectiveness to support their viewpoints—this despite the fact that the complexities of school student inputs, the teaching and learning process, and school outputs and outcomes have not been convincingly researched (Colvin, 1989). Part of the problem stems from the question of how nonquantifiable results can be analyzed through the cost-benefit approach or production function studies. Some successful learning processes and outcomes (such as students who learn to enjoy reading by deviating from the standardized curriculum) are not readily measurable. Nonetheless, some have tried to show the relationship between spending and student achievement. Notable among these researchers are Walberg and Fowler (1987), who investigated the question of school district size and achievement test scores in relationship to the socioeconomic status (SES) of the district. Essentially, they asked, "Are larger and higher spending districts more efficient?" (p. 5). Walberg and Fowler found that low-spending districts on average achieve as well as high-spending districts of the same SES, and larger districts were less efficient than smaller districts with respect to achievement. Their analysis of the results led them to speculate that educational policies and classroom practices had a more important impact on student achievement than resources spent on schools.

A similar conclusion was reached by Childs and Shakeshaft's meta-analysis of research on the relationship between educational expenditure and student achievement (1986). Their analysis indicated that higher resources were important but not the deciding factor in increasing student achievement. Childs and Shakeshaft (1986) also called for educators to examine how well dollars are spent for education in the schools with regard to promoting achievement, particularly since large increases in state and local spending do not appear to be forthcoming. Hanushek's (1989) review of the "educational production function" studies yielded similar results with respect to the relationship between expenditures and student performance (for example, achievement test results, dropout rates, college entrance rates). His analysis indicated "no strong or systematic relationship between school expenditures and student performance" (p. 47). Even though he urged caution in interpreting these results, he also reached conclusions similar to other researchers who called for more attention to be paid to the interrelationship between resource utilization and school achievement. For Hanushek, school finance policy decisions at the legal, legislative, or district/school level need to concentrate on how to effectively use the funds already available. The previously mentioned studies and reviews of the research on resources and student/school achievement have pointed to the "effective" utilization of dollars for improvement in the schools and students, particularly in terms of achievement on standardized tests. Mann and Inman (1984) also called for improving public schooling through increased emphasis on an "instructionally effective schools" approach to improvement. Although they agreed that more funds for public schools would be desirable, their reading of the political climate during the previous decade indicated that generous amounts of funding for the public schools simply were not forthcoming. Furthermore, the schools reviewed for the study indicated a strong utilization of a production function model that centered on achievement as a function of six distinct variables. Specifically:

$$Y = f(X_1, X_2, X_3, X_4, X_5, X_6)$$

Where:

Y = IES (achievement)
X_1 = Teacher characteristics and behavior
X_2 = Administrator characteristics and behavior
X_3 = Student body composition
X_4 = School learning climate
X_5 = Pupil evaluation

$$X_6 = \text{Curriculum material}$$
(Mann & Inman, 1984, p. 266).

They concluded their review with a set of policy implications for schools and administrators. They recommended that administrators strongly emphasize instructional leadership, with a de-emphasis on business management skills. They also called on school administrators to promote instructional effectiveness by taking the risk of setting high instructional goals that might indeed challenge a school staff who had low expectations of students, particularly urban minority pupils. Finally, Mann & Inman (1984) argued for administrators to invest their limited resources on retraining the teaching staff to expose them to "the process and product factors linked to the efficacy of their work with children" (p. 268).

However, critics have pointed out that such retraining of teachers requires dollars for education that the public schools in urban areas simply do not have. Long (1986), for example, stated that policy initiatives to improve the working conditions of teachers, particularly those in urban areas, additional staff training, and increasing instructional leadership all cost more money. He cited a state study of school plant facilities in New Jersey that estimated a cost of over $3 billion to upgrade the run-down conditions of schools in poor urban districts such as Newark or Camden (p. 331). Long also posited that defining the principal as instructional leader was not without cost. These principals take on activities such as observing teachers and meeting with teachers to discuss evaluation procedures and to plan for instructional improvement. These activities in turn take the principal away from the business management function of school operations. Mann and Inman (1984) argued strongly for just such a tradeoff. But Long (1986) asserted that evidence from school finance court challenges has uncovered advantages for wealthy districts on this point. The districts with higher property tax and per pupil wealth are able to spend more on "clerical support, office equipment, counselors and other administrative support necessary to give the principal time to perform leadership functions" (p. 336). Long (1986) concluded that the actual resource inequities in the districts' means to support this instructional leadership role for principals was related to differences in community wealth.

Wealth and power issues were central to the critique of "effective schools" leveled by Dantley (1990). Dantley asserted that schools that have adopted a resource-efficient "effective schools" approach have essentially failed to confront the fundamental exploitive nature of the political economy and cultural hegonomy in the United States that fosters the conditions of poverty, racism, sexism, violence, and so on in urban areas (p. 591). Furthermore, school effectiveness has concentrated so heavily on the mastery of basic skills through the effective use of resources that the movement has failed to ensure increased upward mobility for urban students, given the pyramidal nature of class and race in the United States. Dantley agreed with Yeaky, Johnson and Adkinson (1986) who maintained that principals and the field of educational administration need an entire new focus to investigate the conditions that have led to the utilization of resources for urban schools in an "effective" manner. For example, Yeakey et al. (1986) urged researchers and practitioners to ask "how some individuals and groups have access to resources and others do not; why some groups are underrepresented and others are not; why certain influences prevail and others do not" (p. 115). Dantley (1990) utilized Yeakey's questions and urged schools to serve as "the preparatory arenas for the makers of political and social change" (p. 595). He also called for viewing the principalship in urban schools as a mission:

> For principals in urban poor schools, schooling must be perceived as a mission. Central to this mission must be the empowerment of students to critically evaluate their present realities, systematically deconstruct the aberrations of democracy currently perpetuated in their society, and proceed to project remedies. Principals in these schools must emphasize to teachers the need to establish a dialogic ambience in classrooms that encourage critical analysis and an articulation of hope with regard to overcoming disempowering conditions. (p. 595)

One of the missions of the urban school principal would be to forcefully argue for more resources. Since the inequities of society abound in depressed urban school areas, principals need to become strong advocates of more resource dollars directed specifically to poor urban schools.

Some historical, theoretical, and empirical works have also examined the issue of increased resource dollars and poor urban schools.

Cronin (1980) provided a descriptive history of this crucial subject and advocated for increased funding. Cibulka (1982) looked at enrollment losses as well as service cuts in the revenues received by urban districts. He found that even though some urban districts did face declining enrollments in the mid 1970s and early 1980s, revenue losses were exacerbated by service cutbacks. Ward (1985) tested various predictors of urban school district stress using econometric methods of correlation and multiple linear regression on samples of major U.S. cities (namely, New York, Philadelphia, Boston, Chicago, Cleveland, Atlanta, New Orleans, Los Angeles). Ward's analysis predicted that the districts that faced the most fiscal stress were those that had a large percentage of older housing units, higher spending on non-educational services, lower levels of educational attainment among the city populace, and lower city noneducation-per-capita expenditures. They were also likely to be located in either the Northeast or eastern North Central regions of the United States. Based on this evidence, Ward drew the following policy implications:

> Local policy makers and public managers have little if any control over the age of city housing, the educational attainment of the city population, or the geographic region in which the city is located. In light of these findings, the "blame the victim" theory of fiscal stress makes no sense. Fiscal problems of large urban school districts seem to be more structural in nature and merit the attention of federal and state decision makers. (p. 103)

Ward's position on fiscal stress and urban school districts, particularly with regard to municipal overburden, was also in consort with a study by Goertz (1983) on school finance in New Jersey. Her findings indicated that the state aid formula for local districts failed to consider the harsh demographic realities faced by urban districts in New Jersey (namely, high proportion of poor people needing assistance, need for public health, fire and other essential services). In 1980 "taxes for education represented 30 percent of total local property tax revenues (city, county and school) in the state's largest cities, but averaged 55 percent of suburban revenues, the statewide average" (p. 488).

Besides the problems of fiscal stress, resource generation, municipal overburden, and their impact on large urban school districts, Choy and Gifford (1980) documented the discriminatory effects of inequitable resource allocation in the Los Angeles school district. Their examination of factors such as aggregate spending per student, pupil/teacher ratio, average teacher salary, experience and training, and the racial composition of teacher turnover indicated great inequities. Their analysis showed a strong connection between the racial and ethnic composition of schools and their allocated resources. They found that schools that were majority African American or Latino received less in terms of resources. The schools of nonwhite, non-English speaking students had lower per-pupil expenditures of regular funds, teachers with less experience and training, and faculties with more minority teachers and substitutes (who were paid less) than majority white schools (p. 49). Since this study, Orfield (1988) has documented how the problem of racial and ethnic demographic polarization in the Los Angeles school system has led to even wider disparities not only in K-12 but in higher education in California as well.

Thus, a strong case can be made for children in poor urban school districts (see for example Kozol, 1991). The students who attend these schools tend to have more problems related to poverty, which in turn have a deleterious influence on their academic achievement (Pallas et al., 1989). The supporters of this side of the debate call for more resource dollars to flow to urban schools because of the higher cost of new "effectiveness" and "excellence" initiatives, as well as the unintended consequences of municipal overburden. However, others have cautioned against increased spending on public education in general. They are unsympathetic to the calls for more funds, particularly for urban schools. If the schools have not done a good job with what we have given them before, why should we give them more money now? Unfortunately, this has been the question that faces many school administrators as they struggle to obtain and creatively use the shrinking dollars available to schools, as the early 1990s indicate severe budget reductions for urban public education. Dantley's (1990) call for critical vision and school leadership is an appropriate one for this chapter to address. To be sure, urban school principals need to see their jobs as a mission to help teachers and students engage in a critical analysis of societal inequities that affect poor urban schools. The problem, however, at a pragmatic level becomes: How does the principal engage in this mission, in the face of budget restrictions and a political climate that may reduce school resources even further? It is within this broader framework of the debate over school resources that urban school principals find themselves. The specific problems of these schools and the various administrative avenues to proceed on this mission will be discussed in the remainder of the chapter.

The Social Conditions of Urban Schooling and Resource Needs

The problems related to urban education are numerous and have been well documented (see Chapter 1). Some are directly related to the obviously poor physical plant facilities that exist in urban schools. Urban school resource needs related to school supplies and safety have also been an issue. As a consequence, these inferior conditions have had a devastating influence on school staffs. For example, the effects of budget cuts were documented in a set of case studies by Ginsberg, et al. (1987):

City wide budget cuts add to unhappiness with the condition of the school building. Throughout the school, paint is peeling from the walls, lights are burned out, garbage is not picked up, window shades are torn, windows are broken and those areas which were painted never matched in other areas. In one room we observed, a large hole in the ceiling was obvious, and the room was cold and uncomfortable. One teacher complained, "How can you teach in conditions like this?" Teachers also related other complaints to budget constraints, including the lack of secretarial support, too much paperwork, lack of time to help young teachers get started, and little money to repair audio-visual and other equipment. (p. 10)

In another inner-city middle school, these conditions were described by Ginsberg, et al. (1987):

Similarly, the building is in constant need of repair. For example, damage due to a fire in one wing of the building was left unfixed by simply boarding off the entrance to the wing; a carpentry shop bench was not secured to the floor so one student held it while another worked on it; the pay phone in the school was out of order for most of our visits; classroom students had been hit by falling plaster. One teacher said, "I

begin to feel as if the school and children don't matter any-
more." Another complained, "It's a dreary place to work
because the building is decaying". (p. 8)

The staffs at these schools describe other stressors and recurrent
themes of the work environment in urban schools. One of the ongoing
problems that had a negative effect on staff and children were budget
cuts in school operations. Reductions in monetary aid led to physical
plant problems and forced school administrators to cut teachers and
various programs. Financial reductions also meant that security personnel, paraprofessionals, clerks, and secretaries were laid off. Those
teachers who were left were forced to make due with fewer books and
supplies, and increased class sizes. The remaining staff also had to cope
with more paperwork due to accountability measures called for by the
state (Ginsberg, et al., 1987).

The increased class size in many urban school districts has stemmed,
in part, from the large increase of immigrant children in U.S. cities. For
example, U.S. Census data confirm that the greatest influx of new
immigrants to the U.S. has occurred in states such as California, which
saw a 28% increase in this population (National Coalition of Advocates
for Students, 1988). In addition, almost 40% of the immigrants counted
in the 1980 census have moved primarily to New York and Los Angeles,
while another 20% have taken up residence in San Francisco (National
Coalition of Advocates for Students, 1988). The effects these numbers
have had on urban districts can be seen through the comments of
Ramon Cortines, the Superintendent of the San Francisco Unified
School District. He estimated that more than one-third of that city's
students do not speak English as their primary language. Furthermore,
those students represent 20 or more different language groups. Within
just one year, the district processed over 6,000 new students, most of
them Chinese, Hispanic, and Filipino (National Coalition of Advocates
for Students, 1988).

These huge increases in immigrant students have been added to
already large percentages of African-American and Hispanic students
residing in big-city school systems. In many urban districts, minorities
are now the majority. Inner-city school districts have to deal with this
new pluralism, while at the same time coping with the effects of
problems such as high dropout rates, drugs, gang violence, teenage
pregnancy, and other issues that have impeded the educational progress

of students (Fine, 1991). As McLaren (1988) has noted, in New York City, 66% of all students who start high school failed to graduate in four years. The dropout rate among African Americans in that city's schools has been about 72%, 80% for Hispanics, and 50% for whites. Eighty percent of teenage mothers and 90% of all special education students in that city's system fail to secure high school diplomas.

New York's public high schools have also evolved into a castelike system of schooling. According to Freedman (1989), the 81 academic high schools in the city fall into three categories: (1) the academic/arts schools, which have strict admissions standards and high per-pupil expenditures; (2) the middle range schools, which offer specialized programs in communications or finance; and (3) the bottom 21 schools, which must cater to all of the students in the neighborhood zones. The latter are the high schools with the most violence and the greatest educational needs in terms of students and school physical plant. On average, these students benefit from fewer per-pupil expenditure dollars ($1,631) as contrasted to their more elite counterparts ($1,795).

The special situation of Hispanic students has also received recent attention relevant to urban education. A report by the Department of Education has indicated that the national dropout rate for Hispanics has increased from just under 30% in 1987 to over 35% in 1988 (Johnson, 1989). Roughly 85% of the Hispanic students in the United States live in the metropolitan areas of California, Florida, Illinois, New York, and Texas. Some evidence indicates that over one-third of these Hispanic students have been tracked into vocational education programs that fail to provide training for current job-market skills. About 40% of Hispanic students have been placed in the general, instead of academic, track programs (McLaren, 1988). Given the state of affairs for these and other students of color, there is a critical need for education that will provide equity in terms of access to knowledge. These students need to attend schools where the social and environmental conditions have not foreclosed their opportunities to acquire knowledge.

Unfortunately, substandard conditions have continued unabated in urban school areas. The effect of residential segregation and lack of resources has manifested itself in the example of Camden, New Jersey. Camden, typical of many urban school districts, has had to face tough issues regarding lack of resources and growing educational needs.

Related to this, one of the most important urban school resource lawsuits was initially decided in 1990 by an administrative law judge in

New Jersey (and the state supreme court on appeal). In the *Abbot v. Burke* case, the plaintiffs consisted of school children from the state's poorest urban districts. They argued that New Jersey failed to adequately fund the public schools according to what had been previously mandated by the state's constitution and the state's school finance support model. In addition, these property-poor urban districts claimed that because of the unique special needs of the urban schools they deserved more state aid. The State Department of Education, however, argued that these urban districts did not need extra resources in order to improve their schools. They claimed that the research on effective schools outlined a number of cost-free means to improve schooling, such as the development of a positive school climate and strong leadership through the principalship.

The *Abbot v. Burke* case highlighted these issues through the examination of conditions of various property-poor districts. The problems associated with urban education were most clearly illustrated in Camden, which was one of the districts joined in the suit against the state of New Jersey. According to 1980 U.S. Census figures, Camden ranked first in poverty cities in the United States within the 25,000 to 100,000 population range. The medium family income was $10,607 and the per capita income was $3,966 in 1980. According to 1985 figures, 34% of the city's population received Aid to Families with Dependent Children, and the overwhelming majority (90%) were Hispanic or African American. Before World War II, Camden had been one of the major centers of commerce in southern New Jersey, with one shipyard, for example, employing 35,000 workers. Now there are only 35,000 jobs left in Camden, as most of the business has moved to the surrounding suburbs. The city also has poor public and private housing quality and a severely deteriorating infrastructure (*Abbot v. Burke,* pp. 15-16). Camden's tax rate in 1987 was $13.54 per $100 of assessed valuation. The rate included $1.85 for schools, $1.15 for the county, and $3.63 for the city. It also has a delinquent tax collection rate of 15%. Finally, the city's taxes have been much higher than its surrounding suburban communities. For example, the tax rates in Cherry Hill and Pennsauken are $5.41 and $4.53, respectively. As a result, Camden homeowners have to pay substantially more in taxes than their suburban counterparts (*Abbot v. Burke,* p. 17).

The impact of this urban blight on the 32 schools and 19,000 students in Camden has manifested itself in a myriad of ways. For example, Camden High School serves approximately 2,000 students in grades 9-12. Almost 75% of these students are African American and 25% are Hispanic. Prostitution and drugs surround the area and some of the students engage in these activities themselves. The park across from this high school is well known as a site for drug dealing. A security force of six is needed to keep the school free from outsiders, particularly related to gang conflicts. Absenteeism averages about 20-25% daily and some programs were designed to increase attendance. One of the programs entailed the use of truant officers to sweep the city, with students being detained until their parents called for them. However, this strategy failed because so many of the parents in Camden do not have phones (*Abbot v. Burke*, p. 32). The Pyne Point Middle School also has a student population of over 94% Hispanic and African American. The school is located in the most property-poor/lowest socioeconomic area in the city. The students at Pyne Point Middle School have to get there by walking through an area where houses have been burned out and boarded up. The area where the school is located has been known as a center for drug traffic in southern New Jersey. The district erected a fence to keep incorrigibles out on weekends, but before this action was taken, the principal (Mr. Dover) noticed a tremendous amount of graffiti, broken glass, and urine around the school's entrance. The principal at this school has commented that while principals in other districts work on improving instructional effectiveness and innovations, he has simply tried to keep his school from being subsumed by the surrounding environment.

Through the evidence supplied by Camden and other impoverished urban areas, the administrative law Judge Arthur Lefelt held the state's financing scheme unconstitutional. The judge noted that this problem was clearly tied to lack of resources due to reductions in aid on the state level, inequitable tax burdens, and the increasing needs of the emerging diverse student majorities. He held that the major source of resources for urban schools should come from the New Jersey state government. On appeal, the New Jersey Supreme Court sided with the property-poor urban districts and legally called on the state to provide them with more funds.

Additional Research

Corcoran, et al.(1988) collected descriptive data on 31 urban K-12 schools, along with extensive interviews with teachers, administrators and other school personnel. The Corcoran, et al.(1988) overview of working conditions in urban schools indicated that urban teachers do not "have the resources to do the job" (p. 23). Teachers and administrators expressed frustration with repeated shortages of textbooks, science equipment, paper, desks, blackboards, and the like. Many of the teachers interviewed claimed they bought supplies out of their own salaries rather than teach without the basic materials they needed. There were also complaints about the lack of computers for instructional purposes. The interviewees in the Corcoran, et al. study also found that some schools had been able to utilize parent groups to organize school fundraisers to supplement existing resources. But aggressive school leadership also played a crucial role in the acquisition of additional resources for urban schools. Some of the interviews revealed that aggressive administrators of specialized or magnet schools were able to secure more resources because these administrators agreed to undertake subsidized pilot programs. However, one principal commented that because of this process the "comprehensive high schools are treated as second-class citizens" (p. 31). Corcoran, et al. summarized the principal's role in resource acquisition:

> Principal leadership also seemed to be the key to building parental support, developing business partnerships, and dealing with area superintendents and other district administrators to get additional resources. The district administrators agreed that principals play a large role in whether a school experiences shortages or has enough supplies for the year. (p. 31)

If the principal's leadership is indeed crucial to obtaining urban school resources, what is the essence of the general and specific urban school problems affecting learning that the principal has to try to improve?

Pallas, et al. (1989) highlighted the increasing numbers of nonwhite students born into poverty. According to their analysis of 1980 U.S. Census data, 16.1% of white children were living in households below the poverty line, while 38.7% of Hispanic children and 46.2% of African-American children were below the poverty line. Furthermore, these latter two groups constitute the fastest growing populations of youth in the public schools. In addition, the poverty rate for these two groups of children in particular and all groups overall will increase from 14.7 million in 1984 to 20.1 million in 2020 (p. 19). This means that these new students will place a heavier burden on urban schools already under tremendous stress (Urban Schools, 1990, p. 47). A survey by the National School Boards Association indicated that all of the major urban school districts provide social services for dropout prevention, drug abuse, and teenage pregnancy. From the specific viewpoint of administrators in urban schools, however, even these measures are not enough to stem the tide of individual failure confronting some students due to lack of resources. For instance, Cutler (1989) related her commentary on one of her students whose family is addicted to crack: Because of this condition the child cannot sleep and seldom gets breakfast or clean clothes. The school he goes to has tried to provide these services for him, yet when school officials tried to call the city drop hotline nothing was done. Furthermore, the school officials tried to get the Child Abuse Human Services to intervene but they were overburdened and underfunded. Unless actual physical abuse took place, the student would have to wait until a hearing could be held on his home life condition. Meanwhile the child cannot stay awake in class. Other students fall further behind in their work because of their transient homeless condition, which gives them no stability and consequently affects their academic achievement.

It is clear that these urban school resource needs translate into diminished school achievement with regard to preparing students for work and adult life. Some urban public schools in low-income minority areas have become basic skills sites "where students are constantly drilled in the lowest level tasks, rather than offered a broader curriculum that assumes they can really learn more complex material" (Mezzacappa, 1990, p. 4). This is important because minority students in poor inner cities have to be given the fundamental academic tools to have even a remote chance of succeeding in their later lives. More resources will be needed to prepare these students for the "information age" and a changing job market that requires more abstract knowledge, inference and higher-order thinking, and communication skills (Mulkeen, 1991). In the past, parents, teachers, and administrators have all assumed that if students were not being drilled, real teaching and learning were not taking place within inner-city classrooms. But this attitude will have to change to allow these students the chance to educationally prepare for a changed economic outlook. And such changes will require more funds in order to "train better teachers, lure the most talented ones into troubled urban areas and upgrade the facilities, books, curriculum and equipment in use at the schools" (Mezzacappa, 1990, p. 4).

Clearly, poor inner-city schools, particularly those with low income African-American, Latino, and other minority groups (such as, newly arrived immigrants from southeast Asia), need more social and academic services from the school. There also needs to be significant improvements in the surrounding environment where these students live and where the school is situated in order for any type of learning to take place, whether in basic skills, higher-order thinking, or critical thinking about society. A key person in the process of school improvement can be the principal, because the principal can spearhead the effort to secure educational resources for the improvement process.

Implications for Urban Principals

One of the most crucial findings of a recent study by Hill, et al. (1989) was that urban schools only succeed if the entire community unites on their behalf. Since educational problems are so strongly related to the larger community and its socioeconomic problems, the schools cannot be helped by a reliance on the existing school bureaucracy. It is important to include parents, local businesses, political, and civic leaders, universities, foundations, and local community agencies in the process of improving urban schools. Hill, et al. looked at six big-city school districts in order to find patterns related to school improvement. The four themes that their research uncovered were:

1. Reaching out to involve the larger community in educational issues

2. Making information about community needs, school resources, and student performance broadly available

3. Creating communitywide agreement and understanding about educational improvement goals

4. Subordinating the traditional roles of school boards, administrators, and teachers to the broad imperatives of systemwide improvement effort (Hill, et al. 1989, p. 37)

These points will be used to highlight the efforts made by some urban schools and principals to secure resources from diverse groups to improve their schools. These efforts include the formation of school-university and school-business partnerships, school-parental projects, and school-community cultural resources.

School-Business Partnerships

Much has been written on this particular topic and its effect on education. Some groups, such as the American Association of School Administrators (AASA), have documented the positive aspects of these partnerships (Lewis, 1986). AASA has presented helpful guidelines and sample forms, letters, and step-by-step prescriptions for obtaining grants from corporations, and devising strategies for adopt-a-school programs or job training programs. But others, such as Spring (1972) and Cuban (1983), argue against viewing this connection as a panacea.

Spring's (1972) work documents the exploitative history behind schooling, and the rise of capitalism and the modern industrial state. He contends that, historically, businesses have used the schools as training grounds for new low-wage workers. The schools not only trained the students of the ethnic working class for manual labor but acted as agents of socialization for the purposes of controlling future workers. Even though this documentation has been the subject of differing interpretations (see Peterson, 1985), there can be little doubt about the past connection between schooling and business interests in some big cities. This history may lead one to question whether businesses truly want to educate students to create an intelligent citizenry and work force or simply aim to enhance economic productivity and nationalistic goals. Furthermore, from a practical standpoint, Cuban (1983) warns that corporate involvement has its problems in terms of unrealistic demands placed on schools to meet business goals. In addition, there has been a history of sudden corporate pullouts when the school-business partnership has not gone as well as expected. Nonetheless, many urban schools are proceeding to secure resources from business interests. A special issue of the *Journal of Negro Education* (1988) focused on successful urban schools. Part of their success was attributed to securing business support.

However, the most crucial problem in securing business partnerships has been getting them to address the long-term structural problems that have plagued the schools. Bailin (1989) asserts that, so far, most school-business partnerships have not addressed school reform issues over the long haul. In order to truly improve the schools, money and resources must be continually devoted to promote real reform. Similarly, Hargroves (1987) stated that one of the most crucial issues facing the future success of the Boston school-business compact is the persistent and multifaceted dropout problem. Addressing this issue requires avoidance of a "magic bullet" solution to a complex problem. Indeed, a caveat for urban principals is that, in the future, more corporations will demand total restructuring of schools in order to award grants for school improvement.

An article in the *Wall Street Journal* highlighted the efforts of businesses to use their own funds to establish awards for schools that wish to restructure totally (Putka, 1989). Some of the reforms addressed issues of year-round classes and greater parental involvement in the management of the school. For example, the Pacific Telesis Group in California has earmarked $2 million to encourage schools to meet restructuring goals, and three elementary schools in urban low-income areas (Irvine, Oakland, and Sacramento) have been chosen to participate.

School-University Partnerships

School-university partnerships comprise a second resource that has been used to improve urban schools. As suggested by Puckett (1989), these partnerships have to expand their agendas to include the revitalization of "at risk" communities. The institutional decline of many minority communities in urban areas has been due to a host of factors related to poverty, crime, drugs, unemployment, and the effects of past and current racism. Puckett has argued for a model of school-university partnerships that calls on the resources of the entire university (not just the colleges of education) to play an active role in trying to help the schools and the surrounding communities.

The Yale University Child Study Center in New Haven has been one of the most successful school-university partnerships. It has incorporated the support of parents and school staff in order to meet students' needs. The Center has formed partnerships with a number of public elementary schools in economically depressed areas of New Haven, where the majority of residents and students are African Americans. The partnership involves teachers, administrators, mental-health professionals, and parents. These groups all form a governance-management team that develops a comprehensive school plan covering academics, social activities, and special projects to foster social and psychological development of students. This in turn has promoted staff, student, and parent bonding to the school and has triggered higher academic achievement among the students (Comer, 1988). Under this model, the principal has to use all of the internal school resources (faculty-staff) as well as external resources (outside professionals, parents) in order to develop a sense of cooperation within the management team. The center worked with principals and education-professional staff to utilize the important community resource of parents to improve the school. Parents were invited from the community and actively encouraged to shape policy, participate in school activities, and attend school events. A special effort was made by the Center, principal, and school staff to include disaffected parents and those who initially protested the planned school-university partnership. Through the Yale University Child Study Center's work with the New Haven minority schools, a successful school-university partnership was forged that has fostered cooperation and creativity in meeting the educational needs of urban minority children.

School-Parental Partnerships

Comer's work in New Haven with school-university partnerships through the center has also placed the spotlight on a third resource that can be used by urban schools and principals, namely parental involvement. Chavkin and Williams (1987) have called for parent involvement at all levels of the educational system. They point out that parents have been a "useful resource to help school administrators implement reform mandates" (p. 183), and that

administrators need to make available the appropriate kinds of resources for parent involvement efforts. In particular, there should be staff, and monetary resources identified and allocated for the implementation of effective parent involvement efforts. The provision of these resources will help emphasize the importance of parent involvement in education and demonstrate a commitment to its success. (p. 182)

In addition, Ascher (1988) has reviewed a number of ways in which this type of partnership can be enhanced. One of the points she stressed was the importance of school-parental involvement with regard to the problem of non-English speaking and immigrant parents (p. 118). Similarly, it would make sense for administrators to use the expertise of university researchers who have done ethnographic and advocacy work with various newly arrived Asian groups. The purpose of utilizing this source of knowledge would be to gain insight into these cultures. Once administrators acquire these cultural sensitivities, they could use cultural cues that foster positive relations with the immigrant parents. This may lead toward increased school achievement among immigrant children.

Community Cultural Resources

Finally, the notion of culture and cultural sensitivity is an urban resource that administrators have used in the past to enhance school improvement for students. Historically, schools have operated under the myth of cultural neutrality, but in reality cultural hegemony has been at work. According to Anderson (1978), this cultural hegemony has taken the form of creating false promises of better jobs and college admission as measures to get African-American students to accept Euro-American culture as necessary for socioeconomic mobility—this despite the fact that schools have not had the determining effect on mass economic mobility for minorities (p. 57). Anderson has placed part of the blame for Euro-American acculturation on school administrators:

> School administrators help to identify and promote the goals of the dominant culture, and they also determine and operationalize the means for modifying and shaping that culture. These actions have little to do with concerns for the ability to read and calculate. The main concern is with the way of life that Euro-America wishes to foster for its own benefit and as a basis for a national culture. The cultural development of Afro-America is viewed as antagonistic to Euro-American hegemony and, therefore, to national unity. (p. 52)

Anderson is not calling for cultural separation, or for neglect of the "basics" (that is, what students need to know with regard to reading, writing, and other academic skills). He is saying that schools should use the culture of minorities to set the "instructional and social standards for evaluating the intellectual and social excellence of children within the context of that culture" (p. 47).

We can already see evidence of this, as a small but steadily increasing number of schools has explored new ways to incorporate more of a multicultural focus in the entire curriculum (Sleeter, 1991). The importance of bilingual/bicultural education should also be stressed. Rodriquez (1989) reported the following positive aspects of bilingual/bicultural education programs:

> High school students in bilingual programs also have significantly higher attendance rates (90%) and lower dropout rates (16%). School administrators report that participation in bilingual programs enhances self-esteem and contributes to a more positive self-concept. Bilingual programs have been doing a good job of keeping students in school—something the regular school system has not been able to accomplish. (p. 148)

However, Rodriquez points out that bilingual/bicultural programs have never been fully supported in the United States. Given the success of bilingual programs, it would be important for school administrators to rely on the resource of student culture to enhance the learning of all students. This could be done in addition to calling for more federal and state dollars for bilingual programs.

School business partnerships, school-university partnerships, parental involvement, and cultural pluralism are just a few of the many urban resources that school administrators can capitalize on to improve inner-city education. Ideally, the principal should establish conditions so that all of these internal (faculty and support staff) and external resources can be used to foster educational achievement among students. The final section of this chapter will provide more specific examples of what some principals have done in terms of enhancing urban education through the use of urban resources.

What Can Be Done to Utilize Resources: Examples

The principal can utilize parents and the surrounding minority community to help turn around a troubled urban school. One important example of this has been demonstrated at the Lincoln Preparatory

School for Humanities Languages and Health Professions in San Diego, California. The principal, Ruby Cremaschi-Schwimmer, has utilized the urban resources of parent groups, the minority community, and foundations. Under her leadership, she has fostered more parental involvement and support through Lincoln's Parents-Teachers Association (PTA). Lincoln's PTA has developed into a growing interested party in the educational and cultural affairs of the school. Principal Cremaschi-Schwimmer has also made outreach efforts to minorities in the community churches. At the Phillips Temple C.M.E. Church, she tried to persuade the congregation to take a more active role in the education of minority students:

> "I'm here because the job is large. These are critical times for black youths. The job is too large and too important, so I need you as a partner. You may not be able to tutor your children in algebra or calculus, but you can provide a quiet place at home to study and show them you expect them to study." (Media History, 1988, pp. 9-10)

She has relied on the Girard Foundation to assist in the funding for education of more than 300 students at the school. Principal Cremaschi-Schwimmer has persuaded R. B. Wooly (the foundation's president) to offer "last dollar" scholarships to these students at Lincoln. To earn the scholarships, the students have to be accepted into a college or university. The foundation will then pick up the costs of a college education that are not covered by university-government financial aid (Griffin, 1987).

The ability to obtain grants and establish ties to the business community are seen as crucial parts of the urban school experience, according to interviews conducted with other principals on the topic of urban resources (Personal interviews with urban principals conducted in December 1989). When asked what courses prepared them for writing grants and establishing contacts with the business community for financial assistance, all said they received no preparation whatsoever. All took their own initiative and learned through on-the-job experience. These principals have encouraged their teachers to write grants as well. Such grants have been written to obtain funds for computers, instructional materials, software, and to bring in outside consultants for staff development.

Harry Silcox, a high school principal in Philadelphia, has had great success in encouraging his staff to write grants. Silcox discussed school finance and resource acquisition from a building principal's perspective (personal communication, Temple University, April 24, 1990). He said that close to 90% of his school budget has already been set by school district officials with regard to teachers salaries, school district allocations for services, and so on, so in reality, he only has authority over 10% of his school's budget. He lets his staff know this, and he encourages them through periodic team meetings to work on ideas to secure outside resources for various educational interests. If the teachers have ideas, Silcox wants them to put those ideas to use by securing outside monies. For instance, if a group of teachers has a plan for an educational project utilizing computers, Silcox will direct them to the proper companies to request support. He sees part of his role as facilitator for helping his staff obtain outside funding. He has kept on file various sourcebooks on how to apply for funding from major corporations, and he shares them with his teachers. He also keeps copies of previously rejected or successful grant proposals, so that he and his teaching staff can improve their skills in this area. Silcox argued for "staff empowerment" to secure more material or monetary resources for improving schools.

Most recent reform reports have called for tighter linkages between the schools and businesses in order to improve the condition of education. This was a strand of thought that ran throughout the interview comments and responses of the UCEA Urban Initiative Select Conference attendees. Thus, it would appear important for administrator preparation to include networking experiences with an emphasis on human relations and the development of financial skills necessary for successful fund-raising. Grant writing and the initiation of resource contacts should be a part of future preparation programs for school administrators. The skills of creating and securing urban resources should also be emphasized.

Continuing Challenges

The business community would do well to stop "bashing" the urban public schools for not doing enough to educate students in inner cities. In fact, businesses have contributed to the "lack of educational skills problem" by reaping the tax rewards of the 1980s when their tax dollars could have gone to help pay for educational programs (Corbett & Lee, 1989). Further, it should be noted that 80% of major companies in a *Fortune* magazine study were found to have assisted *higher* education instead of the inner-city public schools where needs were greatest (Kuhn, 1990). Some larger companies are trying to reverse this trend (Kuhn, 1990).

Also, business leaders should be encouraged to visit inner-city schools to experience the complexities of the situation firsthand (Perry, 1990). ARCO's president, Robert Wycoff, learned this when he went to Manual Arts High School in south central Los Angeles. He observed a positive climate among most of the teaching staff and the principal. But he also saw a world around the school that did not offer much hope. He acknowledged that solving the inner-city problems that negatively affect schools would not be easy.

If school-business partnerships are to be beneficial, they must coincide with a large-scale restructuring of the political economy, ensuring high school graduates that they can obtain decent jobs or go on to bonafide four-year colleges. The 1980s saw larger economic disparities between rich and poor in many urban areas. Until businesses do more to help reduce these and other urban inequities, then the short term school-business partnerships in training, counseling, placement, or adopt-a-school plans will not be able to offset the long-term problems that need to be addressed in the political economy (Apple, 1989). The business community appears convinced that a stronger connection between business and schooling will improve the political economy, particularly in urban areas, because schools will be forced to teach basic work skills and habits. These claims do not match reality, given projections concerning occupations with the largest absolute growth (Apple, 1989, p. 214). The rhetoric of those who want to see closer ties between the schools and business should be carefully examined.

Practitioners' Perspectives

I put the question of what skills are needed to develop strong ties to the business community and other urban resources to principals at the UCEA conference and others. They said it was important for school administrators to have an educational vision for their schools through a "team-based" approach to school governance. They said it was important to communicate effectively and have "people skills."

It is fairly obvious that changes are warranted in how educational administrators are prepared to address the resource problems in urban schools. First of all, urban school administrators have to be trained to initiate and develop contacts with the business, social service, and cultural interests in their communities to secure needed assistance with school improvement. For example, one of the principals interviewed said that he engaged in extensive personal contacts with business groups over a long period of time in order to establish career counseling programs and to provide calculators for all of the 1,400 students at his middle school (personal interviews with principals conducted December 12, 1989). He was also able to secure a U.S. Department of Agriculture grant designed to enlighten students about scientific principles and to motivate them toward further study in math and science. Another key resource that this principal mentioned was parents. Repeated meetings with individual parents concerned about their children's education interested other parents. Word spread that there was a middle school principal who sincerely cared about the children in this predominantly poor Puerto Rican area of the city. After building trust, he was able to get the parents together to work on projects with national Latino groups. Their joint work secured assistance from national groups, exposing the children to Hispanic culture and history. The programs started by these joint ventures also included leadership development skills projects, career education opportunities, and bilingual education.

The terms *tenacity* and *trusted contacts* emerge repeatedly in interviews with practicing principals. Tenacity for the urban principal means taking risks and bending rules to secure resources. Taking risks sometimes means failures in securing grants or making contacts with business leaders or parents. These same terms also emerged in case studies of urban school resources by Seashore Louis and Miles (1990). They observed that urban school teachers and principals demonstrated proactiveness, ingenuity, and the use of trusted contacts to obtain needed resources. Seashore Louis and Miles found that money was indeed the most crucial resource because it was used to buy other resources (staff, technical equipment, and assistance). Most funding sources totaled $800, but some of the five urban high schools garnered $50,000 to $1,000,000 a year for substantive school improvements. Seashore Louis and Miles said that these figures were the approximate "floor" monies needed yearly for tangible improvement efforts to take hold, though moderate changes were achieved with fewer dollars. More important, Seashore Louis and Miles argued that resource allocation was the crucial factor in influencing the improvement of the school. Their case studies of five urban high schools indicated that money going to assistance and coordinative efforts (for example, special innovative teaching projects, and organized change attempts to improve the curriculum) had more of an ameliorative effect on the school than the add-on salaries or stipends "that will not continue after the improvement funds stop" (p. 242).

Seashore Louis and Miles (1990) also saw structural resources such as time, personnel, space, and equipment as important issues for urban high schools. They found that when administrators spent more time, dealing with problems and program success were more complete. The survey data from Seashore Louis and Miles's study also indicated that the time-use resource was spent mostly on task force work, training and staff development for teachers, classroom observation and coaching, and collecting and utilizing school data for improvement (p. 244). The personnel resource was important in terms of the principals having staff members who shared a vision of school improvement. In addition to the obvious resources such as time or money, Seashore Louis and Miles found that various forms of assistance were crucial, such as training, "ongoing consulting and coaching, managing/coordinating and capacity building" (p. 251). Overall, the inclusion of coordinators or outside consultants for intensive needs-specific implementation of new plans was important for urban high school improvement. Finally, the psychosocial resources (such as encouragement, enthusiasm, sympathy, and control over decisions) were also important elements for urban high school improvement (pp. 254-256).

Based on this research by Seashore Louis and Miles (1990), as well as personal accounts of the principals interviewed and those in attendance at the UCEA Select Conference, three patterns of successful urban principals emerged with regard to resource acquisition and utilization. First, successful principals were able to find money through securing grants or encouraging their staff to secure grants. Second, time and tenacity were crucial with regard to cultivating the right monetary and nonmonetary sources of assistance. Various resources were relied on to stimulate and secure other resources. For example, principals got parents involved in working together to obtain services for their students. Parents were a community resource that was utilized to get other resources from cultural agencies and companies. Third, successful urban principals allowed individuals and groups to use their energies to push for school resources.

Conclusion

The central question remains, however: What will resources be used for, critical leadership as Dantley (1990) suggested or reinforcing basic skills instruction through effective schools plans? Principals have to ensure that students master basic and higher-level academic skills but also that they become able to think about the society in which they are immersed. Delpit (1986) echoed this conclusion in her article about progressive black education:

> Students need technical skills to open doors, but they need to be able to think critically and creatively to participate in meaningful and potentially liberating work inside those doors. Let there be no doubt: a "skilled" minority person who is not also capable of critical analysis becomes the trainable, low-level functionary of dominant society, simply the grease that keeps the institutions which orchestrate his or her oppression running smoothly. . . . Yes, if minority people are to effect the change which will allow them to truly progress we must insist on "skills" within the context of critical and creative thinking. (p. 384)

If urban school administrators and youth service workers wish to adhere to the ideas set forth by Dantley and Delpit, they will not only have to take individual risks to secure urban resources, but they will have to take collective risks to challenge local, state, and federal governments, private businesses, and society at large. The challenges have to be in the form of an increased national effort to provide more resources to public schools, especially those in poor areas. A report (U.S. is said to Lag, 1990) issued by the Economic Policy Institute Fund found that during the 1980s the United States did not spend lavish amounts of money on schooling as asserted by Presidents Bush and Reagan. The Institute Fund report claimed that for elementary and secondary education the United States was close to the bottom of the group of 16 industrial nations studied in terms of the percentage of national income spent on public schooling. Furthermore, based on the downturn in the U.S. economy, more urban school districts will have to make drastic budget cuts. New York City, for instance, faced $90 million in school budget cuts for the 1990-91 school year, which meant cutting funds from budgets for textbooks and office equipment and the layoff of paraprofessionals and teachers (Yarrow, 1990). When compared to other nations our funding has been smaller, and budgets for big-city school districts are being cut at a time when urban school districts desperately need money to sustain the improvements that some of them have made. In addition, more funds are needed to address the societal problems (drug abuse, homelessness) that in turn have an impact on the children who attend public schools in urban areas.

The urban school principals and youth service workers participating in the UCEA Select Conference were doing a tremendous job in the face of impossible odds with respect to garnering resources to improve the lives of urban school children. There are probably many other urban school administrators and teachers who are putting forth the same effort. To be sure, there are many inner-city students for whom the system of schooling works well. But those students who fall through the cracks will face individual problems, and we as a society will face future problems with those who turn to dropping out of school, drugs, or violence. Pallas, et al.(1989), for example, estimated that the cost in foregone lifetime earnings of the approximately 500,000 dropouts per year is about $50 billion.

Certainly, urban school principals have to take steps to secure resources to improve their schools and to minimize the effects of impending budget cuts on children. However, all of these approaches will be of little value if the broader institutional powers and our society fail to provide more resources for schools, to restructure the political economy, and to change the dominant ideology so as to enhance the importance of education for children who live in poor urban areas. As underscored by Pallas, et al.(1989), the human capital needs of students in our inner cities are great, but they will become even greater in terms of their financial and social costs if the United States continues to ignore them.

References

Abbot v. Burke, State of New Jersey—Office of Administrative Law: Initial Decision OAL DKt. No. EDU 5581085. Agency DKt. No. 307-8/85.

Anderson, J. D. (1978). Black cultural equity in American education. In W. Feinberg (Ed.), *Equality and Social Policy* (pp. 42-65). Urbana: University of Illinois Press.

Apple, M.W. (1989). American realities: Poverty, economy, and education. In L. Weiss, E. Farrar & H. G. Petrie (Eds.), *Dropouts from school: Issues, dilemmas and solutions* (pp. 205-224). Albany, NY: SUNY Press.

Ascher, C. (1988). Improving the school-home connection for poor and minority urban students. *The Urban Review, 20,* 109-123.

Bailin, M. (1989, August 17). School and business partnerships haven't passed the test yet. *Philadelphia Inquirer*, Sec. F, 7.

Brimelow, P. (1990, May). American perestroika? Forbes, 82-86.

Chavkin, N. F., & Williams, D. L. (1987). Enhancing parent involvement: Guidelines for access to an important resource for school administrators. *Education and Urban Society, 19,* 164-184.

Childs, T. S., & Shakeshaft, C. (1986). A meta-analysis of research on the relationship between educational expenditures and student achievement. *Journal of Education Finance, 12,* 249-263.

Choy, R.K.H., & Gifford, B. R. (1980). Resource allocation in a segregated school system: The case of Los Angeles. *Journal of Education Finance, 6,* 34-50.

Cibulka, J. G. (1982). Response to enrollment loss and financial decline in urban school systems. *Peabody Journal of Education, 60,* 64-78.

Colvin, R. L. (1989). School finance: Equity concerns in an age of reforms. *Educational Researcher, 18,* 11-15.

Comer, J. P. (1988). Educating poor minority children. *Scientific American, 259,* 42-48.

Corcoran, T. B., Walker, L. J., & White, J. L. (1988). Working in Urban Schools, Washington, DC: Institute for Educational Leadership.

Cronin, J. M. (1980). Big city school bankruptcy (Policy Paper No. 80-C3). Stanford, CA: Stanford University, Institute for Research on Educational Finance Governance.

Cuban, L. (1983). Corporate involvement in public schools: A practitioner academic's perspective. *Teachers College Record, 85,* 183-204.

Cutler, P. (1989, October 13). Dear Mr. President: Two letters from a city teacher. *Philadelphia Inquirer*, Sec. A, 21.

Dantley, M. E. (1990). The ineffectiveness of effective schools leadership: An analysis of the effective schools movement from a critical perspective. *Journal of Negro Education, 59,* 585-598.

Delpit, L. D. (1986). Skills and other dilemmas of a progressive black educator. *Harvard Educational Review, 56*, 379-385.

DeYoung, A. J. (1989). *Economics of American education*. New York: Longman.

Fine, M. (1991). *Framing dropouts: Notes on the politics of an urban public high school*. Albany, NY: SUNY Press.

Freedman, S. G. (1989, September 17). Snapshots of hope and hopelessness: Inside a New York City high school. *The New York Times Magazine* 57, 72.

Ginsberg, R., Schwartz, H., Olson, G., & Bennett, A. (1987). Working conditions in urban schools. *The Urban Review, 19*, 3-21.

Goertz, M. E. (1983). School finance in New Jersey: A decade after *Robinson v. Cahill. Journal of Education Finance, 8*, 475-489.

Griffin, S. F. (17 December 1987). 300 at Lincoln High get college aid now. *San Diego Union*, Sec. B, 1, 4.

Hanushek, E. A. (1989). The impact of differential expenditures on school performance. *Educational Researcher, 18*, 45-51.

Hargroves, J. S. (1987). The Boston compact: Facing the challenge of school dropouts. *Education and Urban Society, 19*, 303-310.

Hill, P. T., Wise, A. E., & Shapiro, L. (1989). *Educational progress: Cities mobilize to improve their schools* (Report No. R-3711-JSM/CSTP). Santa Monica, CA: The Rand Center for the Study of the Teaching Profession.

Jackson, M. (1989, July 16). Schools in D.C. separate and unequal. *The Washington Post*, Sec. B, 8.

Johnson, J. (1989a, March 8). Curriculum seeks to lift blacks' self-image. *The New York Times*, A1, B8.

Johnson, J. (1989b, September 15). Hispanic dropout rate is put at 35%. *The New York Times*, A12.

Journal of Negro Education (1988). Urban schools that work. 57, 3.

Kozol, J. (1991). *Savage inequalities: Children in America's schools*. New York: Crown Press.

Kuhn, S. E. (1990, Spring). How business helps schools. *Fortune*, 91-106.

Lewis, A. C. (1986). *Partnerships connecting school and community*. Arlington, VA: American Association of School Administrators.

Long, D. C. (1986). An equity perspective on educational reform. In Van D. Mueller and Mary P. McKeown (Eds.), *The fiscal, legal and political aspects of state reform of elementary and secondary education* (pp. 325-344). Boston, MA: Ballinger Press.

MacPhail-Wilcox, B., & King, R.A. (1986). Resource allocations studies. Implications for school improvement and school finance research. *Journal of Education Finance 11*, 416-432.

Mann, D., & Inman, D. (1984). Improving education within existing resources: The instructionally effective schools' approach. *Journal of Education Finance 10*, 256-269.

McLaren, P. (1988). *Life in schools: An introduction to critical pedagogy in the foundations of education*. New York: Longman.

Media History. (1988, January). Media history of *Lincoln Preparatory School for Humanities, Languages and Health Professions*. San Diego, CA.

Mezzacappa, D. (1990, June 10). Turning dollars into school success. *Philadelphia Inquirer*, Sec. C, 1, 4.

Mulkeen, T. (forthcoming). The evolution of the one best system. In T. Mulkeen & N. Cambron McCabe (Eds.), *Democratic leadership: The changing context of administrative preparation*. Norwood, NJ: Ablex.

National Coalition of Advocates for Students. (1988). *New voices: Immigrant students in U.S. public schools*. Boston: National Coalition of Advocates for Students.

Ogbu, J. U. (1978). Minority *education and caste: The American system in cross-cultural perspective*. New York: Academic Press.

Orfield, G. (1988). Exclusion of the majority: Shrinking college access and public policy in metropolitan Los Angeles. *The Urban Review, 20*, 149-163.

Pallas, A. M., Natriello, G., & McDill, E. L. (1989). The changing nature of the disadvantaged population: Current dimensions and future trends. *Educational Researcher, 18*, 6-22.

Perry, N. J. (1990, Spring). Being principal for a day. *Fortune*, 65-68.

Peterson, P. E. (1985). *The Politics of School Reform, 1870-1940*. Chicago: University Chicago Press.

Puckett, J. L. (1989). Book review: School-university partnerships in action: Concepts, cases and concerns. K. A. Sirotnik and J. I . Goodlad (Eds.), *American Journal of Education, 97*, 443-448.

Putka, G. (1989, June 6). Learning curve: Lacking good results, corporations rethink aid to public schools. *The Wall Street Journal*, A1, A10.

Rodriquez, C.E. (1989). *Puerto Ricans: Born in the U.S.A*. Boston: Unwin Hyman.

Seashore Louis, K. & Miles, M. B. (1990). *Improving the urban high school: What works and why*. New York: Teachers College Press.

Sleeter, C. E. (1991). Multicultural education and empowerment. In C. E. Sleeter (Ed.), *Empowerment through multicultural education* (pp. 1-26). Albany, NY: SUNY Press.

Spring, J. H. (1972). *Education and the rise of the corporate state.* Boston: Beacon Press.

Taylor, L. L., & Pinard, J. R. (1988). Success against the odds: Effective education of inner-city youth in a New York City high school. *The Journal of Negro Education , 57,* 347-361.

Urban schools are providing more social services (1990, February 11). *New York Times,* Sec. A, 47.

U. S. is said to lag in school spending. (1990, January 16). *New York Times,* Sec. A, 23.

Walberg, H. J., & Fowler, W. J., Jr. (1987). Expenditure and size efficiencies of public school districts. *Educational Researcher, 16,* 5-15.

Ward. J. G. (1985). Predicting fiscal stress in large city school districts. *Journal of Education Finance, 11,* 89-104.

Yarrow, A. L. (1990, December 17). Painful task: Meeting goal to cut costs for schools. *New York Times,* Sec. B, 1, 2.

Yeakey, C. C., Johnson, G. S., & Adkinson, J. A. (1986). In pursuit of equity: A review of research on minorities and women in educational administration. *Educational Administration Quarterly, 22* (3) 110-149.

7

Governing
Urban Schools

MARILYN TALLERICO

At the UCEA-Danforth Select Conference,[1] three veteran urban principals expressed the following insights related to governing urban schools:

> Principal A: Urban school districts are generally *large*. Therefore, the issue of site-based management—decentralization–is peculiarly important in urban settings. Site-based management means *autonomy*.

> Principal B: The *roadblocks* are different in urban settings. There are different *procedures* to go through [to accomplish goals].

> Principal C: The single best thing that prepared me for the principalship was my experience at the central office level, first. ... to gain familiarity with how things get *done* [in the city system].

Such statements echoed the sentiments and experiences of other principals at the conference. In addition, the following emerged from group discussion and prioritization of initial ideas:

1. Of the 115 urban school problems of practice generated by conference participants, "the process of sharing responsibilities and decisions" was one of five responses rated most important.

2. Of the 101 ideas concerning most useful previous learnings about urban school leadership, "shared decision making" was rated second most important of the top five responses.

3. Of the 99 items generated in response to the question of imaginable administrative tools for creating successful urban school environments, conference participants rated "site-based management" and "flexibility of resources, funding, curriculum, calendar, scheduling, and so on" as the first and second, respectively, of the five highest-priority responses among all group members.

Taken together, these data point toward a critical problem of practice in urban education. The essence of the problem is that a pervasive *tension* exists between school-level autonomy and systemwide uniformity/coordination (Finn, 1984). Since governance may be defined as the control and authority over decision-making processes (Dejnozka, 1983), this tension can be viewed as the product of a dynamic balance of power within large, complex urban educational systems. The student-centeredness of the problem concerns the issues of *where* and *how* decisions are made that affect teaching and learning. The link to students is also reflected in the connection between control of decision making and allocation of resources (including, for example, instructional materials, personnel, time, and facilities).

The goal of this chapter is to integrate and present useful information that may help current and aspiring urban school principals to examine and understand the complexities associated with the tension between school-site autonomy and centralized control. This review of the extant knowledge-base is organized around three central elements: (1) theoretical and conceptual underpinnings related to the identified problem of practice; (2) relevant research, including an historical perspective; and (3) examples of promising intervention strategies. Two themes that surface throughout the discussion are (1) implications for principals and (2) relevancy to the peculiarities of governing *urban* schools.

What We Understand

A brief overview of relevant conceptual frameworks may be helpful in illuminating the control-autonomy dilemma in urban school
systems. Wiles, et al. (1981) explicate the underlying tension with
simple, and colorful, language:

> The issue [of governing schools] is couched in many terms and
> reflects basic issues found in all large, complex organizations:
> What is the sum? What are the parts? And how do they relate?
> Common terms used to describe the issues include centraliza-
> tion and decentralization or autonomy and coordination . . . .
> The politics of the principalship concerns how to cope with
> multiple and shifting decision boundaries that affect the local
> school poker playing . . . . The boundary determines the shape
> of competition for scarce resources and the rules for playing.
> (pp. 87-89)

Along with the need to understand and be able to work with untidy
decision boundaries, other phenomena add to the complexity of this
dilemma. For example, Borman and Spring (1984) point out that the
size and hierarchical structure of city school systems afford abundant
opportunity for educational (and other) decisions to be reinterpreted
and changed as they travel the expansive terrain populated by central
office staff, principals, and teachers —all of whom have the potential to
shape how decisions ultimately reach students. Thus both the formal
structure and the "informal organization created by the actions of
individuals" relate directly to the issues of where and how decisions
that affect students are made (Borman & Spring, 1984, p. 75).

Several theories or models, each based on distinct sets of assumptions, have been used to describe and explain modern organizations.
They may be useful for analyzing urban school systems.

Bureaucracy

Weber's (1947) classic model emphasizes the bureaucratic nature of
formal organization. The basic components of his "ideal type" bureaucracy are: a hierarchy of authority, division of labor and specialization
of functions, an impersonal orientation, and formal rules and regula-

tions. Such a system is intended to maximize rational decision making and administrative efficiency.

During the past 25 years, a number of researchers and theorists have utilized selected aspects of Weber's model to interpret behavior in urban educational organizations. Gittell and Hevesi (1969), for example, describe city school systems as impersonal, centralized bureaucracies, largely nonresponsive to their environments: "In every large city, an inbred bureaucratic supervisory staff sits at headquarters offices holding a tight rein on educational policy" (p. 363). More recently, a Carnegie Foundation Special Report (1988) strongly exhorts the abolishment of "the excessively centralized, bureaucratic control of urban schools," arguing: "In most cities, the school is viewed simply as one more administrative 'unit' to be controlled rather than inspired. Principals are crippled by mindless regulations" (pp. xii, xvi). Such applications of Weber's ideal-type of bureaucracy often emphasize the dysfunctional potential of the model's components (for example, *excessive* rules and regulations, *impenetrable* hierarchies of authority), rather than the positive (for example, potential for increased efficiency).

The utility of bureaucratic theory has been criticized on a number of counts: oversimplification of the variety and complexity in educational organizations (Corwin, 1974), underestimation of school and teacher autonomy within the system (Bidwell, 1965; Lortie, 1977), and neglect of the importance of the informal organization (Borman & Spring, 1984; Iannaccone, 1962). Hills (1966) recommends that instead of debating the question of whether educational organizations are or are not bureaucracies a more useful focus is to analyze the *extent* of bureaucratization within schools.

Loose Coupling

In contrast to the rational structural and behavioral properties of Weber's model of bureaucracy, other theorists emphasize the structural looseness and nonrational aspects of educational organizations (Bidwell, 1965; Meyer & Rowan, 1978; Weick, 1976). Campbell, et al. (1985) find loose-coupling models compatible with the view of educational organizations as "open" systems, with external forces continually impinging on and affecting the system. March and Olsen's (1976) depiction of educational organizations as "organized anarchies" also counters the bureaucratic perspective of tightly connected hierarchical relationships and rational processes. School systems as organized anarchies are characterized by unclear and diffuse goals, uncertain technologies, loosely connected structural elements, nonrational decision making behaviors, and fluid participation of organizational members, patrons, and clients.

To relate these theoretical perspectives more concretely to the tension between school autonomy and systemwide uniformity, school districts may be viewed as federations of schools, which in turn represent federations of classrooms (Corwin & Borman, 1988). Finn (1984) explains loose coupling in educational organizations as follows:

> movement at one point in the system [does] not rapidly or reliably lead to movement elsewhere . . . . Teachers tend to function with considerable autonomy in their classrooms, as do schools within their systems, and local school systems within their states. (p. 518)

An assumption underlying this perspective is that administrators and teachers, as professionals, enjoy broad discretionary power within the organization.

Complex Organization Models

Other researchers and theorists challenge the notion of treating educational organizations as either full-fledged bureaucracies or inherently loosely coupled. Bidwell (1965), Griffiths (1979), Willower (1980), and others argue that educational organizations exhibit a distinctive combination of structural looseness and bureaucracy. Whereas ties may be weak, loose, and infrequent between some elements or functions in the organization, they may be strong and tight between others. Thus, "variable," rather than "loose" coupling may more accurately describe the organization of schools and school systems.

Corwin and Borman (1988) point out that an alternative to both the bureaucratic model and loose coupling perspectives is found in the social science literature. This alternative, the "complex organization model," depicts organizations as composites of bureaucratic, professional, and political variables (Corwin, 1974, p. 70). Aspects of hierarchical order (the bureaucratic perspective), collegiality, and personal autonomy (the professional perspective) and conflicts among interest groups (the political perspective) become merged in the complex organization model. Dual decision-making systems (centralized and decentralized) may coexist, with the relative dominance of each dependent on particular contexts (Corwin, 1974, p. 71).

Cultural Perspectives

Although not clearly formulated as theory, contemporary analyses have focused on what have come to be termed the *cultural* or *symbolic* dimensions of organizations. Bolman and Deal (1984), for example, suggest that one way organizations can be understood is through the symbols, beliefs, and meanings that are shared by members of the organization. In contrast to the structural or political emphases of other frameworks for understanding organizational life, the cultural perspective ascribes great importance to the traditions, rituals, ceremonies, heroes, and stories that transmit the values of the organization. One assumption underlying this perspective is that values are continually negotiated and renegotiated through social interaction. Another assumption is that shared values drive human behavior. Symbols, traditions, and shared beliefs—though difficult to measure—may in fact be the "glue"that holds together loosely coupled organizations.

Drawing on studies of noneducational settings, Peters and Waterman (1982), Deal and Kennedy (1982), and others have focused on the cultures of modern successful corporations. The implications for practice inherent in their views are that organizational leaders can and do indeed affirm and *shape* culture. Such leadership, however, involves framing organizational challenges not solely as technical (rational-bureaucratic), interpersonal (human relations), or political (conflicts of interest) problems but rather as related to deeply ingrained sets of values, beliefs, and norms. According to Firestone and Corbett (1988), "culture helps to clarify what is important and what is not, as well as what to do about both" (p. 335).

The notion of individual school culture currently enjoys wide popular appeal and acceptance. Willower (1984), however, challenges the idea. He points to the distinct constituent *sub*cultures within schools (teachers', students', administrators'), which likely constrain the development of a peculiar schoolwide culture.

Irrespective of Willower's (1984) caveats, the concept of school ethos or culture continues to influence contemporary educational scholarship. The concept can be extended to the tension between autonomy and control in governing urban schools. If schools each have a unique (gluelike, but malleable) culture (Goodlad, 1984; Sizer, 1985), and if school improvement for increased student achievement is viewed as *cultural transformation* (Firestone & Corbett, 1988), then it follows that problem finding and problem resolution are apt to be most appropriately anchored at the local level (Guthrie, 1986). Such reasoning represents a strong argument for increased control and authority over decision processes by individual schools, rather than central offices, state agencies, or federal policymakers. In other words, site-based, group decision making may be important, since it is the organizational members' socially shared values and beliefs that comprise the ethos and underlie the functioning of the school.

Participatory Decision Making

The evolution of quality circles (Ouchi, 1981), interest in the management of Japanese corporations, and widespread success of bestsellers such as *In Search of Excellence* (Peters & Waterman, 1982) and *Passion for Excellence* (Peters & Austin, 1985) combine to popularize an important link between effective leadership/management and the democratization of decision making in modern corporations. This enthusiasm in the corporate world has been paralleled in educational settings. Calls for decentralization of decision making and increased school-level autonomy are generally accompanied by advocacy for "participatory decision making," "teacher empowerment," "shared governance," and "restructuring."

It is important to note, however, that much of the literature related to participation in educational decision making is nontheoretical and hortatory in nature. Firestone and Corbett (1988) cite Conway's (1984) observation that "such exhortations may be based more on myth than fact and that there is no overwhelming evidence that involving two or more actors in the process of reaching a choice produces greater productivity or job satisfaction" (p. 332). Estler (1988) concurs and points out that traditional thinking about participatory decision making is driven primarily by values, beliefs, and views of teacher professionalism, not by conclusive research results or comprehensive explanatory theory.

Despite the absence of an overarching framework to guide understanding of participatory decision making, there are several conceptual models that are relevant to this general topic. For example, Barnard (1938), Simon (1957), and Bridges (1967) have developed the concept of "zones of acceptance/indifference." The zone may be thought of as a range on a continuum, within which subordinates accept superordinates' decision making authority. The idea is that subordinate participation in decision making is desirable when the decision falls outside of the zone of acceptance. The dilemma, of course, is that it is difficult to know or anticipate which decisions fall where on the continuum. Bridges (1967) and Hoy and Miskel (1982) suggest that it may be possible for school administrators to gauge zones of acceptance (and, hence, desirability of teacher participation) by evaluating subordinates' personal stake in (the "test of relevance") and capability of contributing to (the "test of expertise") particular decision areas. These authors recognize, however, the elusiveness and situational variability of acceptance zones, the limitations of the model, and the need to consider not only *when* participatory decision making is appropriate but also *how* and *to what extent* teachers should be involved.

Conway (1984), similarly attentive to situational variability, has developed a contingency model for participatory decision making. The model focuses on two dimensions: need for staff acceptance and need for decision quality. When both needs are high, joint staff-administrative participation in formal committee work is desirable. When both needs are low, the decision may be considered routine and, therefore, not warranting shared decision-making effort. When the need for staff acceptance is high, but the quality of the decision is not critical, staff decision making is appropriate, with or without administrative participation. When the priority of those needs is reversed, Conway's (1984) model supports minimal/informal staff participation.

What We Know

In addition to considering theoretical and conceptual frameworks, the tension between school-level autonomy and district control can be better understood by examining selected aspects of the history of urban education, as well as the results of research.

History

It is important to consider at least three developments in the past 30 years that have significantly affected contemporary governance of urban schools: (1) judicial and social mandates for desegregation, (2) the concomitant push for community control of schools, and (3) the growth of teacher unionism. Though Chapter 1 elaborates these conditions in detail, the following brief review is intended to emphasize their specific connections to issues of autonomy and control of urban school decision processes.

Desegregation. In the wake of the 1954 *Brown vs. Board of Education* Supreme Court decision, calls for racial integration provided an impetus for centralized, district-level decision making in urban environments. Prompted by court orders to desegregate schools in the 1960s and 1970s, city districts developed systemwide reforms and reconfigurations of attendance and transportation zones in an attempt to achieve racial balance within individual schools. From the perspective of the principal, a core variable in the life and work of the enterprise (the definition of clientele; the assignment of students) was reaffirmed as the decision domain of central office and school board, not local school site.

In the 1980s, with continuing demographic changes in inner cities and decreased federal commitment to school integration, segregation of Hispanic students and resegregation of black students both increased (Orfield, 1988). According to the Network of Regional Desegregation Assistance Centers (1989), "The trends are toward more and more severe racial and class isolation in inner-city schools" (p. 36). In any case, however, issues and decisions related to desegregation, busing, magnet schools, "choice" plans, and the like, remain largely centralized at the district-level.

Community Control. The civil rights movements of the 1960s also gave birth to what Dentler, et al. (1987) call a "twin sister to school desegregation": the press for political decentralization and community control. This press was not limited to education, but rather was part of impassioned demands for increased minority (particularly black) participation in American institutions in general (Gittell & Hevesi, 1969).

Altshuler (1970) draws an important distinction between "administrative" and "political" decentralization. Administrative decentralization involves delegating authority downward and outward from superordinates to subordinates within the system. In contrast, political decentralization is the redistribution of authority and jurisdictional powers of elected officials to a greater number of individuals, as in home rule or local community control.

In education, public interest in decentralization focused attention on the *school* rather than the *district* as the locus of improvement (Dentler et al., 1987, p. 39). Political decentralization took the form of various structural mechanisms for increased parental and citizen participation in school affairs (for example, citizen advisory councils) (Wissler & Ortiz, 1986). Reinforcing this movement were a variety of federally funded initiatives (Chapter 1, bilingual education) that mandated citizen consultation/participation in program planning, implementation, and evaluation (Campbell et al., 1985). These developments, at least partially, influenced school site autonomy, providing both opportunities and constraints on the work and independent decision domains of school principals.

Wirt and Kirst (1989) emphasize that, although there was widespread administrative decentralization in large urban school systems throughout the 1970s, there was little political decentralization (that is, community control). Viteritti (1986) agrees that political decentralization efforts failed to achieve their purported egalitarian goals: "Control remained with those populations and institutions that had primary discretion over funding, and it was not minorities" (p. 242). But others contend that both political *and* administrative decentralization failed to achieve their goals. Wissler and Ortiz (1986), for example, state that "the essential decision making apparatus was retained by the superintendent and central office" (p. 285). And Ornstein (1989) advances the notion that, all told, decentralization may have been more myth than reality, "a fading echo of administrative and urban reform ideas of the past," as we move into the 1990s (p. 235). Irrespective of the level or degree of decentralization, however, it is crucial to note that "no research to date has established a generalizable connection between decentralization and [student] learning outcomes" (Dentler et al., 1987, p. 41).

Teacher Unionism. Beginning in the 1960s, the push toward centralization of urban district decision making to enhance racial equity and the simultaneous but countervailing pull toward decentralization for increased local community control were further complicated by the concomitant growth of teacher unionism. The burgeoning power and militancy of organized teacher unions were especially intense in large urban areas. In 1968, these two developing phenomena (decentralization and unionism) resulted in a critical confrontation in New York City: a citywide strike, based largely on disagreements over the extent of powers granted to three decentralized school districts that had been established a year earlier. Gittell and Hevesi (1969) describe the crux of the issue: "Did the [decentralized, local community] school board have the power to hire and fire administrators and teachers in the district?" (p. 306).

With regards to site autonomy "versus" centralized control in a more general sense, district-union negotiated contracts altered the authority and discretionary decision making of principals (at least *formally*, that is). The provisions of collectively bargained agreements were intended to be honored and applied systemwide, creating a press for consistency among administrators and uniformity/equity among individual work-site conditions. Thus, from the perspective of school principals, their line authority became subject to yet another set of centralized influences.

Kerchner (1980) describes the increasingly complex governance styles that have resulted from collective bargaining as "multilateral" decision making. The number of players with whom central office and principals must bargain (formally and informally) has multiplied. Kerchner (1980) points to evidence of building (union) representatives being able to exert more influence than principals, to obtain certain concessions or resources from district offices. The Council of the Great City Schools (1988) underscores these new complexities with the example that "suggesting we lengthen our school day is little help to a school district that must negotiate with *20 unions* to keep a building open" (p. vi). According to Frymier (1987), "These negotiated agreements became another layer of authority within the bureaucracy" (p. 11).

However, this additional "layer of authority" is not consistently viewed as a negative development. McDonnell and Pascal (1988), Hill et al. (1989), and others note that strong union leadership can play an indispensable role in mobilizing teachers' attention and actions toward school improvement and classroom implementation of innovations.

Recent Developments. By the early 1980s, each of the three aforementioned trends evolved into quite different forms than originally construed: (a) the thrust for racial desegregation lost considerable momentum, including diminished federal enforcement and interventions for integration (Borman & Spring, 1984; Oakes, 1987); (b) "decentralization of schools and citizen involvement in educational decision making appeared to slow" (Campbell et al., 1985, p. 135), with a number of cities (for example, Detroit) abandoning [political] decentralization plans that had been put into place in the 1960s and 1970s; and (c) the focus of collective bargaining expanded beyond economic concerns to issues of professionalism, collegial governance, and teacher participation in policy making and school management (McDonnell & Pascal, 1988).

What the Research Says

In addition to the historical developments that have influenced the governance of city schools and the work of urban principals, it is also important to consider selected findings from a broader literature. Research related to issues of control, coordination, and autonomy in urban school systems may be drawn from diverse sources, including political science, organizational studies, and educational administration. A brief overview follows.

Effective Schools. The literature labeled "effective schools research" originated in urban elementary settings (Brookover, et al., 1979; Edmonds, 1979). The resultant theme of this work was essentially optimistic: given the right conditions, urban schools in even the most depressed locales have been able to increase student achievement (Oakes, 1987). Although the limitations of these studies have been widely documented (Good & Brophy, 1986), this literature delineates a number of characteristics of effective schools that are pertinent to urban educational governance. Purkey and Smith's (1983) comprehensive review includes (among others) the following attributes of effective schools: school-site autonomy, collaborative planning, collegial relationships among teachers and between teachers and principals, sense of community, instructional leadership on the part of the principal, and district support of building-level management. The implications for practice that they (Purkey & Smith, 1983) draw from this research emphasize the needs to: expand opportunities for collaborative planning, increase involvement of teachers in decision making, and foster flexible improvement strategies that reflect the uniqueness of individual schools.

Thus, as related to the current discussion of centralized control versus school-site autonomy, the effective schools literature leans heavily toward supporting the latter (Brown, 1987; Kirst, 1983). An important caveat, however, is that though this research yields a number of descriptors, conspicuously absent is specific evidence about *how* schools *become* effective (e.g., Oakes, 1987) or whether the identified characteristics are the *cause* or *result* of effectiveness.

The "Excellence" Movement. Whereas the effective schools research came to the fore in the 1970s, the decade of the 80s spawned a related "educational excellence" movement, this time driven largely by state-level mandates. Prompted by the publication of *A Nation at Risk* (National Commission on Excellence in Education, 1983), initial foci of this reform movement were increased academic standards, as a means of countering the alleged mediocrity of America's schools. Just a few years later, the "second wave" of reform replaced initial foci with emphases on "professionalizing teaching" and "restructuring schools" (Boyd, 1988a; Corcoran, et al., 1988). This second set of themes was forcefully articulated in reports that enjoyed considerable media coverage: for example, *Time for Results* (National Governors Association, 1986), *A Nation Prepared* (Carnegie Forum on Education and the Economy, 1986), and *Tomorrow's Teachers* (The Holmes Group, 1986).

Whereas the first wave was readily convertible into concrete activities that could be monitored at the state level (additional requirements for graduation, longer school days, and higher teacher certification standards), considerable complexity and ambiguity accompanied the subsequent interest in teacher professionalism and school restructuring. The latter seems to fall within the definition of *administrative decentralization*, that is, the redistribution of decision-making authority within school systems, from superordinates to subordinates.

Although the vagueness of the concept of restructuring has led to diverse applications and implementation strategies, the simultaneous press for teacher professionalization has precipitated widespread interpretation of this idea as a shift of decision-making authority and responsibility from the school district to individual schools and their staffs (David, 1989). This shift is often articulated in terms of "teacher empowerment," "school-based management," and "shared decision making" (shared primarily, that is, by administrators and teachers). Whereas advocacy for political decentralization in the 1960s was largely prompted by concerns for increased citizen involvement and control, the 1980s trend toward administrative decentralization was wedded to pressures for teacher participation/power. Dentler et al. (1987) view school-based management, coupled with shared decision making, as "the most 'advanced' version of the policy idea of administrative decentralization" (p. 41).

As alluded to previously, the literature related to "excellence" in the corporate world also influenced this reform movement in education. Specifically, for example, concepts popularized by Peters and Waterman (1982) augmented interest in new relationships between "management and labor." Their research reported that successful corporations develop means for allocating authority to lower and lower levels, to encourage workers at those levels "to assume responsibility for what they do and thus to strive harder" (Frymier, 1987, p. 13). A major premise of the movement was that "an enterprise functions best if all stakeholders participate in decisions affecting their work" (Corcoran et al., 1988, p. 4). That premise was readily translatable into a set of assumptions applicable to education:

> (a) The farther decisions are removed from the classrooms and schools where they will be implemented, the less sensitive they will be to the needs of students and schools; (b) the school must take responsibility for educational outcomes. . . . sharing "ownership" of them; and (c) it is important to avoid *underutilization* of the talent of the school-based teaching force. (Levin, 1987, p. 73)

These issues relate directly to governing schools in that questions underlying current reform trends include: Who controls educational policy and practices that affect teaching and learning? How are authority and responsibility shared between the district and its schools? Are teachers valued for their expertise and, accordingly, afforded professional autonomy, authority, and responsibility for their work? To some extent, however, there are mixed messages conveyed by the teacher professionalism movement and the effective schools research emphasis on "strong leadership" by the principal. That is, how can both be "in charge"? Elmore (1988) points out that the answers to such questions harbor hitherto unexamined implications not only for roles and responsibilities within schools, but for the size, organization, and roles of central office staff. The principal is positioned at a pivotal juncture of these conflicting dynamics.

How does this background information relate particularly to urban educational environments? As is elaborated in the ensuing section, the above described dilemma is more acute in city schools: First, recent research has demonstrated that when compared to their suburban/rural counterparts urban teachers have less authority and receive less administrative support in their daily work. Second, city schools' increasing reliance on federal and state categorical programs, each with "separate special controls and funding subsystems," has contributed to fragmentation, inconsistency, increased conflict, and administrative overload in urban districts (Wirt & Kirst, 1989, p. 186). And third, in later sections of this chapter it is shown that city school districts are the ones that are currently "setting the stage" and conducting large-scale innovations in school-based management/shared decision making models of governance.

In some cases, teacher union leadership and top-level school administration fashioned new coalitions to jointly spearhead these initiatives (Hill et al., 1989). Such partnerships may reflect a departure from previous adversarial strategic relationships between management and instructional staff.

In other cases, external forces prompted reform initiatives in urban school systems in the 1980s. Business/industrial leadership, often centered in cities, voiced increased concern for the quality of graduates who would comprise the future workforce (Borman & Spring, 1984). The private sector not only provided funds for innovative restructuring of urban schools, but it also served "in raising educational problems to the top of the local public agenda" (Hill et al., 1989, p. vi). Thus, governance reform in urban schools is linked to both a set of internal structures and actors, and a much wider set of external factors and dynamics. Accordingly, Viteritti (1986) and others advocate a multidimensional, *open systems approach* to the study of leadership and governance in urban school districts.

Shared Decision Making. Although the *theory* related to participative decision making has been reviewed in a previous section of this chapter, it is also important to consider related *research* findings. Cuban (1984) points out that interest in this issue is not new; the theme of participative decision making in schools has surfaced repeatedly since the early 1900s, largely as a function of the legacy of teacher professionalism.

Duke, et al. (1980) found that teacher participation in decision making did not necessarily mean shared influence, and that participation was often perceived as a formality or an administrative attempt to create the illusion of teacher influence (p. 104). Those same researchers conclude that what is needed to ensure that the benefits outweigh the costs of involvement is some *evidence* that teachers' participation actually makes a difference in decision outcomes. Otherwise, participation leaves teachers both unsatisfied and reluctant to venture future involvement. A more recent study of urban schools (Corcoran et al., 1988) likewise reports that teachers perceive themselves as genuine participants in decision making primarily when their advice and expertise are respected and used regularly, rather than selectively or intermittently.

Conversely, other researchers have found that when real authority and resources accompany participatory decision making teachers report increased satisfaction and, at times, enthusiasm (Clune & White, 1988; David, 1989). Although not focused specifically on education, Kanter (1983) points out that participation in planning committees that lack adequate information, authority, or specific charge for action increases participants' frustration.

Gregory's (1980) synthesis of case study research on successful urban elementary schools reports that in order for decisions to endure the staff who are affected by the decisions must feel a sense of ownership in them. He (Gregory, 1980) recommends the establishment of decision making structures that provide for genuine teacher involvement. But Corcoran et al. (1988) emphasize that the existence of formal participatory structures does not ensure that teachers will be involved in decision making or collegial planning. To be successful, such structures must be accompanied by district support and commitment of time and other resources (Corcoran et al., 1988, p. 130). Firestone (1977) similarly identifies as a barrier to teacher participation in decision making the unequal distribution of time and skills between teachers and administrators.

A recent national study (Carnegie Foundation, 1988) reports that teachers in urban schools are three times as likely as nonurban teachers to feel uninvolved in basic educational decisions such as setting goals and selecting books and materials. "They are twice as apt to feel they have no control over how classroom time is used or content selected" (Carnegie Foundation, 1988, p. 6). Corcoran et al. (1988) cite survey research conducted by PACE (Policy Analysis for California Education), which found that teachers are more satisfied and effective when they are allowed to decide issues related to organizational policies, curriculum, student discipline, teaching assignments, and teacher selection. However, only 30% of urban teachers "have significant decision making authority in academic curriculum matters" (Corcoran et al., 1988, p. 150).

Frymier's (1987) study of urban teacher's perceptions of their workplace likewise confirms that teachers feel left out of decision making within their schools. Frymier (1987) infers that "centralizing routine decisions and decentralizing significant decisions *maximizes* participants' motivation" (p. 14). Of course, judgments vary widely as to which educational decisions are "routine" and which "significant." Moreover, David (1989) emphasizes that schools' decision making authority often is limited by union contracts and federal, state, or district regulations. She proffers an insightful illustration:

> Whether or not school site budgeting equals autonomy depends on how much freedom from restrictions is allowed. For example, a school can receive a lump-sum budget for all expenditures including staff, yet have no decision making authority because of rules governing class size, tenure, hiring, firing, assignment, curriculum objectives, and textbooks. (David, 1989, p. 47)

All told, the research on participative/shared decision making is inconclusive and tends to be more focused on indirect effects (teacher satisfaction, morale) than on student outcomes (Brown, 1987; Duke et al., 1980; Estler, 1988; Hoy & Miskel, 1982; Winfield, 1990). Participatory models of decision making are often based on values and beliefs, not on empirical research. Estler (1988) cites Greenburg's (1975) analysis of the different assumptions that can underlie such beliefs, including valuing participation (a) as a means of increasing productivity, (b) based on ethics and human growth potential, (c) as an end in itself, and (d) as a means of educating participants toward a revolutionary consciousness (p. 309). In sum, "the benefits of participation are [often] viewed as a given rather than as an empirical question" (Estler, 1988, p. 309).

Distribution of Power and Control. There are several now-classic studies related to governing urban schools. In one, Rogers (1968) found that the New York City school system functioned like an authoritarian bureaucracy, with excessive centralization and emphasis on formalized hierarchy. Rogers reported that decision makers in the central bureaucracy were removed from, and unresponsive to, the unique problems and communities of individual schools within the system. Moreover, the lack of communication and coordination among city schools fostered "passive sabotage" by principals and field supervisors. This sabotage, for example, took the form of reinterpreting central office directives, consistent with what principals perceived to be their greater familiarity with the needs and workings of their schools. The implication is that school-site autonomy could only be approached surreptitiously.

Another widely cited study (Gittell & Hollander, 1968) also depicted urban school systems as insulated from the public, with decision making squarely in the hands of professional bureaucrats. These researchers concluded that multilayered bureaucratic structures inhibited or precluded the discretion and input of teachers, principals, and parents. Confirming this perspective, the Council of the Great City Schools (1988) reports that urban principals spend more hours working after school, are more frustrated, and are more dissatisfied with what they perceive as insufficient authority and control over their own schools, largely due to the highly centralized management structure (p. 27). However, McGivney and Haught (1972) caution that formal structures are not the sole explanation of how city school districts function; they found that informal networks also shape organizational members' behaviors.

In their study of Chicago school principals, Morris, et al. (1981) found evidence of activities similar to the passive sabotage documented earlier by Rogers (1968). They identified and elaborated these phenomena in terms of "discretionary insubordination" and "counterbureaucratic behavior" (Morris et al., 1981). Such activities are described not only as necessary for individual and system survival but also as a means of humanizing the effects of the large, impersonal organization. Creative disobedience, rule-bending, and disregard of centralized directives were reportedly driven by principals' interest in making the system work for the benefit of children—thus, school-site autonomy "corrects" the faults of the central system.

Related to the above, McPherson et al. (1986) reports finding two distinct types of principals, each of whose decision making is grounded in a different set of values. One type is largely concerned with *policy-*

delivery, and defines responsibility in terms of allegiance first to the school system, then to the school (p. 75). The other type is more concerned with *service-delivery*, and defines responsibility in terms of allegiance first to the school, then to the system (p. 75). It is this second type of principal who is most likely to engage in the kinds of creative insubordination and "civilized disobedience" described by Morris et al. (1981).

Borman and Spring (1984), however, point out that principals' discretionary insubordination can also be viewed much less positively than the interpretation by Morris et al. (1981). They (Borman & Spring, 1984) argue that such intentional delinquency may ensure that the total system fails to function optimally, and that attempts to implement systemwide reforms may continually be aborted by individual schools/ principals. From this perspective, then, school-site autonomy exacerbates, rather than ameliorates, the weaknesses of the centralized system.

Research conducted in Chicago by Crowson and Porter-Gehrie (1980) documents a wide variety of "coping mechanisms" and discretionary decision-making powers of principals, in an attempt to show that urban school districts are not "as centralized and monolithic as some believe" (p. 45). They conclude that, despite numerous regulations and centralized influences, large educational systems are, in fact, loosely coupled (thereby allowing principals' discretionary decision making). In a re-analysis of this same data five years later, Crowson and Morris (1985) reported that, although loosely structured, systemwide control is maintained through formal structures related to finance, personnel, scheduling, and pupil behavior. They found that the technical core activities of classroom teaching were less subject to systemic formal controls (p. 57), and that approximately half of the principal's workday focused on attending to the central hierarchy's rules, reporting procedures, regulations, and directives (p. 67). This re-analysis thus tempered their earlier inferences concerning city principals' widespread application of creative noncompliance with the formal controls exercised by central office.

In a similar vein, Corcoran et al.'s (1988) study of urban schools concludes that "it is probably more accurate to think of schools as being co-managed by district and building administrators, although the balance of power and authority in this partnership varies enormously from district to district" (p. 97). Their study also reports that, even in districts implementing school-based management models, centralized control is exerted via accountability mechanisms, construction and maintenance priorities, allocation of time and resources, and negotiated agreements regarding teachers' workload.

The issue of the degree of influence that negotiated agreements wield has been widely debated. McDonnell and Pascal (1979), for example, report considerable variation in contract management at the school-site level. They found that while some principals "use the contract both to manage their building more systematically and to increase teacher participation in decision making" others view the contract "as an obstacle to a well run school" and "an excuse for poor management" (McDonnell & Pascal, 1979, p. 81). This variability in contract implementation and idiosyncratic re-interpretation at the school level are confirmed in other studies as well (Johnson, 1988). Nonetheless, Johnson (1988) concludes that although formal contract provisions may yield variable outcomes, collective bargaining generally seems to have expanded the informal influence of teachers on school policy and practices.

Implications for Principals

The preceding overview of theory, history, and research underscores the crucial connections between the immediate practical problem of "school autonomy-systemwide uniformity" and broader organizational and political issues that influence city school governance. Much of the available information clearly relates more to structures and processes than to effects on student learning or other variables.

What are the implications of all this for urban principals? First, it is undeniable that there exists a sense of isolation and a "separation between 'downtown' and the schools" (Corcoran et al., 1988, p. 101). However, whether city school districts are tightly coupled bureaucracies or loosely knit confederations, the reality remains that principals stand at a pivotal point of interchange between central office-school board decision makers and teachers, parents, and students. Second, due to this critical positioning, an important role of urban principals is to both buffer teachers/ students from the pathological aspects of large organizations and to use the system's established channels effectively to acquire resources for their schools (Corcoran et al., 1988, p. xv).

Third, since principals are in a unique position in terms of their connections to (and potentially high visibility within) the local community, they can capitalize on resources both internal and external to the system. Borman and Spring (1984) refer to this as an "entrepreneurial" style that involves the ability to negotiate with a wide variety of actors. This perspective rings true to Kerchner's (1980) emphasis on the contemporary *multilateral nature* of educational decision making.

Fourth, though formal structures and teacher unionism may be viewed as burdensome constraints on the principal's work, in most systems there exists wide latitude within which informal networks/mechanisms may be exercised to advance school-site individuality. McPherson, et al. (1986) observe that "there are many ways of coming to grips with constraints and many postures toward the system which can be adopted.... [it is] the principal's perception of the system [which] becomes tantamount to the reality that will be observed in the local school" (pp. 77, 73). Principals must "live out a schizophrenic role" that involves both loyalty to and insurgency within the urban school system (McPherson et al., 1986, p. 84).

Lastly, it is important to be mindful of some of the inconsistencies in attempts to apply research results to practice. For example, it is not uncommon to find calls for implementation of the research on decentralization or site-based management to be translated into practice as the formation of a school planning committee. Good and Brophy (1986) warn, "Too much of the current school improvement activity naively proceeds as though the existence of a school *plan* that is widely accepted will positively influence achievement outcomes" (p. 586). In like manner, Finn (1984) points to misapplications of research and erroneous oversimplifications by decision-makers who are "tempted to take the superficial attributes of 'effective schools' and *order* all schools to display those attributes" (p. 524).

Tools of Analysis

What tools can principals use to find and/or frame problems related to the tension between school-level autonomy and centralized control? Unfortunately, precise measurement instruments and useful analytical devices for confronting this dilemma have yet to be fashioned.

However, Stevenson (1987) recommends a form of the "backward mapping" process described by Elmore (1979-80). According to Stevenson (1987), the process begins with teachers delineating desirable school characteristics and then working backwards to identify the specific activities and structures needing to be changed in order to facilitate those desirable conditions. Ideally, participants could isolate those areas considered to be crucial for autonomous school authority and decision making and those for which centralized control is warranted. The goals of this "bottom-up" backward mapping process are to first specify, then focus attention and action on obstacles to be removed, internal/external resources and other forms of support to be provided, responsibilities to be divided between district office and school, and "activities and organizational actors most likely to produce the desired behaviors and practices" (Stevenson, 1987, p. 369). This model is grounded in the assumptions that school staffs are willing and able to identify the kinds and amount of autonomy needed at the building level in order to foster improvement.

Other tools mentioned in the literature are less specific than that presented above. Wiles et al. (1981), for example, stress the need for principals to engage in a kind of "situational analysis," to identify and define the boundary that "pinpoints the demarcation of local school concerns from system (environment) concerns" (p. 104). Yet these same authors acknowledge the politically dynamic, shifting nature of those boundaries—thus, clearly complicating (if not making impossible) the assessment task. Nonetheless, several of their recommendations for principals seem viable: for example, to stay attuned to observable indicators such as patterns of upward communication, threat of veto of school-site decisions by the district, and system-level support of local initiatives. These suggestions underscore Wiles et al.'s (1981) premise that these decision boundaries determine how scarce resources are allocated and what the rules are for "playing the game" (pp. 89, 87).

In a related vein, the tools referred to by McPherson et al. (1986) focus less on assessing decision boundaries and more on attempting to predict the magnitude of risk associated with principals' "discretionary insubordination" and "civilized disobedience" of district directives. According to McPherson et al. (1986), principals engage in situational analysis and critical self-examination through questions such as: "Which of these problems before me are real? Which are not? How do I differentiate? How willing am I to act?" (p. 77).

It may be observed, however, that the previously described approaches represent technical-rational attempts to understand a complex and somewhat unpredictable organization. Borman and Spring (1984) emphasize the importance of analyzing both the organization's formal mechanisms of control, as well as the (less readily observable/ measurable) informal mechanisms of power (p. 70). The specific tools for doing so, however, remain illusive.

Intervention Strategies

How are city districts contending with the countervailing presses for school-site autonomy and central coordination? What is presently being done to govern urban schools in new and different ways? What are some examples of changes implemented to ameliorate the tension between centralized control and decentralized authority? The purpose of this section is to review the concept of school-based management and to elaborate a number of related interventions that are being tried in urban school districts.

School-Based Management

Ideas and issues related to *school-based management* have surfaced repeatedly throughout this chapter, although frequently not specifically labeled as such. Preceding discussions of theory and research about decentralization, site autonomy, the distribution of power and control, the restructuring of school governance systems, and participatory or shared decision making are all integral to the notion of school-based management. The crux of the concept is the individual school as the primary unit of decision making (Lindelow & Heyndrickx, 1989). The reason for revisiting the concept here is that, currently, school-based management is being viewed as (a) an effective "response to what many educators perceive as an overcentralization of power within school districts" (Lindelow & Heyndrickx, 1989, p. 109) and (b) a promising intervention strategy for the improvement of urban schools (Oakes, 1987; Winfield, 1990).

Guthrie (1986), for example, while emphasizing that the concept has existed for at least 20 years, advocates school-based management as the "next needed educational reform" in order to revitalize individual schools, "unleash productive local initiatives," and sustain the momentum of the educational reform movement in general (p. 306). More importantly, he views school-based management as a means of resolving the tension that currently exists between state-imposed policies and local control (p. 309). Guthrie recommends four specific intervention strategies to transform the authority and problem-solving capabilities of local schools:

1. Recognize the principal as chief executive officer (for example, via symbolic and economic incentives such as salaries higher than those of central office administrators; via the authority to approve or veto the assignment of all teachers to his or her school).

2. Establish parent and teacher school councils. These councils would have strictly advisory status regarding policy, planning, hiring, and resource allocation, but would have the authority to evaluate the principal.

3. Institute school-site budgeting and accounting, as a means of both increasing local school resource-allocation discretion and ensuring accountability.

4. Require annual planning and performance reports, developed jointly by school advisory councils and the principal. These reports would serve as assessment and communication vehicles for the various school constituencies.

Site-based planning is frequently a key component of school-based management endeavors. Some city school districts "have initiated such programs on a voluntary basis; others (Milwaukee) have mandated them for some of their schools (typically the lowest achieving ones); others (Atlanta) have required all their schools to initiate site-based improvement programs" (Oakes, 1987, p. 15). Oakes (1987) also notes that the intent of these initiatives is often to achieve greater goal consensus among faculties and higher expectations for students. School-based planning teams are typically encouraged "to survey their current needs, develop improvement goals, and plan specific strategies for meeting those goals" (Oakes, 1987, p. 14). But sometimes, there exist serious conflicts between what a school staff wishes to pursue and the improvement planning vision of the district (Louis, 1986). Miles, et al. (1986) found that district-level pressures to standardize improvement planning diverted considerable time and energy from school-based initiatives. Purkey and Smith (1985) advocate planning designed at the school-level, coupled with district-level mandates and incentives that press schools to improve.

Not surprisingly, however, interpretations and applications of the general concept of school-based management vary widely. In Brown's (1987) estimation, "school-based management is a remarkable mix of organizational and financial arrangements for districts and schools" (p. 38). As will be seen in subsequent examples drawn from urban settings, decision making authority can be distributed among principals, site councils, and communities in ways quite distinct from those recommended by Guthrie (1986). There exist multiple variations in (among other things) the membership of site councils, the relative authority of councils and principal, the decision domains delegated to the site (curriculum, personnel, budgeting) or maintained by central administration (transportation, maintenance, data processing), and the structures and processes for shared decision making at the school level (Clune & White, 1988; Lindelow & Heynderickx, 1989; Wirt & Kirst, 1989).

Although the following examples illustrate some of these variations in intraorganizational relationships, Brown's (1987) conclusion that there is a lack of empirical research on school-based management is a crucial one. Likewise, it is important to note Corbett's (1989) caveats that (a) school-based management initiatives often focus intently on restructured decision making relationships, but neglect "consideration of the staff and student outcomes desired (results) that are substantially different [from the current ones]" (p. 13) and (b) broadened empowerment may be "hollow" when increases in authority (the right to make decisions) are not accompanied by increases in ability to influence others to adhere to the decisions made (p. 13).

Dade County, Florida

One of the most highly publicized recent experiments with decentralized decision making is that of Dade County (Miami), Florida. A major goal there is to give principals, teachers, parents, and community leaders more discretionary authority in school management and more control over local schools, as a means of encouraging innovation and school improvement (Hill et al., 1989). The project began as a large, three-year pilot, initiated in 1987 and involving approximately 10% (32) of the district's 259 schools (Council of the Great City Schools, 1988). A notable aspect of this venture was the closeness with which the then-superintendent (Joseph Fernandez) and teacher union president (Pat

Tornillo) worked on the project. Some interpreted their close collaboration as an indicator of an era of new collegial partnerships in hitherto adversarial relationships in large urban contexts (Hill et al., 1989). This somewhat unprecedented level of collaboration was also viewed as a crucial element in the potential success of the pilot. The notion was that, because of the power of their offices, they were in strategic positions for garnering the internal and external support needed to sustain the experiment.

One of the unique features of the Dade County model is that the union (an affiliate of the American Federation of Teachers) agreed to waive selected provisions of the teachers' contract, in order to facilitate school-based management and shared decision making. Similarly, for its part, the district office attempted to relieve individual schools of excessive centralized regulation by "eliminating complex administrative processes for purchasing and staff hiring" (Hill et al., 1989, p. 16). The Council of the Great City Schools (1988) reports that certain school board rules and state department of education regulations had also been waived, and that school-based teams together decide how to allocate funds, teach students, and structure the school's curriculum and programs.

Rather than imposing any one model of school-based management/shared decision making, the district encouraged participating schools to develop bottom-up plans of their own. Each school formed a committee of teachers and staff "to propose to the Board of Education structural, regulatory, and instructional changes needed to improve performance and student achievement" (Council of the Great City Schools, 1988, p. 56). At least two-thirds of the faculty had to approve (by vote) the site-developed proposals to participate in the project (Dreyfus, 1988). The program includes parent and community involvement components, and schools are allowed discretionary decision making in approximately 80-90% of their budgets. Training conferences were initially provided for school teams comprised of the principal, union steward, and three elected representatives from each participating school (Dreyfus, 1988). Ongoing training is also an important part of the model, for school teams as well as entire faculties.

Although this innovative pilot project earned considerable national media attention in the late 1980s, it should be noted that since the mid-1970s the Dade County teacher union had been very active in expanding collective bargaining beyond bread-and-butter issues and in seeking changes in school policies and procedures. At that time, largely due to union pressure, "faculty councils" were established at every school to consult with the principal (Finn, 1985, p. 334). Dreyfus (1988) points out, however, that though the school board granted increased discretion in budget decision making at the school level in the 1970s, it decided against "full implementation of school-based management in 1975" (p. 12). Some 10 years later, however, the 1986 collective bargaining agreement focused intensely on the professionalization of teaching.

In Miami, as in other major American cities, the Urban League has played an important role in fostering political and community support for school improvement initiatives and increased salaries for teachers. The League assists directly in one of the district's experiments with school-based management: the Partners in Education project (Snider, 1988). Other community agencies and corporate sponsors have also contributed to specific site-based innovations.

Rochester, New York

Collaboration between teacher union (affiliate of the American Federation of Teachers) and top-level district administration facilitated reform of governance and decision making structures in Rochester, New York as well.[2] As in Dade County, these initiatives have received national attention, but in the case of Rochester that attention focused largely on the city's path-breaking (and high-paying) teachers' contract. However, then-Superintendent McWalters (1988) emphasized that school board leadership, multiyear preplanning, and community involvement were all equally crucial to Rochester's reforms. The contract, "which has attracted so much attention, is really only one item on a much larger agenda for reform that started in Rochester in the late 1970s" (McWalters, 1988, p. 13).

Spurred by a communitywide initiative led by the Urban League of Rochester and the Center for Educational Development (a nonprofit foundation), city and educational system mobilized to jointly focus on improving the schools. Between 1985 and 1988, numerous changes in curriculum and support programs were implemented. Simultaneously, attention and resources were directed to school-based planning, shared decision making, and a restructured salary system for teachers. All three components were incorporated into the negotiated agreement signed in August 1987.

Contractual agreements provided for a four-tiered career advancement and incentive system for teachers, and a shared governance process for decision making at the school level (Urbanski, 1988). School improvement planning teams, chaired by school principals, include parents, teachers, administrators, and, in secondary schools, students. The teams range in size from eight to 28 members, and teachers comprise the majority of membership. (The number of teachers is determined by adding one to the total number of all other members selected for the team.) Teachers, parents, and students elect their representatives to the team, while principals may appoint members. Teams operate by consensus and have decision-making authority over "school budgets, school dynamics, instructional goals, and other important matters" (Urbanski, 1988, p. 52). The team's plan must be shared with the school's community, and be submitted to the central office "for review, approval, and facilitation" (McWalters, 1988, p. 15). As in Dade County, teams may request special waivers from school board policies or provisions of the negotiated contract. Central office administrators are "expected to assist school-based planning teams by supporting their requests for waivers and working to remove the barriers that impede them from accomplishing their goals" (Guidelines, 1988).

Underlying much of these reforms is the vision of transforming teaching into a financially rewarding profession with increased autonomy —*and* accountability for student achievement. An illustration of the latter is that "in exchange for higher salaries, Rochester teachers agreed to work a longer school year and to expand the Home Base Guidance program," a program in which teachers essentially become case managers, responsible for home contacts, personal attention, and general supervision of approximately 20 students during their stays in their schools (Urbanski, 1988, p. 52). According to McWalters (1988), "Issues of decentralization in decision making and the role of the central office are directly tied to getting the best answers to questions of how to aid students" (p. 15).

It is not uncommon that, over time, "flagship" local teacher organizations (often in large urban districts) set the pace and establish the precedents for changes in major contract provisions. Thus, McDonnell and Pascal (1988) suggest that "we cannot expect all districts to look like a Rochester or a Dade County within the next ten years, but we can expect them to move in a similar direction" (p. 52).

Boston, Massachusetts

Boston is another example of a large city school system in which the teacher's union contract incorporates agreement to give individual schools increased authority in hiring, curriculum, and budget decision making. The agreement was originally approved in the fall of 1989. (As in Dade County and Rochester, the Boston teachers' union is an affiliate of the American Federation of Teachers.)

According to the three-year contract, each school[3] that elects to participate in the restructuring must develop an annual plan specifying its educational goals. A "school-site council" of teachers, parents, the principal, and (at the high school level) students is to set these goals. The council's other responsibilities include designing instructional programs, budgeting, fundraising, purchasing, scheduling, staffing, hiring, and parent-teacher relations (Bradley, 1989). Councils are allowed to recruit teachers from other Boston schools without regard to seniority (Gold, 1989).

Decentralization of decision- making authority, however, is tied to centralized accountability mechanisms. For example, the central administration is to use the site-developed goal statements as measures against which to assess the school's progress each year. A variety of assessment indicators are to be used, including dropout rates, student test scores, evaluations of school climate, and measures of parental involvement (Bradley, 1989). If progress towards goals is unsatisfactory, and if the school does not improve its performance after receiving a year's assistance from a joint labor-management team, then some or all of the school's administrators and teachers could be replaced or reassigned (Gold, 1989).

Interestingly, approximately one year prior to the contract agreement, business leaders had announced that they would not renew the "Boston Compact" unless the city's schools increased the pace of reform. (Under the partnership compact, initiated in 1982, businesses pledged employment and college aid for high school graduates, in exchange for the school system's agreement to improve student achievement, work preparation, and school operations.)

Chicago, Illinois

In Chicago, the mandate for decentralized, school-based management (initiated in the fall of 1989) is found not in the union contract but in Illinois state law. The law, drafted by a coalition of business, parent, research groups, and the late Mayor Washington, dissolved the existing Chicago school board, and required the mayor to appoint future boards from a list of candidates to be developed by a new nominating commission (Snider, 1989). Decision-making authority was shifted, but in different ways than in the cities previously described; in Chicago, the emphasis is on increasing *parents'* (rather than teachers') power to influence city school governance.[4]

The Illinois law specifies that each of Chicago's 600 schools will have an 11-member council, consisting of six parents, two teachers, two community residents, and the principal. Unlike past local school councils that served purely advisory roles, each of these councils is to have broad authority, including the power to allocate the school budget, to select its own principal, and to decide whether or not to renew the principal's four-year, performance-based contract (Chicago alternative, 1989). Pursuant to this reform law, half of the city's principals were to lose their tenure in 1990, and half in 1991.

Teachers Advisory Councils were also established at each school. Although teachers are expected to be held more accountable for their performance, they also are to have increased authority over their school's educational policies, via the Advisory Councils. An example of one mechanism aimed at increasing accountability is that teachers whose performance is judged unsatisfactory are given 45 days to improve (not one year, as had been the practice), prior to facing dismissal.

Summary

Although examples cited in this section focused solely on Dade County, Rochester, Boston, and Chicago, other urban school districts (for example, Cincinnati, Cleveland, Houston, Portland, San Diego, Seattle, St. Louis, Tulsa, and more) likewise are instituting changes in the way their schools are governed and in the distribution of power and authority among central office, schools, principals, teachers, parents, and communities. These four examples, however, illustrate the variety of forms that "school-based management" or "decentralized decision making" can take. They also demonstrate the increasingly complex web of forces—internal and external to the schools—that shape local educational decision making.

From the perspective of the school principal, such forces contribute to the ambiguity and complexity of his or her workworld, as well as to a sense of uncertainty as to the potential viability of any of these reformist strategies to restructure educational decision-making authority. A report of the Council of the Great City Schools (1988) emphasizes that "as these examples make clear, any change in decision making authority must walk a fine line between competing interests" (p. 35). Those interests are, of course, unique to particular settings. Nonetheless, Hill et al. (1989) point out that although improvement initiatives are often so specific to individual communities that they could not be duplicated elsewhere the dissemination of information about such models can be useful "as a frame of reference within which local [improvement] activists can build their own strategies" (p. 9).

It is important to note that the changes described in the four cities included in this section are so recent and ambitious that implementation and evaluation results are as yet incomplete. Thus, it is impossible to present any definitive conclusions about the value of these initiatives. Although each set of interventions is considered promising by some, evidence of success in implementation or concomitant and sustained improvement in student learning both remain to be seen. The thread that holds these examples together, and that perhaps is illustrative of a future long-term trend, is that emphasis is placed on encouraging school-level responsibility, rather than increasing centralized control and uniformity (Corcoran et al., 1988).

Questions Remaining

In this chapter, an overview of the extant knowledge-base related to the tension between school-level autonomy and systemwide control in urban school districts has been presented. Discussion included: (a) what is understood about this problem of practice, in terms of relevant theory and conceptual frameworks; (b) what is known about the problem, including its historical underpinnings and selected research findings; (c) implications of this theory, research, and tools of analysis for the work of urban school principals; and (d) selected examples of intervention strategies utilized by several large urban districts, as related to innovations in governing schools. The importance of these issues is grounded in the quintessential question of *where* and *how* decisions are made that affect teaching and learning—that is, in the

locus of control of decision-making processes, (including the allocation
of resources), as related to *children*.

Though various forms of decentralized decision processes appear
to be driving many of the recent reforms in education, there exists
tremendous imprecision in terms and ambiguity of meanings attached
to the concepts of "shared governance," "school-based management,"
"teacher empowerment," "community control," "participatory decision
making," "restructuring," and the like. In order to facilitate the sharing
of ideas and innovations in these regards, a number of urban school
districts have increased efforts to communicate and collaborate. These
efforts include, for example: (a) the dissemination of printed information about promising innovations in urban education (Council of the
Great City School, 1987 & 1988); and (b) the formation of an Urban
District Leadership Consortium, a coalition resulting from an unprecedented national "summit" meeting of teacher union presidents, superintendents, and school board members from 19 urban school districts
(Following Summit, 1989).

Nonetheless, numerous questions about governing urban schools
remain:

1. Is *governance* reform *educational* reform? Gittell and Hevesi (1969)
   underscore that "there is, as yet, little empirical evidence to prove
   systematically that maximum public participation will automatically lead to maximum educational quality" (p. 14). Some 20
   years later, that evidence is still lacking, whether related to *public*
   participation or *teacher* participation. Moreover, Dentler et al.
   (1987) remind us that, over the past decade, the issue of administrative decentralization of decision processes has become
   "freighted with every hope and fear carried by every group with
   a stake in the institution of schooling" (p. 40).

2. Even if there were agreement that centralized control at the
   district level should be diminished and site-based authority
   increased, how can school autonomy and teacher autonomy be
   reconciled? Both terms are open to broad interpretation, leaving
   unclear the relative degrees of authority over decision making to
   be exercised by principals, parents, teachers, community members, or others. The question of who *should* control America's
   schools (professional educators or laypersons) is as old as public
   education itself (Zeigler & Jennings, 1974). Which decision

domains are best left to which specific (combination of) key players? Good and Brophy (1986), for example, state that "although we believe that some consensus on school goals and use of resources across an entire staff is necessary, there can be too much as well as too little school-wide planning" (p. 588). Furthermore, of course, participatory structures do not guarantee influence (Corbett, 1989; Corcoran et al., 1988). This issue concerns how the meaningfulness of any form of shared decision making can be ensured.

3. How can the central educational objective of *equity* be guaranteed in a decentralized educational structure? Historical experience (for example, racial segregation) demonstrates that harmful inequities may be perpetrated in the absence of centralized constraints (Swanson, 1969). In addition, economies of scale and cost effectiveness may be attributed to certain centralized practices in large organizations. Given current enrollment declines and the fiscal retrenchment affecting urban school districts (Oakes, 1987), how can such economies be reconciled with decentralized control of budgeting and staffing?

4. Despite the emphasis of recent research and reform on individual schools as critical cultural and decision systems, will this "fundamental shift in educational governance [be] lost in the popular focus upon district versus state (and federal) control issues" (Wiles et al., 1981)? Are principals' responsibilities and authority being simultaneously eroded both "from above" and "from below"? If so, is it unreasonable to expect that this basic tension can *ever* be fully reconciled? How can broadened power distributions be capitalized on and accepted as strengths, rather than obstacles?

5. What can principals do to ensure that school-based management works to the advantage of students at the local site? How can they exercise leadership so that shared decision making will lead to improvements in teaching and learning? What can be done to ensure that restructured authority relationships are sustained long term? How can individual schools make central offices, boards of education, state agencies, or federal authorities more aware of their needs, their perceptions of the negative impact of certain regulatory practices, their commitment to accountability, and the like?

Conclusion

With every "major educational movement" there is always the possibility that the hoopla and flurry of activities undertaken in the name of the movement will actually combine to create an immense *diversion* from issues most directly relevant to children's learning. The same may apply to the issues of school autonomy and centralized control discussed in this chapter. What is to prevent, for example, the attention to revising decision boundaries between and among teachers and administrators to become viewed as an end in itself, rather than a means to increase responsiveness to students' needs? Does the emphasis on reformed *processes* of decision making in urban districts divert attention from the more important issue of improved *products* and *outcomes* of decision making?

Mann (1985) poignantly underscores the point that "the politics of school leadership has been too much about adult working conditions and too little about children's learning conditions" (p. 16). Cuban (1989) warns that it is simply incorrect to assume that "changes in school governance, district boundaries, curriculum, or decision making authority automatically lead to classroom changes in urban schools" (p. 29). Moreover, tracing the potential impact of the loosening of centralized control and decision making from urban school boards through district offices, union contracts, principals' memoranda, and teacher or parent committees to classrooms, may, in fact, be impossible.

Nonetheless, there are at least two reasons for continuing to study, deliberate, and debate issues related to how and by whom schools are governed. First, as Sergiovanni et al. (1987) remind us, the current reality is that:

> Educating youngsters for productive lives in the twentieth century requires organization, and organizations require governance. Governance includes such things as setting some priorities among all the possible objectives of the organization, allocating resources to meet those objectives, and coordinating the activities of members of the organization to accomplish the objectives more effectively. (p. 183)

In addition, from the perspective of the principalship, as any changes in governing schools occur (for example, collegial self-government by teachers), it is inevitable that the roles of those with managerial responsibilities will also change (Campbell et al., 1985). New or different skills may need to be developed, in order to be able to understand and behave proactively and appropriately to the changed context of urban school leadership. For these reasons, it is hoped that the synthesis of information and questions raised in this chapter will be helpful to current and aspiring principals in city school systems.

Notes

1. The purpose of the Urban Initiative Select Conference was to identify critical problems of practice that could serve as foci for the organization of a knowledge-base relevant to urban school administrators. The conference was sponsored jointly by the Danforth Foundation and the University Council for Educational Administration. Ten principals of urban schools, six representatives of metropolitan youth-serving agencies, and eight educational administration professors from urban universities participated in the Conference, which was held in Mesa, Arizona in April 1989.

2. The Rochester City School District has 49 schools and serves approximately 32,000 students.

3. There are 123 schools in Boston, and a total of 4,575 teachers (Gold, 1989).

4. The Chicago model seems to conform to Altshuler's (1970) definition of *political decentralization*, in contrast to *administrative decentralization*. This distinction among terms is in an earlier subsection of this chapter, "Community Control."

References

Altshuler, A. (1970). *Community control: The black demand for participation in large American cities.* New York: Pegasus.

Barnard, C. I. (1938). *The functions of the executive.* Cambridge, MA: Harvard University Press.

Bidwell, C. E. (1965). The school as a formal organization. In J. March (Ed.), *Handbook of organizations* (pp. 972-1022). Chicago: Rand-McNally.

Bolman, L. G., & Deal, T. E. (1984). *Modern approaches to understanding and managing organizations.* San Fransisco: Jossey-Bass.

Borman, K. M., & Spring, J. H. (1984). *Schools in central cities: Structure and process.* New York: Longman.

Boyd, W. L. (1988). How to reform schools without half trying: Secrets of the Reagan administration. *Educational Administration Quarterly, 24*(3), 299-309.

Bradley, A. (1989, May 31). Contract in Boston calls for site-based management. *Education Week,* 5.

Bridges, E. M. (1967). A model for shared decision-making in the school principalship. *Educational Administration Quarterly, 3,* 49-61.

Brookover, W. B., Beady, C., Flood, P., Schweitzer, J., & Wisenbaker, J. (1979). *School social systems and student achievement: Schools can make a difference.* New York: Praeger.

Brown, D. J. (1987). *Preliminary inquiry into school-based management.* (ERIC Document Reproduction Service No. ED 284 331).

Campbell, R. F., Cunningham, L. L., Nystand, R. O., & Usdan, M. D. (1985). *The organization and control of American schools,* 5th ed. Columbus, OH: Merrill.

Carnegie Forum on Education and the Economy. (1986). *A nation prepared: Teachers for the 21st century.* New York: Author.

Carnegie Foundation for the Advancement of Teaching. (1988). *An imperiled generation: Saving urban schools.* A Carnegie Foundation Special Report. Lawrenceville, NJ: Princeton University Press.

The Chicago alternative. (1989, March 29). *The Village Voice,* 16.

Clune, W. H., & White, P. A. (1988). *School-based management: Institutional variation, implementation, and issues for further research.* New Brunswick, NJ: Center for Policy Research in Education, Eagleton Institute of Politics, Rutgers.

Conway, J. (1984). The myth, mystery, and mastery of participative decision-making in education. *Educational Administration Quarterly, 20*(3), 11-40.

Corbett, H. D. (1989). *On the meaning of restructuring.* Unpublished manuscript, Research for Better Schools, Inc. Philadelphia.

Corcoran, T. B. Walker, L. J., & White, J. L. (1988). *Working in urban schools.* Washington, DC: Institute for Educational Leadership.

Corwin, R. G. (1974). *Education in crisis.* New York: Wiley.

Corwin, R. G., & Borman, K. M. (1988). Schools as workplace: Structural constraints on administration. In N. L. Boyan (Ed.), *Handbook of research on educational administration* (pp. 209-238). New York: Longman.

Council of the Great City Schools. (1987). *Challenges to urban education: Results in the making.* Washington, DC: Author.

Council of the Great City Schools. (1988). *Teaching and leading in the Great City Schools.* Washington, DC: Author.

Crowson, R. L., & Morris, V. C. (1985). Administrative control in large-city school systems: An investigation in Chicago. *Educational Administration Quarterly, 21*(4), 51-70.

Crowson, R. L., & Porter-Gehrie, C. (1980). The discretionary behavior of principals in large-city schools. *Educational Administration Quarterly, 16*(1), 45-69.

Cuban, L. (1984). *How teachers taught.* New York: Longman.

Cuban, L. (1989). At-risk students: What teachers and principals can do. *Educational Leadership, 46*(5), 29-32.

David, J. L. (1989). Synthesis of research on school-based management. *Educational Leadership, 46*(8), 45-53.

Deal, T. E., & Kennedy, A. A. (1982). *Corporate cultures.* Reading, MA: Addison-Wesley.

Dentler, R. A., Flowers, C., & Mulvey, K. (1987). Decentralization in the Cleveland public schools: An evaluation. *Equity and Excellence, 23*(1-2), 37-60.

Dejnozka, E. L. (1983). *Educational administration glossary.* Westport, CT: Greenwood Press.

Dreyfus, G. (1988). Dade County opens doors to site decisions. *The School Administrator, 45*(7), 12-18.

Duke, D. L., Showers, B. K., & Imber, M. (1980). Teachers and shared decision making: The costs and benefits of involvement. *Educational Administration Quarterly, 16*(1), 93-106.

Edmonds, R. (1979). Effective schools for the urban poor. *Educational Leadership, 37*, 15-24.

Elmore, R. F. (1979-80). Backward mapping: Implementation research and policy decision. *Political Science Quarterly, 95*, 601-616.

Elmore, R. F. (1988). *Early experiences in restructuring schools: Voices from the field.* Washington, DC: National Governors' Association.

Estler, S. (1988). Decision making. In N. L. Boyan (Ed.), *Handbook of research on educational administration* (pp. 305-320). New York: Longman.

Finn, C. E., Jr. (1984). Toward strategic independence: Nine command-ments for enhancing school effectiveness. *Phi Delta Kappan, 65*(8), 518-524.

Finn, C. E., Jr. (1985). Teacher unions and school quality: Potential allies or inevitable foes? *Phi Delta Kappan, 66*(5), 331-338.

Firestone, W. A. (1977). Participation and influence in the planning of educational change. *Journal of Applied Behavioral Science, 13*(2), 167-187.

Firestone, W. A., & Corbett, H. D. (1988). Planned organizational change. In N. L. Boyan (Ed.), *Handbook of research on educational administration* (pp. 321-340). New York: Longman.

Following "summit," reform-minded urban districts form a network. (1989, May 10). *Education Week*, 5.

Frymier, J. (1987). Bureaucracy and the neutering of teachers. *Phi Delta Kappan, 69*(1), 9-14.

Gittell, M., & Hevesi, A. G. (Eds.). (1969). *The politics of urban education.* New York: Praeger.

Gittell, M., & Hollander, T. E. (1968). *Six urban school districts.* New York: Praeger.

Gold, A. R. (1989, May 23). Boston's teacher pact to decentralize schools. *New York Times*, A16.

Good, T. L., & Brophy, J. E. (1986). School effects. In M. C. Wittrock (Ed.), *Handbook of research on teaching*, 3rd ed. (pp. 570-602). New York: MacMillan.

Goodlad, J. (1984). *A place called school.* New York: McGraw-Hill.

Greenburg, E. S. (1975). The consequences of worker participation: A clarification of the theoretical literature. *Social Science Quarterly, 56*, 12-21.

Gregory, L. L. (1980). Synthesis of the case studies. In Phi Delta Kappa, *Why do some urban schools succeed?* (pp. 132-142). Bloomington, IN: Author.

Griffiths, D. E. (1979). Intellectual turmoil in educational administra-tion. *Educational Administration Quarterly, 15*, 43-65.

Guidelines for school-based planning. (1988). Rochester, NY: Roches-ter City School District.

Guthrie, J. W. (1986, December). School-based management: The next needed educational reform. *Phi Delta Kappan, 68*(4), pp. 305-309.

Hill, P. T., Wise, A. E., & Shapiro, L. (1989). *Educational progress: Cities mobilize to improve their schools.* Santa Monica, CA: RAND.

Hills, J. (1966). Some comments on James G. Anderson's "Bureaucratic rules: Bearers of educational authority." *Educational Administration Quarterly*, 2, 243-261.

The Holmes Group. (1986). *Tomorrow's teachers.* East Lansing, MI: Author.

Hoy, W. K., & Miskel, C. G. (1982). *Educational administration: Theory, research, and practice* (2nd ed.). New York: Random House.

Iannaccone, L. (1962). Informal organization of school systems. In D. Griffiths et al. (Eds.), *Organizing schools for effective education* (pp. 227-293). Danville, IL: Interstate.

Johnson, S. M. (1988). Unionism and collective bargaining in the public schools. In N. L. Boyan (Ed.), *Handbook of research on educational administration* (pp. 603-622). New York: Longman.

Kanter, R. M. (1983). *The change masters.* New York: Simon & Schuster.

Kerchner, C. T. (1980). Unions and their impact on school governance and politics. In A. M. Cresswell and M. Murphy (Eds.), *Teachers, unions, and collective bargaining in public education.* Berkeley: McCutchan.

Kirst, M. W. (1983, Winter). Effective schools: Political environment and educational policy. *Planning and Changing*, 234-244.

Levin, H. M. (1987). New schools. *Teacher Education Quarterly*, 14(4), 60-83.

Lindelow, J., & Heyndrickx, J. (1989). School-based management. In S. C. Smith and P. K. Piele (Eds.), *School leadership: Handbook for excellence* (pp. 109-134). Eugene, OR: ERIC Clearinghouse on Educational Management.

Lortie, D. C. (1977). Two anomalies and three perspectives on school organization. In R. G. Corwin and R. Edelfelt (Eds.), *Perspectives on organizations: The school as a social organization.* Washington, DC: American Association of Colleges for Teacher Education.

Louis, K. S. (1986). A survey of effective schools programs in urban high schools. Paper presented at the annual meeting of the American Educational Research Association, San Fransisco.

Mann, D. (1985, December 18). Principals, leadership, and reform. *Education Week*, 5(16), 16.

March, J. G., & Olsen, J. P. (1976). *Ambiguity and choice in organization.* Bergen, Norway: Universitetsforlaget.

McDonnell, L. M., & Pascal, A. (1979). *Organized teachers in American schools.* Santa Monica, CA: RAND.

McDonnell, L. M., & Pascal, A. (1988). *Teacher unions and educational reform*. Santa Monica, CA: RAND.

McGivney, J. H., & Haught, J. M. (1972). The politics of education: A view from the perspective of the central office staff. *Educational Administration Quarterly, 8*(3).

McPherson, B. R., Crowson, R. L., & Brieschke, P. A. (1986). Marjorie Stallings: A walk through a mine field. *Urban Education, 21*(1), 62-85.

McWalters, P. (1988). New realities call for new rules. *The School Administrator, 45*(8), 13-15.

Meyer, J. W., & Rowan, B. (1978). The structure of educational organizations. In M. W. Meyer et al. (Eds.), *Environments and organizations* (pp. 78-109). San Fransisco: Jossey-Bass.

Miles, M. B., Louis, K. S., Rosenblum, S., Cipollone, A., & Farrar, E. (1986). *Lessons for managing implementation*. Center for Survey Research: University of Massachusetts.

Morris, V. C., Crowson, R. L., Hurwitz, E., & Porter-Gehrie, C. (1981). *The urban principal: Discretionary decision making in a large educational organization*. Chicago: University of Illinois.

National Commission on Excellence in Education. (1983). *A nation at risk: The imperative for educational reform*. Washington, DC: U.S. Department of Education.

National Governors Association. (1986). *Time for results*. Washington, DC: Author.

Network of Regional Desegregation Assistance Centers. (1989). *Resegregation of public schools: The third generation*. Andover, MA: Author.

Oakes, J. (1987). *Improving inner city schools: Current directions in urban district reform*. Santa Monica, CA: RAND.

Orfield, G. (1988, February). School desegregation in the 1980s. *Equity and Choice*, 79-93.

Ornstein, A. C. (1989). Centralization and decentralization of large public school districts. *Urban Education, 24*(2), 233-235.

Ouchi, W. (1981). *Theory Z*. New York: Avon.

Peters, T. J., & Austin, N. (1985). *A passion for excellence*. New York: Random House.

Peters, T. J., & Waterman, R. H., Jr. (1982). *In search of excellence*. New York: Harper & Row.

Purkey, S. C., & Smith, M. S. (1983). Effective schools: A review. *Elementary Schools Journal, 83*(4), 427-452.

Purkey, S. C., & Smith, M. S. (1985). School reform: The district policy implications of the effective schools literature. *Elementary School Journal, 85,* 353-389.

Rogers, D. (1968). *110 Livingston Street.* New York: Random House.

Sergiovanni, T. J., Burlingame, M., Coombs, F. S., & Thurston, P. W. (1987). *Educational governance and administration,* 2nd ed. Englewood Cliffs, NJ: Prentice-Hall.

Simon, H. A. (1957). *Administrative behavior,* 2nd ed. New York: Free Press.

Sizer, T. R. (1985). Common sense. *Educational Leadership, 42*(6), 21-22.

Snider, W. (1988, November 23). A "collaboration": Urban League gains quiet reform role. *Education Week,* 1, 18.

Snider, W. (1989, May 31). Mayor names new members to revamped Chicago board. *Education Week,* 1.

Stevenson, R. B. (1987). Autonomy and support: The dual needs of urban high schools. *Urban Education, 22*(3), 366-386.

Swanson, A. D. (1969). The governance of education in metropolitan areas. In T. V. McKelvey and A. D. Swanson (Eds.), *Urban school administration* (pp. 177-196). Beverly Hills, CA: Sage.

Urbanski, A. (1988). The Rochester contract: A status report. *Educational Leadership, 46*(3), 48-52.

Viteritti, J. P. (1986). The urban school district: Toward an open system approach to leadership and governance. *Urban Education, 21*(3), 228-253.

Weber, M. (1947). *The theory of social and economic organization.* New York: Oxford University Press.

Weick, K. E. (1976). Educational organizations as loosely coupled systems. *Administrative Science Quarterly, 21,* 1-19.

White, P. A. (1988). *Resource materials for school-based management.* New Brunswick, NJ: Center for Policy Research in education, Eagleton Institute of Politics, Rutgers.

Wiles, D. K., Wiles, J., & Bondi, J. (1981). *Practical politics for school administrators.* Boston: Allyn & Bacon.

Williams, M. R. (1989). *Neighborhood organizing for urban school reform.* New York: Teachers College Press.

Willower, D. J. (1980). Contemporary issues in theory in educational administration. *Educational Administration Quarterly, 16,* 1-25.

Willower, D. J. (1984). School principals, school cultures, and school improvement. *Educational Horizons, 63*(1), 35-38.

Winfield, L. (1990). *Restructuring schools: Organizational practices that impact school culture.* Paper presented at the meeting of the American Eduational research Association, Boston, MA.

Wirt, F. M. & Kirst, M. W. (1989). *The politics of education: Schools in conflict,* 2nd ed. Berkeley: McCutchan.

Wissler, D. F., & Ortiz, F. I. (1986). The decentralization process of school systems: A review of the literature. *Urban Education, 21,* 280-294.

Zeigler, L. H. & Jennings, M. K. (1974). *Governing American schools.* North Scituate, MA: Duxbury.

8

Effecting Change in
Urban Schools

WILLIAM J. KRITEK

Over the last 10 years the demands for change in the way schools are structured and in the quality of their product have become louder and louder. Presidents and governors, chief state school officers and school board members, business leaders and educational professionals have all decried the present state of the educational enterprise and have called for dramatic improvement in educational quality and equality. The list of problems facing the schools include everything from a failure to address the country's need for creative scientists and mathematicians to a failure to teach anything at all to children of poverty and color. The proposed solutions run the gamut from privatizing the system of public schools to a tighter governmental rein on who should be allowed to teach and what should be taught. Whereas all schools are included in the charges of incompetence and all have become targets of the various

AUTHOR'S NOTE: Dr. Naida Tushnet of the Southwest Regional Educational Laboratory, Dr. Kery Kafka of the Milwaukee Public Schools, and Dr. Belkis Santos, Mr. Jerome Brandl, and Dr. Albert Weiss, formerly of the Milwaukee Public Schools, provided helpful critiques of earlier drafts of this chapter.

waves of reform, urban schools have suffered the harshest criticism and are most often identified as needing substantial change.

The urban principals who participated in the UCEA-Danforth Select Conference feel the public pressure for change and school improvement in ways that few do. All too often, they and their colleagues across the country are the ones blamed for what is perceived as the sorry state of education. Yet these same urban principals have the clearest picture of the magnitude of the problem and the best understanding of the need for change. The Select Conference participants produced long lists of problems facing urban schools and equally long lists of potential solutions. And they explicitly accepted part of the responsibility for bringing about school improvement. In doing so, they were not much different from other principals who worked in less turbulent times or who are working today in less turbulent settings.

The change-agent role for urban principals at the end of the 20th century is, at once, more difficult, more urgent, and more crucial to their schools' survival and the survival of our young people and our society. The days of the "one best system" (Tyack, 1974) have disappeared since the time of the baby boom, the civil rights marches, and the Vietnam war. Whereas urban schools at one time had more resources, better-educated teachers, and a broader curriculum than nonurban schools, many urban schools are now characterized by discipline problems, low academic achievement, and disaffected teachers. Many urban schools are mired in a culture of poverty, and in some cases surrounded by violence and drug addiction. Thus, the demand for change in urban schools has grown more insistent.

Consider Evelyn Jones Rich, who became principal of Andrew Jackson High School in New York City in 1980. According to her account,

> Jackson in August, 1980, was indisputably the most difficult school in Queens. Its outside walls were covered by graffiti. Beer and whiskey bottles lay on its grounds and around the periphery. Some of the buildings across the street from the school were empty. The police no longer responded to calls for assistance. Inside the school, large numbers of students spent the day in the halls. The cafeteria was a haven for peddlers of drugs. Certain stairways were declared off-limits for staff and students. An atmosphere of fear permeated the building. At

the beginning of each new term, parents would bring pressure on the Superintendent's office to have their newly assigned youngsters transferred to some other Queens high school. . . . Newly assigned teachers and support staff often refused to appear.

At the first faculty conference, in September, 1980, I shared with the staff my stated goals for the year. They were to change the public image of the school, to improve school tone, to improve basic skills, to expand career and occupational education programs, and to establish minimal standards for the entire staff.

Now things are different at Jackson. Not only is there grass growing on the athletic field, but there is new hope and expectation evident among students, staff, and community about the school and its future. Inside, the building is clean. Most of the 3,050 minority students go to classes in an orderly fashion. Many carry books. Supervisors are overseeing an instructional process that is gaining credibility. The custodial and cafeteria staffs have a newfound feeling of achievement and commitment. Secretaries, para-professionals, teachers, supervisors, and the principal believe that the school is on its way to becoming a successful educational institution. And so does the community that earlier had written off the school, that had increasingly refused to send its children to the school. (1983, p. 40)

Andrew Jackson High School may be an extreme case of the problems facing urban education, but it serves to point out dramatically the need for change and school improvement. Unbelievably high dropout rates and unconscionably low achievement test scores, especially among poor children and children of color, are only the most visible indicators of serious educational problems. Behind the classroom door one too frequently finds low expectations for students, a minimalist approach to teaching, and a hodgepodge of ill-conceived policies, programs, and rules imposed by local school bureaucracies—all conspiring to limit the likelihood that poor children will maximize their learning potential (Goodlad, 1983; Keating & Oakes, 1988).

Some of the remedies prescribed for the ills of urban schools have become part of the problem. Not only must schools cope with students who bring the problems of society to school with them, they must also cope with efforts to help. Urban principals are caught in the crossfire of federal programs such as Chapter 1, PL 94-142, and enticements to establish magnet schools; court-ordered desegregation plans; state-mandated programs to provide for children-at-risk; local communities that think business partnerships are important; and the central office that has its own list of essential projects and programs that need to be mounted right now. All the while, principals are told to keep out gangs, weapons, and drugs, and in some cases, to "turn the school around"— that is, recapture it from chaos.

This chapter addresses the need of urban principals to be agents of productive school change. It will draw on three separate but interwoven strands of research and knowledge about change and school improvement. Each of these strands—the literature on school effectiveness, the various models of the change process, and the more recent focus on school culture—has already been linked with the other two. The treatment here will make its own connection by an explicit reference to the role of teachers in each of the strands. Although the chapter is addressed to urban principals, the focus on teachers seems appropriate for two reasons. First, underlying all the changes that urban principals are supposed to accomplish is the fundamental charge to improve the teaching available to all children and to increase the learning of those children; second, principals will be able to accomplish little without the active cooperation of the school's teachers.

At the end of almost 500 pages of detailed analysis of a set of 12 ethnographic studies of planned school improvement projects, Huberman and Miles (1982) comment:

> [A]dministrators and teachers, though they live in different worlds and have different agendas, can, under the right circumstance, complement each other's efforts productively. . . . If administrators and users can successfully work together to meet their differing agendas, using good quality, substantial innovations, there will be clear student impact. Schools can, it seems, improve, and we can now see more distinctly just how they do it. (pp. 477-478)

"Working together," of course, is easier said than done. It requires a willingness to adjust one's actions to take the other party's needs and concerns into consideration, but perhaps more important, it requires an understanding that there is more than one perspective on the reality of the school. This chapter seeks to contribute to that understanding.

The Literature on School Effectiveness

The "effective school movement" raised the hopes of parents, teachers, and principals who long for schools where poor children perform as well as middle-class children on measures of basic school achievement (Edmonds, 1979a). Based on instances of exceptional urban schools where poor children perform better than their socio-economic status would predict, the movement drew on Edmonds's belief that if one such school could be found, all schools could be made effective. Researchers and practitioners sought to identify the characteristics of effective schools and to replicate them in other sites.

The earliest lists of characteristics contained the now familiar entries of an orderly school climate, an emphasis on the basic skills, high expectations, a system to monitor student achievement, and strong instructional leadership on the part of the principal (Edmonds, 1979b; Brookover & Lezotte, 1979; Venezky & Winfield, 1979). Other characteristics appeared with varying degrees of frequency. For example, some writers included parental involvement and support while others, following the lead of Edmonds, pointedly omitted the need for parental involvement in order to focus responsibility for student achievement on the school.

As an antidote to the "schools don't make a difference" conclusion drawn from the Equality of Educational Opportunity research (Coleman et al., 1966), the early school effectiveness studies did much to reestablish the belief among school people that their efforts did make a difference in children's education. In particular, the effective school movement raised the consciousness of urban school principals about the importance of their role. To be sure, the principal's role has always been linked to leadership and change (Sarason, 1982; Lipham, 1981), and it is a rare individual who embarks on the job without optimistic beliefs that, at last, he or she is in a position to make an impact on a significant part of the educational landscape. However, with the effective schools movement, principal leadership took on a new urgency and new significance.

During the early 1980s, there were few studies that did not hang their conclusions on the word *effective*. Indeed, as Wimpelberg et al.,

(1989) note, effective schools research moved from its urban (elementary) school focus and an explicit concern for equity to a more implicit concern for efficiency by considering other school levels and other socioeconomic contexts. Consequently, the lists of characteristics of effective schools multiplied and the broad call for principal leadership spawned lists of its own. Many of these lists, even those intended for urban elementary schools, simply repackaged earlier lists of characteristics and added to the confusion about what items should be included in *the* definitive list. The lists were seductive in their simplicity and their optimism. Few gave any indication that the elements were open to an infinite variety of interpretations (for example, different people have dramatically different ideas about what constitutes basic skills); few pointed out that it was relatively easy to proclaim high expectations for children, but very difficult to embody those expectations in the curriculum and in instructional practices; few acknowledged that *making* a school effective is an entirely different issue than describing such a school's characteristics. Eventually, however, the focus shifted from identifying characteristics to the process of creating effective schools. As a result, greater attention was paid to the role of the teacher in efforts to improve schools.

For example, Persell (1982), in a review of a large number of studies, identified nine behaviors of effective principals, repeating the standard effective schools list but including encouraging staff growth and development and facilitating the participation of teachers. McCormack-Larkin and Kritek (1982) singled out efforts to change the belief structures of principals and teachers and a strong emphasis on inservice education as contributing to the initial success of Milwaukee's Project RISE. In their comprehensive review of the literature, Purkey and Smith (1983) explicitly highlighted a set of factors needed to create an effective school: collaborative planning, collegial relationships, schoolwide staff-development, and district support.

Even more specific suggestions became available. For example, principal Barbara Ferguson (1984) reported on strategies she used to turn around one of the three lowest-achieving New Orleans elementary schools. Her approach included the reassignment of some teachers, grade-level faculty meetings, and formation of a staff task force on school improvement.

Blase's (1987a) two-and-one-half-year case study in an urban biracial school that experienced a change in principals resulted in a set of factors that characterized effective school leadership *in the eyes of teachers*. Included were accessibility, consistency, follow-through, fairness/ equitability, and willingness to delegate authority. However, teachers characterized ineffective principals as arriving late and leaving early, "arrogant, condescending, aloof, authoritarian" (Blase, 1987b, p. 209).

The earliest school effectiveness studies were also largely silent about the concurrent research agenda on teacher effectiveness. Beginning in the mid-1970s, many studies linking teacher behavior to student achievement were completed (Rosenshine, 1983, and Brophy & Good, 1986, provide syntheses of these studies). Another set of studies described effective practices in classroom organization and management (Emmer & Evertson, 1981, and Doyle, 1986, provide syntheses). Although the effective-schools and effective-classrooms research strands have remained separate, eventually connections between school effectiveness and the work of the teacher were made.

Leithwood and Montgomery (1982) explicitly include classroom-related factors along with school-related factors in their model linking principal behavior to student learning. Bossert et al., (1982) indicate that principals "can play an important management role by making decisions about school-level factors that fundamentally shape classroom instructional organization" (p. 42). Cohen (1983) argues that effective teaching and a coordinated and well-managed instructional program are essential to school effectiveness. And Bossert (1988) notes that since instruction is the core technical activity of the school, "an effective school principal manages a school in the same way as any other production manager, by crystallizing production goals, managing interdependencies in the workflow, and 'buffering' production processes from external influences" (p. 347). Thus, an effective principal links management activity to instruction in the following six areas: "instructional time, class size and composition, instructional grouping, curriculum pacing and articulation, student evaluation, and classroom task characteristics" (p. 347).

During the decade of the 1980s, the school-effectiveness studies instilled a belief that all schools can successfully educate all children. Moreover, the literature made progress in identifying school characteristics that were empirically linked to effectiveness and started to provide principals and other school people with an understanding of how to bring about school improvement. However, if the increased dismay about the condition of education in the nation's cities is any indication, a decade of efforts in the tradition of Edmonds and others has not been particularly successful. According to Louis and Miles (1990), effective schools programs have had more of an impact on the "cosmetic and administrative side" of schools than on student achievement (p. 49). Certainly, societal conditions have created more severe problems for urban schools over the last few years. An unanticipated consequence of the effective schools movement may have been to create unrealistic expectations about what principals could accomplish—especially if the interpretation was that they had to do it by themselves.

Although there are some principals who beat the system (Borman & Spring, 1984; Watson, 1979) or who, like inner-city elementary school principal Marjorie Stallings, create their own system for getting things done (McPherson et al., 1981), there are definite constraints on what principals can accomplish. Principals cope with uncertain environments and, particularly in urban schools, operate in a straitjacket of central office regulations and union prohibitions. The principal's middle-manager role often results in a tendency to play it safe and to overlook the fairly extensive discretionary opportunities they have. Furthermore, the work of a principal is fragmented, episodic, and in most instances removed from the work of the classroom (Sproull, 1981). The principal is supposed to be the school's instructional leader, but, as McNally (1974) noted in summing up a year-long series on the principalship in the National Elementary Principal, the "way it is" is quite different from the "way it spozed to be."

Still, it is the middle manager who bears much of the responsibility for insuring that schools improve. This responsibility has never been clearer than in Chicago where school principals, unprotected by tenure and appointed or terminated at the pleasure of each school's governing council, must manage the creation of schools where all the children can learn (Walberg et al., 1988). But Chicago's principals, like principals in other urban schools, will need much more than a list of effective school characteristics and a bank of prescriptions for exerting leadership. They will need a thorough knowledge of strategies for addressing the needs of disadvantaged students (for example, those included in Natriello et al., 1990; Wehlage et al., 1989; and Slavin et al., 1989) and they must understand the processes and the variables that impact on change and instructional improvement efforts in the school. Fullan (1985) calls it a "leadership feel for the improvement process" (p. 400). Simple formulations and easily understood suggestions are wanted and needed but unfortunately cannot be copied from one school to another. There is no guarantee that what worked for one principal will work for another, or that what worked for a principal in one school will work for that same principal when he or she moves to another building. As Firestone and Corbett (1988) note, "There are no *universal rules for changing organizations*" (p. 333). What is required is that principals draw on an understanding of the context and the problem and constantly reinvent their own lists of approaches to fit the situations in which they find themselves. To begin to address that need, let us next consider the change process.

The Process of Change

Much like the cumulative nature of the research on effective schools and effective principals, knowledge of the change process in education has been accumulating over the years. The first part of this section will review several approaches to understanding the process of planned change. The latter part will focus more directly on the teacher in relation to the change process.

Perhaps the most fundamental conception of change comes from the work of Kurt Lewin who saw individual and organizational behavior as a balance between opposing forces. Change takes place through a process of "unfreezing" the balance between the restraining forces and the driving forces and then "refreezing" in a new dynamic balance. The Lewinian model identifies one of the first imperatives for change: recognition that something must be given up or unlearned before new behavior can be acquired (Schein, 1969). Fullan (1982) provides a succinct version of this conception of change by noting that the rewards of changing will at least have to be equal to the costs. That is, change will inevitably require principals and teachers to let go of established ways of doing things, to let go of established relationships, and maybe even to let go of long-established beliefs. None of this will happen without the expectation of a payoff in student learning, in a teacher's feeling of competence, in a lessening of the burden of classroom work, or in some other dimension. In urban schools, where teachers and other professionals already feel severely overburdened by large numbers of students with serious educational deficits, the perceived payoff will have to be significant.

The family of strategies that traces its roots to Lewin, along with various related approaches, has been termed "normative/re-educative" by Chin and Benne (1969) or "problem-solving" by Havelock (1971). The *problem-solving model* (to use Havelock's terminology) focuses on the individual or group or organization that will be the ultimate user of an innovation—whether that be a new process or a new structural arrangement or a new curriculum. The main thrust of this approach is to make change likely because of the close connection of a solution to a user's definition of the problem. Thus, Havelock identifies a derivative strategy in which teachers screen and evaluate new teaching practices and then share them with each other. T (training) groups are a manifestation of the problem-solving strategy as is organization development (OD), which places the focus on the system in which some change is desired rather than on the individual. The goal of OD is to develop more adequate system functioning so that ongoing coping with a changing environment can take place.

> Organization development attempts to facilitate that release of energy by helping school people learn productive ways of working on their problems, improving their organizational capabilities, achieving new ways of interacting despite frustration, and becoming confident in their own ability to understand themselves, assess their own circumstances, identify their goals, and perform the functions to which they have committed themselves. (Schmuck et al., 1977, p. 3)

Chin and Benne and Havelock have also provided syntheses of another tradition of planned change: the *research, development and diffusion* (RD&D) approach. This highly rational strategy assumes that significant educational change can be expected only if extensive research is conducted on some means of addressing an educational problem; the innovation is developed and packaged in a way that will make it appealing to the user; and the product is then disseminated through information networks, demonstrations, or administrative edict. The system of federally funded R&D centers based in universities and regional educational laboratories is derived explicitly from the RD&D model. Many curricular and instructional innovations have been developed by the labs and centers and disseminated to schools and school districts.

Essential to this model is the linkage connecting one system, such as a research and development organization, with the potential user system that is searching for ways to solve a problem. An example is the National Diffusion Network, a U. S. Department of Education program that links school people to new educational programs that have been demonstrated to be effective in some other site. State facilitators, located in state education agencies, help schools and teachers clarify their needs and identify programs and products that may be helpful.

One of the virtues of the RD&D model, the availability of quality educational products and processes, at the same time has been a source of problems for urban schools. For a variety of reasons, urban schools have been a prime setting for experiments with new curricula, instructional strategies, and organizational structures, and for studying the change process itself. A large number of specialists based in a central office provide RD&D organizations relatively easy access to many schools. The availability of a diverse student population is an additional attraction for researchers and developers. At the same time, the constant search for programs and strategies to address the needs of urban children, the lure of federal money for innovative programs, the need of central office specialists to appear innovative, and vulnerability to political pressures lead urban educators to jump on virtually every opportunity that comes along. In the process, only scant attention has been paid to the users in the schools and their definitions of the problems they face.

Our understanding of the change process itself went through a major rethinking with the publication during the mid-1970s of the reports of the Rand Corporation on federal programs supporting educational change. The Rand Study (Berman & McLaughlin, 1978) focused on the processes by which innovations became operating realities in schools and school districts. The authors identified three overlapping phases of innovation: mobilization, by which an innovation is introduced into a school district; implementation, involving the translation of a proposal into practice; and institutionalization or the incorporation of the innovation into a regular part of school or district functioning. According to Berman and McLaughlin, "top-down" mobilization typically leads to implementation problems and eventual discontinuation of the innovative practice. The path to institutionalized change leads from grass-roots support (as characterized by an enthusiastic, committed staff in a single school) or broad-based support (where all levels of a district back a project) through mutual adaptation during the implementation phase. The concept of "mutual adaptation," in which both the innovative project and the school or school district undergo change, is perhaps the most cited contribution of the Rand Study.

> Mutual adaptation could involve a variety of adjustments to the project itself—for example, reduction or modification of idealistic project goals, amendment or simplification of project treatment, downward revision of ambitious expectations for behavioral change in the staff or of overly optimistic effects of the project on students, and so on. Concomitant with these modifications in project design or objectives, new behaviors were required by project staff, as well as new attitudes necessary for integrating project strategies into classroom practices. (Berman & McLaughlin, 1978, p. 16)

The authors' list of elements that support mutual adaptation include "concrete, teacher-specific, and on-going training; classroom assistance from project or district staff; observation of the project in other classrooms or districts; regular project meetings; teacher participation in project decisions; local materials development; and principal participation in training." They go on to identify the quality of working relationships among teachers and the active support of the principal as essential for project implementation and continuation. "In general, the more supportive the principal was perceived to be, the higher was the percentage of project goals achieved, the greater the improvement in student performance, and the more extensive the continuation of project methods and materials" (p. 31).

One other component of the Rand study seems particularly descriptive of urban schools. The study of Title VII Bilingual Projects (Sumner & Zellman, 1977) focused attention on political influences that affected program implementation. The term political was used by the authors to describe "influences and constraints on decision making that may be independent of educational needs" (p. 7), including bureaucratic elements as well as constituency demands. Although not all the sites included in this study were urban, the reality they describe is clearly characteristic of big-city schools. The political influences the authors discovered in the initiation, design, and operation of bilingual projects are also present in other programs that are typically urban, namely, desegregation, dropout prevention, and magnet schools. One of Sumner and Zellman's findings was that due to political influences, bilingual education projects, unlike other innovations, often were continued despite low perceived success.

The value and significance of mutual adaptation were challenged and qualified by a comprehensive study, completed by The Network, Inc. in 1983, entitled *People, Policies and Practices: Examining the Chain of School Improvement* (Crandall & Loucks, 1983). This 10-volume study of state and federal efforts intended to improve schools and classrooms used information from over 4,000 questionnaires, almost 500 interviews, and year-long field studies in 12 sites. The model used to guide data collection and analysis indicates that contextual features, such as prior history of innovative practices and organizational norms, influence how an innovation is adopted and then transformed during implementation. Also, the nature and quality of the innovation itself influence adoption and any transformations that occur. Finally, the nature and quality of the innovation, the transformations it underwent, and the assistance provided to users of the innovation all affect eventual outcomes. The field study part of the research found that, as far as implementation is concerned, "neither 'fidelity' nor 'adaptation' necessarily makes for student impact. The question is whether a program is well-designed in the first place—and whether adaptations made strengthen or weaken that design" (Huberman & Miles, 1982, p. 223).

Even though the study's data and conclusions apply more directly to school-district-level administrators than to principals, two of the major findings of the entire Network study are significant in the context of this chapter:

1. Forceful leadership is the factor that contributes most directly and surely to major effective changes in classroom practice that become firmly incorporated into everyday routines.

2. New practices entailing a significant amount of change live or die by the amount of personal assistance they receive. (Crandall & Loucks, 1983, pp. 10-11)

Both of these conclusions are discussed further later in this section.

The flip side of the importance of assistance to the ultimate full implementation and incorporation of educational innovations is the importance of the user who is being assisted. Implied in The Network's second conclusion cited above is that productive school change is dependant on the teacher who is the user of the innovation. As Elmore (1983) comments: "If school district administrators are smart, they will. . . . design their implementation strategy around maximizing the individual teacher's control of the instructional process" (p. 357). This provocative statement calls into question some widely held assumptions about the best ways to bring about change in schools. For example, the highly managed RD&D approach to educational change contributed to the belief that the classroom teacher could essentially be bypassed on the route to school improvement. Outside change agents became the key people, so-called teacher-proof materials were designed, and "resisters" were labeled and stigmatized. Obviously, not everyone makes these assumptions, as evidenced in efforts to professionalize teaching and in the generally accepted belief that it helps to involve the user in planning change. However, the need for immediate improvement in some urban schools and the call for strong principal leadership have contributed to a tendency for principals to ignore teachers as they try to force schools into shape.

In the long run, of course, forcing change simply will not work. Teachers make the ultimate decisions about what is covered in the classroom and how it is covered. Teachers are the policy brokers and "street level bureaucrats" who decide how much time will be devoted to instruction, what topics will be taught, to whom they will be taught, when and how long each topic will be taught, and how well the topics are to be learned (Lortie, 1975; Weatherly & Lipsky, 1977; Charters, 1981; Schwille et al., 1983). In short, teachers make most of the important choices in instructional matters. Each teacher meets a proposed innovation with personal strengths and weaknesses, with a personal belief system, and with personal preferences about how to teach.

An intensive observational study by Carew and Lightfoot (1979) of four teachers in a city they call Conroy illustrates the uniqueness of teacher beliefs and predispositions. Two of the teachers taught at Inner School located in a neighborhood diverse in race, culture, and education. Ms. Allen, a first-grade teacher, describes her teaching as "'teacher directed, more structured at the beginning of the year, then gradually coming more open, free and flexible as the year progresses" (p. 113).

She had experimented with more truly "open" methods and with team teaching but "has returned to her own blend because she simply feels more comfortable with it personally and has confidence that it works for her" (p. 113). At the same time, Ms. Allen was skilled in responding to children's unique temperaments and abilities and had a strong desire to meet the needs of individual children: "I think that the worst thing you can try to do is to make the child a carbon copy of what you are. I don't want to take their personalities away in trying to have them meet the school situation"(p. 114).

The other Inner School teacher, Ms. Prima, also taught first grade. The authors note:

> Her choice of teaching strategies and curricular goals stresses those aspects of the educational process that emphasize her best qualities and make her feel most comfortable. She is aware that she is fast-moving, impatient, and nonreflective, that she thrives on organization and structure; thus, she creates a class-room environment that supports those aspects of her character. Ms. Prima purposely does not venture into the more complex and 'messy' world of open classrooms because she knows that would match neither her skills nor her temperament. Likewise, she focuses on intellectual content and ignores the psychosocial issues of classroom life because she devalues those dimensions of interaction and feels uneasy searching out the motivations and personalities of children. (p. 156)

Given such differences between two first-grade teachers, it is little wonder that a school's teachers will greet a proposed change with dramatically different reactions. Further, most innovations involving instruction increase the demands on teachers who need stable routines to insure an orderly classroom and to conserve a limited amount of energy (Weinshank et al., 1983; Doyle, 1979). What looks like resistance may well be a rational response to irrational demands or a firmly held belief in different educational ends and means. Cuban (1984) sums up an historical look at instructional innovation by observing that it may be more productive to try to improve marginally what teachers already are inclined to do rather than try to force something foreign into their teaching repertoire. According to Duke et al., (1981), teachers will weigh the potential costs of "time demands, loss of autonomy, risk of collegial disfavor, subversion of collective bargaining, and threats to career advancement" against "feeling of self-efficacy, a sense of ownership, and advancing the cause of workplace democracy" (p. 331). As Fullan (1982) notes, teachers will decide to become involved in a change effort if they see that it addresses an instructional need, if it is relatively clear in terms of what is required, and if personal costs are not too great. Teachers will also become involved in changes that address a school need that they perceive as relevant to their work, such as changes aimed at reducing disorderly student conduct that poses a threat to teacher safety or that interferes with classroom teaching.

Elmore (1987) claims that persisting in standard ways of teaching is a reaction to "reforms that make teachers into passive receivers of advice and knowledge from external rulemakers and experts; that use external prescriptions on content and performance to control what teachers teach; and that define the teacher's role as next-to-the-lowest subordinate in a vast hierarchy of rules, procedures, and sanctions."(p. 75). In essence, teachers cope with a threat to their own sense of personal power by refusing to be cast in the role of a nonprofessional subordinate. Elmore goes on to note that benign reforms look much the same as menacing ones from the vantage point of the one being imposed upon. And, according to Fullan (1982), involving *some* teachers in the change process does not automatically insure acceptance by other teachers. To those others, the innovation looks just as externally imposed as if it came from some distant administrator.

Principals themselves often compound the problem. Sarason (1982) points out, "Those who want change do exactly that for which they criticize others" (p. 232). That is, they *tell* them what is the "right" way to act and think. In situations where they are charged with turning a school around and leading it through crisis, principals frequently act in an authoritarian fashion and maintain tight control over all aspects of the school's functioning (Tewel, 1987). This version of "strong leadership" may enable them to bring order into a chaotic situation but it may also leave them isolated and unable to move the school along toward more intrinsic improvement that must then deal with classroom realities.

When change is forced by administrators, some fallout is inevitable. In some cases teachers will implement some aspects of an innovation, usually the more visible aspects, while silently withholding support for the more subtle and often more intrinsic aspects of the change. Staff morale is most vulnerable and that has implications for the enthusiasm with which teachers approach improving instruction.

Based on a study of three schools that were among the 202 recognized by the Ford Foundation in the City High School Recognition Program for having transformed violent, crime-ridden, racially torn schools into calm and peaceful places and having improved educational performance, Tewel (1987) has noted the following dilemma:

> In their rush to introduce change, however, these principals sometimes ran roughshod over faculty members who stood in their way, damaging their relationships with those teachers who would be needed to initiate, implement, and sustain instructional innovations and planting the seeds of future alienation and factionalism.
>
> With the passing of time, communication among teachers with different views deteriorated as faculty morale dropped. Fewer staff members supported efforts to develop innovative programs if it meant additional work or adjusting to new roles.
>
> The divisions within the staff frequently impeded further improvement efforts. The principals, committed to change and successful in improving climate, plowed ahead, leaving many staff members even further behind. (p. 107)

It is not only in matters that take place behind the classroom door that teachers are key. New programs dealing with school discipline, with structural arrangements such as site-based management, or with integrating desegregated schools are dependent on teacher willingness to embrace the innovation. The implementation of site-based management, for example, will result in role changes for both teachers and principals and the need for new skills of consensus decision making and cooperative planning.

The key role that teachers play in the process of change does not detract from the role of the principal. As noted above, The Network study concluded that "forceful leadership" or "administrative pressure," as it is called by Huberman and Miles (1982), is necessary if major, effective changes are to become incorporated into classroom practice. This emphasis on leadership and pressure is consistent with the findings of the effective schools studies (Edmonds, 1979; Leithwood & Montgomery, 1982; Venesky & Winfield, 1979) and is consistent with the "initiator" style of change facilitator that Hall and Hord (1987) link to implementation success at the classroom level. In their description,

"Initiators push; they have strong expectations for students, teachers and themselves, and they push to see that all are moving in goal-oriented directions" (p. 230).

Huberman and Crandall (1982) take pains to clearly delineate what they mean by "forceful leadership":

> It is important to stress that we are *not* advocating knee-jerk authoritarianism as the royal road to school improvement. . . . The *least* successful scenario in the field study was that of the administrator-as-thug: ramming a poorly designed project down the throats of recalcitrant, ill-prepared users and trying to keep it in place by raw, mindless power. (p.26)

Rather, forceful leadership that is productive takes the form of securing resources, becoming personally knowledgeable about the innovation, providing encouragement, supporting coalitions of enthusiastic teachers, expecting teachers to implement the innovation, monitoring implementation and student performance, and holding people to the task over the long term. Finally, the second conclusion of The Network study that was cited above must be added: administrative pressure must be accompanied by assistance.

The purpose of assistance is to help teachers master new instructional techniques and thus increase their commitment to the new practice and ultimately to have an impact on student outcomes. In essence, there is a reciprocal positive relationship: mastery leads to commitment; commitment leads to mastery. Assistance can facilitate both.

> [I]f initial commitment was low, it tended to be boosted by the presence of district-level and peer assistance, by the experience of mastery and the resulting change in practice, and by gradually-improving classroom or building fit. As the level of commitment rose, so did further practice mastery and, ultimately, stabilization of use. (Huberman & Miles, 1982, p. 455)

Mastering a new instructional technique is not an easy task. A teacher is not only faced with trying to learn something new, he or she must also continue to maintain order in the classroom and instruct children. Energy and enthusiasm are finite. Change will require an understanding of the rationale behind the new teaching method, observation of demonstrations of the method, and personal practice with feedback, supported by coaching (Joyce & Showers, 1982; Showers, 1983). It can sometimes take a couple of years for a teacher to feel that a new method of teaching is firmly embedded in his or her active repertoire of skills. Further, teachers' needs and concerns change as they become more involved with an innovation and get experience utilizing it in real classroom situations (Hall & Hord, 1987). Assistance in the form of inservice training, visits from outside experts or central office personnel, visits to other sites, peer coaching, the provision of relevant materials, and the occasional suggestion or word of advice is needed over the long term, not only in the start-up or early implementation phase of a new program. Principals need not deliver assistance personally, of course, but they must arrange for it to be available and must facilitate its use. For that matter, principals need not be the sole source of administrative pressure either; other district personnel can contribute leadership in conjunction with the principal. It is clear, however, that both pressure and assistance must be present if meaningful change is to happen.

One other component of forceful leadership and assistance seems important in urban schools. As noted above, urban schools are particularly vulnerable to what seems like a never-ending barrage of new programs. Fullan et al. (1990) sum up the result of this constant bombardment of new programs and processes: "In our view, the greatest problem faced by school districts is not resistance to innovation but the fragmentation, overload, and incoherence resulting from the uncritical acceptance of too many different innovations which are not coordinated" (p. 19). The principal's task is to protect the school and the teachers from this onslaught of innovations, maintain focus, and develop competence in a unified set of strategies.

Just as a school that embodies the effective school's characteristics will have a certain "feel" or "tone" or "atmosphere," so will a school in which forceful leadership (administrative pressure) and assistance are consistently prominent features. In essence, these characteristics and features constitute, or at least contribute to, the unique "culture" of the school.

The Culture of the School

The early school-effectiveness studies explicitly refer to the importance of a school's culture, although they sometimes use a comparable term such as "climate" or "atmosphere" or "ethos." Brookover et al. (1979) define *school climate* as the "normative social-psychological environment" that is rooted in the perceptions of students, teachers, and the principal about what is expected of themselves and of each other. In their model, school climate is directly related to student outcomes, including academic achievement and self-concept. Rutter et al. (1979) use the term "ethos" to mean the norms, values, and standards of behavior that characterize a school. Their data indicate that a school's ethos has an effect on student outcomes that is not explained by individual processes or features of school life. In their review of a number of school-effectiveness studies, Purkey and Smith (1983) conclude that "an academically effective school is distinguished by its culture: a structure, process, and climate of values and norms that channel staff and students in the direction of successful teaching and learning" (p.68).

Studies of excellent corporations that were completed at roughly the same time (Peters & Waterman, 1982; Deal & Kennedy, 1982) highlight the importance of a "culture" of excellence. According to Peters and Waterman, "Without exception, the dominance and coherence of culture proved to be essential qualities of the excellent companies.... In these companies, people way down the line know what they are supposed to do in most situations because the handful of guiding values is crystal clear" (pp. 75-76). They go on to identify eight basic characteristics of the culture of excellence, phrasing them as aphorisms such as "close to the customer," "autonomy and entrepreneurship," and "productivity through people."

Although effective schools and excellent corporations have been characterized as having strong positive cultures, every organization has a unique culture (and probably several subcultures unique to the subgroups within the organization) that embodies the core norms, values, and beliefs of the social system's members. Thus the characteristics that typify an effective school define its culture while the quality of life in other schools may be described by terms such as *divisiveness, apathy,* and *low expectations for staff and students*. Clearly, the culture of a school can either facilitate or hinder school improvement.

Rossman et al. (1988) have provided an in depth cultural perspective based on extensive case studies of three schools. They argue that some aspects of school culture, defined as "the set of shared expectations about what is and what ought to be" (p. 4), are "sacred" and almost impervious to change attempts; other aspects, the "profane," while they may be defended, are more easily altered to accommodate educational innovations.

For example, in the Westtown High School, accountability changes that required extra work for teachers were resisted because the extra work cut into planning time and other classroom-related activities. The sacred belief of "classroom as capitol" had been violated. In the words of one of the teachers, "'There was a time when the classroom was the capitol; the administration existed to serve the teacher performing in an excellent manner—everything was done with learning as the ultimate goal'" (Rossman et al., p. 76). At the same time, some innovations are compatible with the sacred aspects of the school culture and meet with little resistance. Consequently, Westtown teachers generally embraced a new instructional program because they saw it as contributing to their conception of their job and the role of the school. Perhaps some minor, "profane" aspects of the culture needed modification and improvement, but the core values were reinforced, not threatened.

The picture is complicated by the existence in most schools of subgroups that have different values and cling to different notions of what is sacred. At Somerville High School in a large urban school system, Rossman et al. identified three subgroups: the "Coterie," a small group intensely loyal to the principal that was a powerful influence on and maintainer of the school's dominant culture; a second group of teachers, the majority, who accepted the dominant culture of the school but were not as closely identified with the principal although they respected him; and a small third group of teachers who were marginally committed to the school and expressed some resentment to the influence of the Coterie.

The dominant values of Sommerville were an emphasis on order and good citizenship, a strong sense of autonomy, and pride in a unique personality that differentiated it from the other city high schools. The school staff had a strong concern for the individual students and stressed preparing them for the world of work. The staff saw the "standardized curriculum as robbing them of their authority to make classroom decisions and as usurping their responsibility to design an educational program for their students" (p. 116). The principal, Mr. P, worked diligently to maintain the school's autonomy by shielding the staff from the policies of a new superintendent who tried to impose a standardized curriculum and pacing schedule.

> In his role as cultural leader, Mr. P served as a buffer from this authoritarian initiative and as an interpreter of it. In words and gestures, he conveyed to teachers that they were "the pros," that he regarded them highly as professionals, and that the central office was very removed from the realities of everyday life in school. In the words of one teacher: "He lets us know that some is rhetoric—there's only so much you can do. He makes us feel that we know the kids best and that what we do on a daily basis is best for them." (p. 119)

From the perspective of the superintendent, Mr. P may well have been considered a resister who stood in the way of change. From the perspective of the staff, he was defending sacred elements of the school culture and not allowing an ill-conceived innovation to destroy the type of school they valued. At the same time, Mr. P worked within those values and tried to strengthen them. He worked especially to "make students feel known and cared for" by walking through the school's hallways and greeting teachers and students. As the authors note:

> Mr. P embarked upon a transformative effort designed to modify the school's culture. This modification was in fact an intensification of themes that already had a sacred quality to both faculty and the community. Through his own statements and manipulations of symbols such as during the graduation ceremony, he clarified existing values of the importance of order, citizenship, decency, and preparation for the world of work. (p. 129)

The example of Mr. P is indicative of a dilemma facing the principal. On the one hand, a school's culture is rooted in the entire organization, or in dominant subgroups, not in any single individual. It is questionable just how far and how fast any principal can get out in front of the professional staff. As Sarason (1982) noted, change efforts run into resistance when they fail to take into consideration the culture of the school and its existing "regularities." On the other hand, however, some schools, and their cultures, desperately need changing. Principal leadership is required to begin the long and painful process of changing the school's values.

It is unrealistic to suggest that this dilemma can be resolved easily—or, in some cases, even at all. But a principal must make the effort if there is to be any hope of an effective school. The principal's role may well begin with a "vision" or image of what the school should be like—a vision that informs all the principal's behaviors. Vaill (1982) refers to the process as "purposing—that continuous stream of actions by an organization's formal leadership that has the effect of inducing clarity, consensus, and commitment regarding the organization's basic purpose" (p. 29). Although an entire chapter in this volume focuses on vision/mission, it is important to briefly mention herein some aspects of vision related to effecting change in urban schools.

Manasse identifies four types of vision: organizational, future, personal, and strategic. *Organizational vision* enables the principal and staff to understand how all the separate elements of the system fit together and protects against inconsistency and counterproductive efforts. *Future vision* "is a comprehensive picture of how an organization will look at some point in the future, including how it will be positioned in its environment and how it will function internally " (Manasse, 1986, p. 157). Future vision can become embodied in symbols and metaphors that capture the spirit of what the organization is desired to become. *Personal vision* involves awareness of personal strengths and weaknesses and allows the principal to capitalize on his or her strengths and rely on other persons who may have the strengths needed to compensate for his or her weak areas. *Strategic vision* "involves connecting the reality of the present (organizational vision) to the possibilities of the future (future vision), in a unique way (personal vision) that is appropriate for the organization and its leader" (Manasse, 1986, p. 162). Strategic vision requires skill in managing the change process and using daily events to further long-term goals. One tactic sometimes used is to talk about the school as if it has already become the school of future vision. Other tactics have been suggested in the prior discussion of the change process.

A principal can use symbols, slogans, rituals, and ceremonies to reinforce a strong positive culture or to convey his or her vision of what the school could become. Symbols, ranging from the neatness of floors and grounds and the clothes worn by staff members to principal attendance at staff development sessions communicate expectations to both students and staff and convey an identity to parents and community. Rituals such as standing by the front door of the school to check for students taking books home and awards ceremonies for staff or students call attention to what is valued in the organization and reinforce those values. Deal and Kennedy (1982) suggest that principals "tell stories" about cultural heroes and heroines—teachers or students who embody the values of the school. Thus, stories could be told about the former student who is now a prominent judge, the student who got admitted to an honors program at a prestigious university, and the teacher whose students always win the academic Olympics in the school district.

An example of cultural leadership is provided by Dwyer (1986) in the person of Frances Hedges, principal of Orchard Park Elementary School in the city he calls Hillsdale. Dwyer's account comes from an extensive case study of this principal of a multiracial school whose children come mostly from low-income or lower-middle-income families. Hedges is described as personable with the staff and students, very well organized, and a strict disciplinarian. She had been at the school six and one-half years at the time of the study. Hedges is known by her staff and superiors for her outstanding instructional leadership.

There seem to be two components to Frances Hedges' vision for Orchard Park Elementary School.

1. Reading is by far our number one priority. I believe that [if] children don't know how to read they really cannot make it in this world. (p. 26)

2. My philosophy is that if we are warm and humane and nurturing we maximize the learning of children, and there is just no way to separate out those basic needs. (p. 64)

This vision is embodied and modeled in her relationships with staff and students. In the words of two of her teachers:

I think I do more because she spends a lot of time. . . . When we have circuit meetings and committee meetings and stuff, she's there giving her input, too. Right now she's helping write the [school plan]. She's giving her input, and it's like we're working side by side. And it's not the principal up here and all of us down there. We're kind of side by side .... I do more. (p. 46)

[Hedges] has a relationship with almost all of the children. .. they may be really on a blacklist in their classroom. If they just aren't living up to behavior, she will find a way to have a relationship with them. If it's your child that's constantly acting out [misbehaving], you almost want her to say "Doggone! Let's give up on that kid." But she really does not. (p. 41)

Hedges also utilized a "hands-on" approach to all curriculum matters. She hired the reading coordinator and thus had a direct effect on the grouping practices for reading in the school. She regularly observed and critiqued teachers' reading lessons. She listened to teachers in arranging for inservice workshops but also included areas she believed were important and was responsive to ongoing situations in the school. Again, in the words of teachers:

She talks to us in faculty meetings about her expectations as far as [writing], reading, [and] math.... She encourages us to share with each other what we're doing. I think she has a very good handle on curriculum development.

[Curriculum] is developed first of all within circuit meetings, and Mrs. Hedges attends about 98 percent of these. She's considered part of the circuit, and she [adds] her ideas and influences. She listens to our ideas first. That's where... what is good for the grade levels [is] reported to the staff and we discuss one another's ideas and then we develop the curriculum from that. (p. 45)

Everyone has in-put on staff development. It is really a program where the teachers decide what it is they would like to do, how they would like to spend the money, what they would like to see in improvement. [Hedges] takes a lot of input from parents and teachers. It's not a school that is run by the principal.

Dwyer sums up:

Much of the leadership that we attribute to Hedges' activities stemmed from the manner in which she organized programs, suggested materials and methods to teachers, and provided opportunities for teachers to develop new skills—all in accordance with her fundamental beliefs about the nature and importance of education. Much of the consensus of purpose that we found at Orchard Park, then, seems to have spread from Frances Hedges. Through observation and interview, we found that she was able to affect both the social and academic goals held by her staff. (p. 30)

Looked at from the perspective of the previous section, Frances Hedges provided administrative pressure and abundant assistance to her staff.

Cuban (1988) provides an example of a high school principal enacting the role of cultural leader—an example that may be particularly relevant to high school principals who find they are unable to maintain the daily contact with teachers and teaching that characterize elementary principals such as Frances Hedges. Bob Eicholtz became principal of Pioneer High School in the Whittier Unified School District in 1979, when it had 2,100 students, mostly Hispanic and low-income, and was considered the "basket-case" of the district. According to Cuban, within three years Eicholtz had turned the school around mainly by developing the conditions for improved instruction: moving staff who he believed stood in the way of improvement, recruiting staff who could develop a better program and delegating responsibility for organizing the instructional program.

Teachers, department heads, and his assistant principals developed ideas for his approval. . . . He approved the total reorganization of the math curriculum (including the transfer of a department head), adding another year beyond the district's graduation requirement, and introducing courses to match student performance and level of instruction. He approved the incorporation of writing into social studies and other subject areas. He approved a flexible scheduling plan designed by a subordinate. . . . He approved the intensive training of teachers for introducing computers, getting non-English teachers to teach writing in their classes, and helping students with limited reading skills. (p. 73)

Eicholtz was well aware of the symbolic power of strategic changes to build and convey what the school stood for. Seeking to demonstrate that the school held high expectations for its students, he established an honors program with advanced placement courses, introduced the Principal's List to honor students who excelled in academics and extracurricular activities, and rewarded with free yearbooks those students who had perfect attendance.

Cuban summarized the instructional leadership role of the principal in cultural terms.

> Through shaping the mission of the school, establishing a climate within the school that communicates a seriousness of purpose and a respect for the members of the school community, designing rituals and daily mechanisms that make tangible the mission and ethos, through communication skills, personal example, and numerous other informal means, the principal invents a personal curriculum of improvements for the school community and teachers. (pp. 69-70)

Cuban also identifies a political role for principals, again in cultural terms. Thus, principals are acting politically when they work to build support among adults in the school community (teachers, parents, central office administrators) for the emerging vision of what the school must become. Again citing the case of Bob Eicholtz, Cuban reports:

> When the school board approved a twelve-foot chain-link fence to be placed around the school, giving it a prison-like appearance, Eicholtz organized parents, staff, and students to install instead a wrought-iron fence covered by fast growing ivy to give the exterior more of a campus-like appearance—for the same price as the chain-link fence. (p. 80)

The essential value of emphasizing school culture in discussions of effecting change and school improvement is to focus attention on the importance of shaping the belief and value systems of the members of the school community. Still, it is an array of concrete actions that will communicate these beliefs and values, lead to their adoption, and strengthen them. The fundamental task of the principal is to orchestrate these actions in the service of the culture he or she wants to establish so that teachers provide appropriate learning opportunities for children.

Implications for Urban Principals

The preceding pages have portrayed the possibilities open to urban principals who seek to bring about school change. They should also have conveyed the reality that this is no simple task. If anything, bringing about instructional improvement is always more difficult than one expects at the start. In urban schools, the barriers are probably more numerous and more difficult to overcome than they are in other settings, but the task is not impossible.

I will conclude with four observations. First, the change process takes time. Modifying a school culture or bringing about changes in instructional methods will not happen in a year. Seeing effects in student achievement will obviously take much longer. Yet, the public and district officials ordinarily will want to see results tomorrow if not yesterday. Some changes have to happen immediately, especially if the safety of students and staff are at stake, and longer-term changes have to start somewhere, but principals need to resist the temptation to go for the quick fix. For example, we've all learned that one-shot inservice sessions do not result in new teaching methods. Unfortunately, neither does a semester's worth. It is probably more likely that several semesters of continuous instruction, support, and coaching are needed for teachers to integrate radically new teaching methods into their repertoire.

Second, a lot of little interventions must accompany the more dramatic efforts needed to bring about change in a school. Cultural change is unlikely to take place unless all the forces are lined up in the same direction, each reinforcing the others. Drop-in visits to class-rooms, short conversations in the hall with a teacher or student, decorations in the building, congratulatory notes to students who make the honor roll, and attendance at inservice sessions with teachers are examples of principal actions that must supplement the appointment of new staff members, securing the transfer of some problematic teachers, instituting a new curriculum, or installing hundreds of computers.

Third, it is unlikely that a principal can secure significant educa-tional change alone. As indicated earlier, the image of a strong leader may contain the seeds of failure if the word strong suggests "I don't need any help." Obviously, very little of substance will happen without the collaboration of a school's teachers. Encouraging teachers to become proficient in new instructional methods and then enabling them to help other teachers, relying on an assistant principal to plan a new program, capitalizing on support staff that may be available from the district office, all help build coalitions of like-minded collaborators, all help extend the vision and the culture throughout the school.

Finally, there is no possibility that a once-and-for-all plan will be sufficient to accomplish any major change. This is not to suggest that no planning is needed; on the contrary, a plan consistent with what is known about effective schools, the change process, and school culture is absolutely necessary. However, change takes place incrementally, in fits and starts. Mistakes will be made and will need to be corrected; new opportunities will crop up that must be capitalized on. There will be unintended roadblocks and unanticipated successes. The necessity and desirability of involving others in the change process adds to the complexity and unpredictability. Since it will be necessary to "muddle through," one ought to do it willingly and intelligently.

Conclusion

Clearly, there is a continuing need for additional research related to effecting change in urban schools. Specifically, studies are needed that describe how urban principals carry out an array of practical tasks that must be accomplished on the road to school improvement. For example, how do urban principals provide time for staff to be involved in program planning and for extensive inservice education? How do they buffer their schools from the proliferation of new programs that are being foisted on them? How can collaboration among diverse subgroups of teachers be facilitated? Where do urban principals get the support and assistance they need as they work to bring about change? Descriptions of ways urban principals solve these problems (and many others) are needed if the call for principal leadership is to be more than a slogan.

References

Berman, P., & McLaughlin, M. W. (1978). *Federal programs supporting educational change*, Vol. 8, *Implementing and sustaining innovations*. Santa Monica, CA: Rand.

Blase, J. J. (1987a). Dimensions of effective school leadership: The teacher's prospective. *American Educational Research Journal, 24,* 589-610.

Blase, J. J. (1987b). Dimensions of ineffective school leadership: The teacher's perspective. *Journal of Educational Administration, 25*, 193-213.

Borman, K. M., & Spring, J. H. (1984). *Schools in central cities: Structure and process.* New York: Longman.

Bossert, S. T. (1988). School effects. In J. Boyan (Ed.), *Handbook of research on educational administration* (pp. 341-352). New York: Longman.

Bossert, S. T., Dwyer, D. C., Rowan, B., & Lee, G. U. (1982). The instructional management role of the principal. *Educational Administration Quarterly, 18*(3), 34-64

Brookover, W., Beady, C., Flood, P., Schweitzer, J., & Wisenbaker, J. (1979). *School social systems and student achievement.* New York: Praeger.

Brookover, W. B., & Lezotte, L. W. (1979). Changes in school characteristics coincident with changes in *student achievement.* (Occasional Paper No. 17). East Lansing, MI: Michigan State University. Institute for Research on Teaching.

Brophy, J. E., & Good, T. L. (1986). Teacher behavior and student achievement. In M. C. Wittrock (Ed.), *Handbook of research on teaching* (pp. 328-375). New York: MacMillan.

Carew, J. V., & Lightfoot, S. L. (1979). *Beyond bias.* Cambridge, MA: Harvard University Press.

Charters, W. W. (1981). The control of microeducational policy in elementary schools. In S. B. Bacharach (Ed.), *Organizational and political dimensions for research on school district governance and administration* (pp. 277-312). New York: Praeger.

Chin, R., & Benne, K. D. (1969). General strategies for effecting changes in human systems. In W. G. Bennis, K. D. Benne, and R. Chin (Eds.), *The planning of change,* 2nd ed., (pp. 32-590). New York: Holt, Rinehart & Winston.

Cohen, M. (1983). Instructional, management and social conditions in effective schools. In A. Odden and L. D. Webb (Eds.), *School finance and school improvement: Linkages for the 1980s.* Cambridge, MA: Ballinger.

Coleman, J. S., Campbell, E. G., Hobson, C. J., McPartland, J., Mood, A. M., Weinfield, F. D., & York, R. L. (1966). *Equality of educational opportunity.* Washington, DC: U.S. Department of Health, Education, and Welfare, Office of Education.

Crandall, D. P., & Loucks, S. F. (1983). *People, politics, and practices: Examining the chain of school improvement*, Vol. 10, *A roadmap for school improvement*. Andover, MA: The Network

Cuban, L. (1984). *How teachers taught*. New York: Longman

Cuban, L. (1988). *The managerial imperative and the practice of leadership in schools*. Albany, NY: State University of New York Press.

Deal, T. E., & Kennedy, A. A. (1982). *Corporate cultures: The rites and rituals of corporate life*. Reading, MA: Addison-Wesley.

Doyle, W. (1979). Making managerial decisions in classrooms. In D. Duke (Ed.), *Classroom management: The seventy-eighth yearbook of the National Society for the Study of Education* (Part 2). Chicago, IL: University of Chicago Press.

Doyle, W. (1986). Classroom organization and management. In M. C. Wittrock (Ed.), *Handbook of research on teaching* (pp. 392-431). New York: MacMillan.

Duke, D. L., Showers, B. K., & Imber, M. (1981). Studying shared decision making in schools. In S. B. Bacharach (Ed.), *Organizational and political dimensions for research on school district governance and administration* (pp. 313-351). New York: Praeger.

Dwyer, D. C. (1986). Frances Hedges: A case study of instructional leadership. *Peabody Journal of Education, 63*(1), 19-86.

Edmonds, R. R.(1979a). Some schools work and more can. *Social Policy, 7*, 28-32.

Edmonds, R. R. (1979b). Effective schools for the urban poor. *Educational Leadership, 37*, 15-18, 20-24.

Elmore, R. F. (1983). Complexity and control: What legislators and administrators can do about implementing public policy. In L. S. Shulman and G. Sykes (Eds.), *Handbook of teaching and policy* (pp. 342-369). New York: Longman.

Elmore, R. F. (1987). Reform and the culture of authority in schools. *Educational Administration Quarterly, 23*, 60-78.

Emmer, E.T., & Evertson, C. M. (1981). Synthesis of research on classroom management. *Educational Leadership, 38*, 342-347.

Ferguson, B. (1984). Overcoming the failure of an inner-city school. *Phi Delta Kappan, 65*, 629-630.

Firestone, W. A., & Corbett, H. D. (1988). Planned organizational change. In N. J. Boyan (Ed.), *Handbook of research on educational administration* (pp. 321-340). New York: Longman.

Fullan, M. (1982). *The meaning of educational change.* New York: Teachers College Press.

Fullan, M. (1985) Change processes and strategies at the local level. *Elementary School Journal,* 85, 391-421.

Fullan, M.G., Bennett, B., & Rolheiser-Bennet, C. (1990). Linking classroom and school improvement. *Educational Leadership,* 47(8), 13-19.

Goodlad, J. (1983). *A place called school: Prospects for the future.* New York: McGraw Hill.

Hall, G. E., & Hord, S. M. (1987). *Change in schools.* Albany, NY: State University of New York Press.

Havelock, R. G. (1971). *Innovations in education: Strategies and tactics.* Ann Arbor, MI: Center for Research on Utilization of Scientific Knowledge, University of Michigan.

Huberman, A. M., & Crandall, D. P. (1982). *People, policies, and practices: Examining the chain of school improvement,* Vol. 9, *Implications for action.* Andover, MA: The Network.

Huberman, A. M., & Miles, M. B. (1982). *People, policies and practices: Examining the chain of school improvement,* Vol. 4, *Innovation up close: A field study in twelve school settings.* Andover, MA: The Network.

Joyce, B., & Showers, B. (1982). The coaching of teaching. *Educational Leadership,* 40(1), 4-9.

Keating, P., & Oakes, J. (1988). *Access to knowledge: Breaking down barriers to learning.* Denver, CO: Education Commission of the State.

Leithwood, K. A., & Montgomery, D. J. (1982). The role of the elementary school principal in program improvement. *Review of Educational Research,* 52, 309-339.

Lipham, J. (1981). *Effective principal, effective school.* Reston, VA: National Association of Secondary School Principals.

Lortie, D. C.. (1975). *Schoolteacher: A sociological analysis.* Chicago: University of Chicago Press.

Louis, K. S., & Miles, M. B. (1990). *Improving the urban high school.* New York: Teachers College Press.

Manasse, A. L. (1986). Vision and leadership: Paying attention to intention. *Peabody Journal of Education,* 63(1), 150-173.

McCormack-Larkin, M., & Kritek, W. (1982), Milwaukee's project RISE. *Educational Leadership,* 40(3), 16-21.

McNally, H. J. (1974) Summing up. *Principal,* 54(1) 6-15.

McPherson, R. B., Crowson, R. L., & Brieschke, P. A. (1981). Marjorie Stallings: A walk through a mine field. *Urban Education, 21*(1), 62-85.

Natriello, G., McDill, E. L., & Pallas, A.M. (1990). *Schooling disadvantaged children.* New York: Teachers College Press.

Persell, C. H., (1982). *Effective principals: What do we know from various educational literatures?* Paper presented at the National Conference on the Principalship. (ERIC Document Reproduction Service No. ED 224 177

Peters, T. J., & Waterman, R. H. (1982). *In search of excellence.* New York: Harper and Row.

Purkey, S. C., & Smith, M. S. (1983). Effective schools: A review. *Elementary School Journal, 83,* 427-453.

Rich, E. J. (1983). Making it happen: Turning a high school around. *Social Policy, 13,* 40-43.

Rosenshine, B. (1983). Teaching functions in instructional programs. *Elementary School Journal, 83,* 335-351.

Rossman, G. B., Corbett, H. D., & Firestone, W. A. (1988). *Change and effectiveness in schools,* Albany NY: State University of New York Press.

Rutter, M., Maughan, B., Mortimore, P., Ouston, J., & Smith, A. (1979). *Fifteen thousand hours.* Cambridge, MA: Harvard University Press.

Sarason, S. B. (1982). *The culture of the school and the problem of change*, 2nd ed. Boston, MA: Allyn and Bacon.

Schein, E. H. (1969). The mechanisms of change. In W. G. Bennis, K. D. Benne, and R. Chin (Eds.), *The planning of change,* 2nd ed., (pp. 32-59). New York: Holt, Rinehart & Winston.

Schmuck, R. A., Runkel, P. J., Arends, J. H., & Arends, R. I. (1977). *The second handbook of organizational development in schools.* Palo Alto, CA: Mayfield.

Schwille, J., Porter, A., Belli, G., Floden, R., Freeman, D., Knappen, L., Kuhs, T., & Schmidt, W. (1983). Teachers as policy brokers in the content of elementary school mathematics. In L. S. Shulman and G. Sykes (Eds.), *Handbook of teaching and policy* (pp. 370-391). New York: Longman.

Showers, B. (1983). *Coaching: A training component for facilitating transfer of training.* Paper presented at the annual meeting of the American Educational Research Association, Montreal.

Slavin, R. E., Karweit, N. L., & Madden, N. A. (Eds.). (1989). *Effective programs for students at risk.* Boston, MA: Allyn & Bacon.

Sproull, L. S. (1981). Managing education programs: A microbehavioral analysis. *Human Organization, 40,* 113-122.

Sumner, G., & Zellman, G. (1977). *Federal programs supporting educational change,* Vol. 6: *Implementing and sustaining Title VII bilingual programs.* Santa Monica, CA: RAND.

Tewel, K. J. (1987). Urban high school principals need a new kind of support system. *NASSP Bulletin, 71*(498), 101-112.

Tyack, D. B. (1974). *The one best system.* Cambridge, MA: Howard University Press.

Vaill, P. (1982). The purposing of high performing systems. *Organizational Dynamics., 11*(2), 23-39.

Venezky, R. L., & Winfield, L. F. (1979). *Schools that succeed beyond expectations in reading.* (Studies on Education Tech. Rep. No. 1). Newark, NJ: University of Delaware. (ERIC Document Reproduction Service No. ED 177 484)

Walberg, H. J., Bakalis, M. J., Bast, J. L., & Baer, S. (1988). *We can rescue our children.* Chicago: URF Education Foundation.

Watson, B. C. (1979). The principal against the system. In D. A. Erickson and T. L. Reeler (Eds.), *The principal in metropolitan schools.* Berkeley, CA: McCutchan.

Weatherly, R., & Lipsky, M. (1977). Street-level bureaucrats and institutional innovation: Implementing special-education reform. *Harvard Educational Review, 47*(2), 171-191.

Wehlage, G. G., Rutter, R. A., Smith, G., Lesko, N., & Fernandez, R. (1989). *Reducing the risk: Schools as communities of support.* Philadelphia, PA: Falmer Press.

Weinshank, A. B., Trumbull, E. S., & Daly, P. L. (1983). The role of the teacher in school change. In L. S. Shulman and G. Sykes (Eds.), *Handbook of teaching and policy* (pp. 300-314). New York: Longman.

Wimpelberg, R. K., Teddlie, C., & Stringfield, S. (1989). Sensitivity to context: The past and future of effective schools research. *Educational Administration Quarterly, 25*(1), 82-107.

9

Establishing the Mission, Vision, and Goals

ROBERT T. STOUT

"Lead, follow, or get the hell out of the way."
Popular bumper sticker

"What the hell, it runs."
Another popular bumper sticker

"Wherever you go, there you are"
Yet another bumper sticker

Because this chapter is about some things called "mission," vision," and "goals," the first step is to attempt to define terms, particularly since my purpose is to suggest how urban school principals might go about establishing them. Unfortunately, the task of definition is not a simple matter. The subject index of the largest compendium in our field, *Handbook of Research on Educational Administration* (Boyan, 1988), contains no entries for *mission, vision, goals,* or *purpose*(s), and the entry *role* has to do with roles that persons fill in organization structures, not the role of the institution in the larger society. Not, it seems to me, a particularly auspicious beginning for research-based advice to urban principals.

Nonetheless, the wisdom of the bumper sticker suggests that as principals you must do something, that you must get about the business of moving the school someplace, particularly if you presume to lead, since to lead presupposes to lead someplace. Or, in a popular phrase in a state I call home, your job is "to get the herd moving roughly west." That task is made tougher because in the landscape in which you operate, "roughly west" may not be easily discerned.

One way to define a word is to discuss some things that it does not mean. Because vision is, perhaps, the most mysterious of the three and because it is much in the popular literature about organizations, I choose to begin with it. In the context of this chapter, vision does not mean a number of things. When Alexander the Great was about to give up in his attack on the city of Tyre he had a dream in which the dominant character was a dancing satyr. His soothsayer, in interpreting the dream (vision), decided that the satyr represented, first, the word "Satyros," and that, second, Satyros could be deciphered to mean "sa Turos" which meant "thine is Tyre." Alexander attacked and captured the city. In this example, the vision "belonged" to Alexander, but the operating instructions were provided by the soothsayer. History is filled with the reliance of leaders on soothsayers who decided for the leader what manner of thing was auspicious and what timing was required to make it right. Modern soothsayers stand ready for any principal who wishes a quick fix for the problems confronting the school. In this chapter, vision will not mean that sort of make believe.

Another form of vision is represented in Puck's last speech in *A Midsummer Night's Dream*. At the end of one of Shakespeare's most fantastic plays, filled with mischief, myths, ethereal creatures, and outrageous happenings, Puck comes out to the audience to ask them to put the play in perspective. He says,

> If we shadows have offended,
> Think but this, and all is mended —
> That you have but slumb'red here
> While these visions did appear.
> And this weak and idle theme,
> No more yielding but a dream,
> Gentles, do not reprehend.

In more than a few urban schools in America, faculty and students alike slumber while a principal puts on a play titled, "We are going to make some changes around here." The gentles have no need to reprehend because they know that their dream will be over, that the principal will go someplace else with her or his weak and idle theme, and that they will continue to slumber undisturbed.

This chapter will not define vision in the way that the Reverend Dr. King was able, nor in the way that major religious leaders through history have done. The dreams of Dr. King and others are more grand and more patently radical than those we can reasonably expect from normal human beings operating in the constraints of public organizations. Notwithstanding much popular discussion of "charismatic leaders," successful urban schools are not often going to be led by charismatic leaders, since, by definition, *charisma* (literally, a spiritual gift or talent regarded as divinely granted to a person as a token of grace and favor) is in restricted supply among mortals.

Nor will this chapter define vision as cheaply as a slogan, although slogans are useful tools for saying something about a vision. Slogans may, from time to time, remind us of what we are about, but they are less likely to keep us focused on what we must do to achieve what we are about.

Finally, for our purposes, vision must not be defined in a highly complex or academic way. Although useful to researchers, the following definition is more complex than it need be to meet the needs of this chapter:

> (Vision is) the principal's ability to holistically view the present, to reinterpret the mission of the school to all its constituents, and to use imagination and perceptual skills to think, beyond accepted notions, of what is practical and what is of immediate application in present situations to speculative ideas and to preferably possible futures. (Bredeson, 1985, p. 44)

For the purposes of this chapter, then, let *vision* mean a statement of a future state that is better than we ever thought we could achieve. Earlier, Barnard had said that leadership

> is that capacity of leaders. . . . to bind the wills of men to the accomplishment of purposes beyond their immediate ends, beyond their times. (1938, p. 283)

Burns(1978) has reaffirmed the notion by arguing that transforming leadership is the act of lifting people into their better selves and that "the ultimate test of practical leadership is the realization of intended, real change that meets people's enduring needs "(p. 461). Vision is the signal to normal people, operating in normal organizations, that they can accomplish ends that are beyond those they thought they could accomplish.

The Mission of America's Schools: History and Perspectives

This has been problematic for the American high school, and for urban schools as well. The first part of the problem has been the difficulty of establishing "roughly west." More than a few people and groups have had fights over the meaning of that. The mission of the American public school system has evolved in fits and starts from something quite simple and consensual into something quite complex and disputatious. In what might be thought of as the first publicly supported schools in America, the citizens of the colony of Massachusetts knew that schools were for teaching all of the children to read well enough to be able to read the Bible, to read the laws propounded by religious leaders (so that if the laws were broken the miscreant could not claim ignorance of them), and to be able to make a living sufficient to stay off the public dole. For a few schools, the mission was to teach young men sufficient Latin, Greek, right behavior, and arithmetic to allow them to become ordained ministers and other powerful figures. Life was simple, with a few declared to be in power and the many prepared to accept the power of the powerful, all supported by God's Will.

Much the same pattern prevailed in the Mid-Atlantic colonies. In the Southern colonies, children of the elite were tutored, allowing them to continue in their roles as definers and protectors of the culture.

Although periodic attempts were made to expand opportunity, and opportunity was expanded, serious efforts were not possible until after the Civil War. Suddenly America had a declared unity, a bustling commercial and industrial sector, fast growing cities, an expanding Western frontier, and aspirations to become powerful. Out of the mix came a need to give serious thought to what the schools should do. By the late 1800s, leading educators had decided that the schools had to do a great deal. John Dewey, in a 1902 speech, said that education must provide "means for bringing people and their ideas and beliefs together, in such ways as will lessen friction and instability, and introduce deeper sympathy and wider understanding " (Spring, 1986, p. 159).

The people of whom Dewey spoke were an interesting collection of enormous diversity. They spoke different languages, they came from different places in the world, they believed in different gods, and most were poor and their children underprepared to live successfully in a modern, industrial world. The schools responded by providing nurses, shower facilities, health care, meals, playgrounds, clothing, day care, and lessons in personal hygiene, nutrition, English and, of course, the American Way. The schools had become a social agency of some magnitude.

By 1892, with perhaps as many as 10% of the 13-16 year olds beginning to attend something called a high school or secondary school, interest developed in trying to decide what such a school should offer in its course of study. Prompted in part by a concern that such schools should contribute to making America a democracy and in part by concerns among high school principals that increasing numbers of colleges required different forms of preparation for admission, the National Education Association formed the Committee of Ten on Secondary School Studies, chaired by the President of Harvard, Charles Eliot. This committee made two revolutionary proposals: that all students should take a comparable course of study in high school (the democratic argument) and that the course of study should be a college preparatory one in the liberal arts tradition.

By 1918, having fought World War I and anticipating an increase in the numbers of young persons in high schools, American educators declared that the curriculum of the Committee of Ten was inappropriate for a modern, world-class, democratic country. In 1918 the Commission of Reorganization of Secondary Education of the National Education Association broke dramatically with the assumptions and programs of the Committee of Ten. In its *Seven Cardinal Principles of Secondary Education*, the commission, in effect, put to rest the notion that the same curriculum could meet the needs of all students. The commission declared that modern high schools in a powerful, industrial, democratic country must provide students with a course of study that taught them good health habits, how to be worthy members of families, how to get and hold jobs, how to participate in civic life, how to make worthy use of leisure time, how to behave ethically, and how to take command of the fundamental processes of reading, writing, and computing. These cardinal principles, and their derivatives, have defined the American comprehensive high school since their publication.

But as evidenced by *James Madison High School* and other alternative courses of study (the list is long and well known to you), tension remains about what direction is "roughly west" for a modern high school and, by implication, the elementary school from which its students come. We have seen the "tracked curriculum" of the 1950s give way to the open, elective curriculum of the 1960s and 1970s, and the subsequent demand for higher standards beginning in the late 1970s and continuing today. The tension is real, has been in the system since the 19th century, represents conflict over important issues, is not resolved, and is unlikely to be in the near future. If, then, vision is something that refers to mission, one must look hard for sources of mission that are clear, steady, and attainable.

The search for mission is further complicated by an underlying, often unstated, mission given to the schools by the larger social order: to produce the right sort of citizen. What, it is possible to ask, is the right sort of citizen? The conventional answer is that the right sort of citizen takes his or her rightful place in the society. That tautology prompts the next question, What is her or his rightful place? In a very general way, two kinds of answers have been offered to this question in the past 200 or so years. The first answer is that people occupy, rightfully, the places they have earned by hard work and careful planning. The second answer is that people occupy the places they do because of accidents of birth; they are born to rich parents, or to Anglo parents, or to other forms of social advantage.

Proponents of both answers point to the American high school as one of the primary instruments by which this sorting and sifting into rightful places occurs. One argument is that the American public school system (particularly the high schools) performs the very necessary function of establishing an arena of competition. If the rules are fair, it is argued, able students of whatever social class or ethnicity will demonstrate their abilities and will be rewarded by assuming adult positions of influence and economic well-being. As one moves down on the "ability" scale, students will sort themselves into appropriate adult roles, thereby assuring that the society will have the most talented persons in the most responsible positions.

The proponents of the other perspective say, in effect, the first answer is simply wrong. They assert, first, that the rules are not fair; certain kinds of students get breaks, other kinds of students get penalties. Second, they argue that the process is a sham, designed to assure only that the sons and daughters of the wealthy and influential sustain their relative advantages into adulthood, and that the sons and daughters of the poor learn to take their lowly (rightful) places in a society that is rigged against them. In this argument, the American high school performs the very necessary role of maintaining a status-driven and unfair society. The high schools dupe the poor into believing that it is their own fault if they do not make it.

The correct answer, of course, escapes us because the evidence required to "prove" either case is so difficult to obtain. However, a quite consistent body of research has developed in which the principal finding seems to be that "American elementary and high schools seemingly transmit these biases [the links between social class and achievement], strengthening them in the process" (Bidwell & Friedkin, 1988, p. 467). And because people believe one or the other answer, public schools are subject to intense criticism for not equalizing opportunity on the one hand or for "coddling" underprepared students on the other. The great civil rights struggles in our history, the press for equality of opportunity, the debate over standards, the fights over school finance, and the strident demands that the schools do this or that in the name of meeting the needs of children are all centered on this unspoken debate. Thus, on the one hand, the primary mission of the school is to preserve status differences. On the other hand, the primary mission of the school is to make sure that every child has a fair chance to be a successful adult.

Up to this point, the problem of goal/mission/vision-setting in urban schools has been discussed as an imbedded problem of the larger social order: How democratic (fair) are we, and how democratic do we want to be? Whatever the answer, urban schools both influence and are influenced by it. Either urban schools perpetuate an unfair existing social order in which the sons and daughters of the wealthy receive advantages, or urban schools become places of great opportunity in which the sons and daughters of the poor find avenues of rapid upward social mobility. As will be argued, the principal of the urban school has something important to say about how the school chooses to define its position on this question.

Aside from the influence of powerful external forces, internal forces work to determine institutional mission as well. Scholarly writing on the influence of internal forces on organizational mission is rich in both prescriptive and descriptive terms. Two general views seem to encompass the writing on this issue. In the first view, the mission is seen as a statement of purpose of such importance that it determines, for all practical purposes, the shape and activity of the organization. It provides a clear criterion against which action strategies are measured: Is the decision to do X and to not do Y consistent with the mission? Resource allocation decisions are made in answer to the question "Will this allocation decision do the most to help us reach our goals/mission?" The purpose of the organization is that which helps determine whether the organization is successful; it is successful to the degree that it meets its purpose. Thus, in this view, the purpose/mission of the organization plays a dominant role in structuring the organization, allocating roles and activities, choosing action strategies, and serving as the measure of success. Also, in this view, one of the major functions of the executive is to formulate and define that purpose. Burns (1978) has captured this position nicely by stating:

> It was long assumed that the fundamental, if not the sole, meaning and justification of organization was purpose, mission, task, or goal. The organization was in essence a means to an end, and the end was a purpose anchored in, and measured by, values defined as preferred end-states that served as both calls to action and guides to behavior. (p 375)

In much of contemporary popular writing on organizations this view is translated to mean that the leader of the organization is responsible for bringing to the organization a vision presumed to be of sufficient power to engage the attention and energy of all the members of the organization. From this perspective, much attention is to be paid to developing the mission statement, to insuring that the key players have contributed sufficiently to it to prompt their "buy in," that patrons and clients know what it is, that members of the organization can repeat it faithfully, and that it gets printed on the organization's letterhead.

A contrary view is that, for all practical purposes, mission statements and articulated goals are meaningless, except as buffers between the organization and its external environment (Baldridge & Deal, 1975).

In this view, the articulation of mission serves to reassure the public that a school, say, is doing something worthwhile, that it is accomplishing something of sufficient worth to justify its continued existence and support. The declared mission is simply a cover for what is really at stake, the continued employment and general comfort of teachers and administrators. This position rests on the assumption that collections of individuals working in an organization will use the resources provided by it to meet their own self-interests, which only coincidentally overlap those of the avowed purpose. From this perspective, the idea of organizational or institutional mission is something of a myth; organizations do not have operational missions, but the people inside them have self-interests which they attempt to satisfy within the organization's boundaries.

The Urban Context

Although these internal and external forces working to shape the school's mission do not influence urban schools exclusively, they do meet in sharper contrast, perhaps, in cities. This is so because cities have become the major collectors of disparate values, social classes, and ethnicities. By whatever measures one wishes to use, schools in America's big cities are simply not as good as schools in the suburbs and smaller cities. If America has an education problem it is, largely, an urban education problem.

Two major shifts have conspired to change city schools from the lighthouse schools they were in the early part of this century to the battlegrounds they have become in the latter part. The first has been the flight of the middle and upper middle classes from the city to the suburbs, and their replacement in the cities by the poor and very poor. America's old and large cities are characterized by:

A predominance of sub-standard housing and old, blighted and abandoned business areas;
A rate of declining school enrollment greater than in the surrounding areas;
Flight of middle class families with children to the suburbs;
High vandalism and crime rates;
High minority youth unemployment;
High percentages of children in poverty;

High school dropout rates;
Concentrations of subsidized housing;
Concentrations of illiterate adults;
High costs of service provision;
Concentrations of homeless persons;
High percentages of youth and young adults who are career criminals. (Briggs, 1987, p. 4)

These conditions do not lend themselves to developing and sustaining good schools. That good schools exist at all in such environments says much about the ambition of children and the dedication of teachers.

A second shift that has affected all schools, but perhaps has had more effect on urban schools, has been the loss of academic credibility of the high school diploma for all students, but most of all for children of the poor. Sedlak and his colleagues (1986), citing the work of dozens of other researchers, have catalogued the decline in credibility of the diploma:

Knowledge is fragmented and incoherent; the concept of a "core" curriculum has receded or been abandoned.
Specialized, narrow, often trivial electives have proliferated.
Course content is often determined by teachers acting in relative isolation and driven by their aspirations to develop classes based largely on their personal predilections, hobbies, outside employment, disciplinary loyalties, and interest in attracting students in a competitive market, with courses designed to appeal to the adolescent's definition of "knowledge" and "relevance."
Students occasionally exert unwarranted and detrimental influence over the curricular content of their high school educations.
However hastily developed in response to special interest group pressure, new courses displace basic academic classes.
Instructional priorities are confused and differ radically by district.
Graduation requirements vary considerably by state and district.
(p. 37)

Thus, it is argued, a "good" high school education has to be carefully crafted by an academically ambitious student and supportive parents, because the opportunities to have a bad one are great. The problem is exacerbated in urban schools with their concentrations of poor children and their reliance on tracking by both subject and ability. As Goodlad (1984) has argued, tracking works an especially disproportionate ill on the poor and minorities because it closes them out of routes to upward social mobility, reinforcing prevailing economic, social, language, and educational inequalities. Imagine, if you will, the "typical" poverty child in America's cities. From the time he or she enters school, options to adult success are systematically stripped away, so that at graduation from high school (if it occurs, as it does not for perhaps as many as 50%) the young adult has few options left. In a recent study (Stout, 1989), even the "best" students from an inner city high school produced SAT scores of about 700 in total. Such students, though aspiring to attend college, were virtually unprepared for the task they faced.

Establishing a mission for an urban school, aside from "hanging on," is no simple task. Because this chapter is written for persons who are attempting to make positive changes in urban schools, however, the task of mission-setting deserves more systematic attention.

Schools as a Special Class of Organization

In order to think about missions of organizations it is first necessary to think about organizations. More particularly, we ask you to think about what an organization is; that is, What kind of place is the organization you know best? It has a number of characteristics that distinguish it from families, or crowds, or a group of people waiting for a bus. It has systems for gathering and distributing resources, for processing information, for sanctioning desirable behavior, for distinguishing between insiders and outsiders, and for getting work done. But in large and important ways, organizations differ from one another in the way such systems are designed and operate. Supermarkets are not like prisons, which in turn are not like engineering firms, which in turn are not like schools. These differences have effects on mission and, in turn, are affected by the mission of the organization. Much of the literature in organizational analysis is devoted to understanding how these structural differences occur and what effects they have (Blau, 1956; Drucker, 1974; Etzioni, 1961; Parsons, 1969). To get a sense of the power of these structural differences one need only think about how an urban principal can and cannot sanction (encourage) desirable behavior, and how her or his available techniques differ from those available to the regional sales manager of a consumer manufacturing firm. The principal can cajole, upbraid, lay on guilt, bluster, supervise closely enough to be on the edge of harassment, give little favors to this or that person, and the like. Teachers will respond or they will not, but the principal's techniques are constrained by the structural fact of a compensation system that is independent of any real measures of teacher performance. The regional sales manager looks at sales figures, makes them public to the sales staff in the region, and fires the lowest-producing salespeople. Whether good or bad, evil or kind, it makes no difference. The tools of the leader are simply different and the difference modifies what is possible.

Another example may serve to enrich the discussion. Urban schools look like urban schools. They do not look like suburban schools and they do not look like high-class department stores. As Corcoran and colleagues (1988) put it, "Teachers [in their study of teachers in urban schools] appeared to accept as normal, and therefore adequate, conditions that were at best bleak and dreary" (p. 12). Most urban schools are ugly, fenced, old, and intimidating to outsiders. They do not invite entry nor praise for their beauty.

Within a class of organizations, (schools as a class or hospitals as a class, for example), organizations also differ in the kinds of places they are. Although metaphors differ by author (Morgan 1986), four can serve to show important differences among types in the same class. For example, some schools are like machines or factories. These "tight ships" are recognizable by their proliferation of rules and procedures, by the obvious power of the principal, by the outward obedience of the members of the organization, by their efficiency in distributing resources, and by their clear answer to the question "Who's in charge here?" On closer examination, these schools may also be recognizable by the undercurrent of resistance among teachers, by their lack of joy, by their lack of extra effort, and by their smoldering resentment. While they may be safe and orderly, they may not be pleasant.

Other schools are more like loose confederations of competing political parties. Teacher cliques compete against one another for whatever spoils the school has to offer (typically good kids and good classes, along with space and materials), powerful teachers work to constrain the principal's discretion, spies and counterspies collect and distribute information, and periodic contests are held to determine "who runs things around here."

Still other schools look and feel like tribes or families or, in more modern terms, cultures. Teachers, parents, and students have deeply held shared values, many of which operate at a subconscious level for the members of the group. Most of the rules are unwritten (they do not have to be written because most of the members "know" them), and obedience to the code is a powerful constraint on individual action. Internal conflict is not tolerated, and norm breakers must be isolated or exiled. Members believe that their actions contribute to the survival of the tribe or to the greater glory of the culture. Persons with authority behave as benign despots and as wise persons, tempering conflict, distributing praise, and guiding the organization toward some end. Insiders feel very good; outsiders feel miserable and isolated. Such schools are more likely to be elementary schools and private high schools than they are to be public high schools.

Finally, some schools may look like the following:

Imagine that you are either coach, referee, player or spectator at an unconventional soccer match: The field for the game is round; there are several goals scattered haphazardly around the circular field; people can enter and leave the game whenever they want to; they can say "That's my goal" whenever they want to, and as many times as they want to and for as many goals as they want to; the entire game takes place on a sloped field, and the game is played as if it makes sense. (Weick, 1985, p. 106)

In a school like this, teachers do their thing, as do students. Principals also do their thing. Coincidentally, perhaps, what students, teachers, and principal do ends up looking as though it makes sense.

The missions of these types of schools may be very different. In the factory model, the mission is efficient movement of children from one grade to the next. Teachers get through the book and the principal oversees the production system. In the political confederation, the mission is to gain and retain control of the system. In the family/tribe/ culture, the mission is to protect the family from hostile external forces pushing the family/tribe to adopt new ways of doing things. In the soccer match, the notion of organizational mission becomes virtually incomprehensible. The major mission is to insure that the game goes on, if, indeed, even that can be called a mission.

To this point in the discussion, the goals of an urban school have been shown to be influenced by powerful external forces: America's ambivalence over questions of social justice and equal opportunity and the role of schooling in promoting them; the generally deplorable state of America's cities; and, the decline in academic credibility of the high school diploma with its disproportionate reduction in opportunities for children of poverty. In addition, it has been argued that the mission of urban schools is influenced as powerfully by intraorganization forces: that schools are a special class of organization and that, within the class, schools are different from one another on a dimension of what is often called "climate" or "feel."

All of these forces interact in a way not yet explained by research, to provide an environment in which some sort of mission gets into place. Sometimes the mission is real, in that the stated mission is the real one. Sometimes the real mission is never stated, is in direct conflict with the stated one, and can only be discovered by careful analysis of what people do and how the resources of the organization are used (Hoy & Miskel, 1982). Sometimes, perhaps, there is no mission other than to keep doing what has been done without attracting attention from the external environment.

Mission Statements

Our discussion of the complexity of establishing a mission would not be complete without some discussion of the vagaries of mission statement language. Some language makes sense and some does not. As an example of the former, the public mission of a high school in a very wealthy suburb of one of America's great cities is "To insure that every graduate has a successful freshman year in college." That is very clear and very powerful language. It sets up expectations for all the players and it provides criteria by which choices can be made among options. Further, it "fits" with public notions about what kind of place that high school is and ought to be.

A little farther down the scale of clarity is the following:

The primary mission of the District is to provide a quality education which affords each student the opportunity to develop to his or her maximum potential regardless of personal handicap, ethnic or socio-economic origin. Quality instruction and effective management will be accomplished using the team approach so that exemplary service to the total community continues to be a hallmark of this school district.

It should come as no surprise to the reader that this is the mission statement of an urban school system, nor that this mission statement took dozens of people about two years to develop and adopt. It should be clear to the reader that such a mission statement is not one that the larger public will understand, nor one that will provide principals with a clear sense of what they ought to do and how they ought to allocate resources.

Underlying the first mission statement is community homogeneity, upper-class aspirations, and the resources necessary to accomplish it. It may be disastrous for some kids, but it says what the school is all about. Underlying the second mission statement is community heterogeneity, the constraints of urban places, and the lack of resources necessary to do much in the way of the pursuit of excellence. It says, in effect, "We pledge ourselves to do the best we can with the resources we have."

The language is acceptable enough to educators but, in general, unacceptable to major constituents, particularly legislators. Legislators want school visions to have punch and meaning and to promise extraordinary things, all of which will be held up for periodic accounting. Thus, it is not surprising, at times, that educators relish the kinds of mission statements that make direct accountability difficult, knowing as they do the immense difficulty of delivering on too-bold promises.

There is another way in which language interacts with ideas in a mission statement. Thompson (1989) has argued that the key elements of a mission statement are that it be understood, that it be articulated, that it be possible, and that it speak to a more desirable future state. Each of these components contribute to the political and operational power of a mission statement. Lacking any of the elements, a mission statement loses it capacity to stir people to necessary cooperation and high energy.

Vaill (1986), in a discussion of high-performing systems (HPSs), says of mission that "the thesis of this essay is that the definition and clarification of purposes is both a fundamental step in effective strategic management and is a prominent feature of every high-performing system I have ever investigated" (p. 85). Further he states, "HPSs are clear on their broad purposes and on nearer-term objectives for fulfilling these purposes. They know why they exist and what they are trying to do. Members have pictures in their heads which are strikingly congruent" (p. 86).

So far we have established both a set of internal and external forces that make problematic the establishment of meaningful purpose statements and directions in schools, particularly urban schools. In addition, we have given some attention to the language of mission statements and its importance. Now we shall step back and take a somewhat broader view of the mission of an organization and its relationship to organizational performance.

Mission and Organizational Performance

On the face of it, an organization attempts to achieve some socially respectable purpose. Indeed, the classic definitions of what an organization is include some reference to its "goal attainment" characteristics. It is hard to imagine an organization without purpose. Further, it can be observed that even in the absence of a declared purpose, organizations take on purpose(s) that correspond to the definitions that their members impose. Parsons (1956) has made perhaps the most direct statement about the purpose of an organization by stating, "As a formal analytical point of reference, primacy of orientation to the attainment of a specific goal is used as the *defining* [emphasis added] characteristic of an organization that distinguishes it from other types of social systems" (p. 33). Having said this is not to say that the goals of organizations are static nor that they are easily derived and sustained. A basic fact of life in organizations is that goals are often messy, they are hammered out through interactions within the organization and between the organization and its environment, and they are sometimes subject to almost imperceptible, but dramatic, change over time. In effect, they bear watching.

The goals of an organization must be publicly acceptable, else the larger social order will withdraw support from it. That is, a successful organization must adopt a set of goals that the larger society can be persuaded to applaud, or at the least support. Thompson and McEwen (1969) have argued that the interaction among an organization seeking support for its efforts and the larger society attempting to decide whether or not to lend support can be described as one of four types.

The first, *competition*, implies rivalry. In this process, organizations of like class put wares in front of the larger social order, which, in turn, declares preferences. Although schools are thought of as near-monopolies, competitive strategies play some part in determining school goals. Public schools compete with one another for teacher talent and with other government agencies for public funds. Public schools compete with private schools for students. Urban schools compete with suburban schools for teachers, students, and middle-class families. Current legislative demands for "choice" are attempts to increase the efficacy of this strategy, viewed by many as consistent with the "American way of life." The demands for parent choice are expected by proponents to force schools to compete with one another on a more explicit basis, providing prospective clients with more information through which to decide their preferences.

The other three interactions through which organization goals are established are forms of cooperation. The first, *bargaining*, is a process in which the provider (schools) and the customer (the public) dicker over an acceptable price for acceptable goods. Endemic in bargaining strategies are such assumptions as the need of each party for the other, the relative strengths of each party, the ability of each party to hide from the other its ultimate price, and the willingness of each party to compromise its most favored position for an agreement. School goals, perhaps, are more a function of this strategy than of any other. Schools and the public are in a constant state of bargaining, in which the schools argue for more resources without promising major increases in school output, while the public argues for additional output without a major increase in resources. Schools have polished this strategy to a fairly high level and the most effective school leaders seem to be those who can generate the greatest levels of public support without promising extraordinary levels of outcome.

The second cooperative strategy is *co-optation*, in which hostile outsiders are absorbed into the internal workings of the organization, making them less of a threat to make unreasonable demands. School superintendents discuss at length their strategies for "educating" school board members (Stout, 1981; Tallerico, 1988). What they are discussing are the processes by which they attempt to blunt the agendas of school board members and to turn the agendas into organization support. Schools also are very good at co-opting parents. This is an effective strategy for stabilizing relationships between the organization and its environment, as long as the persons who are targets of co-optation are willing to be drawn in. The cost of such strategies, however, is that that organization may be forced to modify itself in part in exchange for support from the co-optation target(s).

The final interaction between an organization and its environment that has an influence on organization goals is the process of *coalition formation*. Although a coalition may be unstable, it nonetheless increases the resources the organization has for dealing with its environment. School leaders have been remarkably successful in coalition formation, particularly with selected clients. Coalitions with Chapter 1 parents, parents of gifted children, parents of handicapped children, Chambers of Commerce, the PTA, and the like are all examples of historically successful coalitions.

Thus, goals may grow out of various forms of interaction between an organization and its environment. Leadership of an organization is obligated to test those interactions and to choose strategies that increase the probability of gaining support. Four strategies have been identified that are available to school leaders for this purpose.

Goals and Goal Displacement

Establishing goals, although a process of constant interaction with an environment, is no less complex than seeing that they stay more or less true to their original intent. Without leadership attention, goals are subject to modification through normal workings of the organization. As Sills (1969) has put it:

> The generic problem of goal preservation may be stated as follows: In order to accomplish their goals, organizations establish a set of procedures or means. In the course of following these procedures, however, the subordinates or members to whom authority and functions have been delegated often come to regard them as ends in themselves, rather than as means toward the achievement of organization goals. As a result of this process, the actual activities of the organization become centered around the proper functioning of organization procedures, rather than upon the achievement of the initial goals. (p. 227)

Five sources of "goal displacement" have been identified and discussed by Sills (1970). None should be surprising to the principal of an urban school, even though she or he may overlook them on occasion. Sills states first that the ultimate source of goal displacement is the process of delegation, in which persons throughout the organization have opportunity to adjust and modify the goals to meet their own needs. Persons with higher status in the organization are likely to have more opportunities to modify the goals than persons with lower status, independent of the formal authority positions which each occupies. Thus, the power of the members of the English Department in a high school may determine, in effect, the goals of the school, notwithstanding the purpose declared by the principal.

The second source of goal displacement rests in the interpretation of organizational rules. Myers (1990), for example, has shown that principals have predispositions to interpret school discipline rules in what she calls "developmental" or "custodial" ways. The same rule, students will not cut classes, for example, can be used by the principal and staff to punish wrongdoers, thereby consigning them to the status of outlaws, or to help students understand something about the relationship between personal effort and ultimate success. Although most schools have as an important stated goal the development of self-reliance and independent thought, how rules are interpreted may bear significantly on the realization of such goals. A school is filled with people in a position to interpret rules and to apply their own interpretations, thus making goals as they go.

The third source of goal displacement occurs when the implementation of routine organization procedures takes on its own momentum, independent of any evidence of its contribution to the original goal. More than a few challenges to organization routine are met with the response, "Because that's the way we do it around here." Although no routine is established as a deliberate impediment to goal attainment, many achieve such a status. Thus, the corner-cutter and the rogue principal are born out of perceived necessity. As one teacher put it, "Custodians are restricted by union work rules and regulations. For example, school custodians can't screw a bolt in the door unless they call central administration. It's a lengthy and bureaucratic process. As a result, we never get anything repaired" (Corcoran et al., 1988, p. 16).

A fourth source lies in the relationships among persons in the organization. Every formal organization has within it groups of individuals which are bound to one another by shared needs and values, not all of which are congruent with those espoused by the organization. Smokers and nonsmokers contend for space. Academic and vocational subject teachers contend for students and the daily schedule. The old-guard contends with the whippersnappers for hegemony. The union activists contend with those who view teaching as a profession. And so it goes, out of which interactions may come goals that bear no clear relationship to the stated ones.

Finally, the relationship between organization members and outside publics influences what transpires inside the organization. Few schools are without the powerful teacher who has outside contacts. Few principals do not have a reputation of some sort for their relationship with parents or the central office. Each of these interactions and relationships has the potential for altering goals, as the insider brings into the organization the influence of the outsiders with whom she or he has an understanding.

Implications for Practice

All of this suggests, at least, that goals are not to be taken for granted. However, it does not suggest that leadership of an organization is in a position to keep track of all of this. Further, as March (1986) states, one of the prevailing but probably inaccurate assumptions about modern organization life is that "intelligent administrative action presupposes clear goals, precise plans, and unambiguous criteria for evaluation" (p. 19). It would be silly to assert that leaders have little or no influence over goals. It would be *as* silly to assert that leaders have the major influence over them. Somewhere in the mix of human interactions that make up a school, in the demands and constraints of the larger social order, and in the preferences of leadership for some outcomes over others, school people decide to do things that they understand are connected in some fashion to outcomes of some sort. All of this appears quite chaotic, and it may be. However, there are some generalizations about leadership, organizations, and organization goals that may be worth discussing as the bases for action:

- The principal is responsible for doing things that make it appear as though the school has purpose.

- The apparent purpose of schools cannot be too far from some general public agreements about what schools are.
- Although many actors can influence, some actors can influence more than others.
- Some general understanding of what the school is about probably serves as a general guide to action and a kind of motivation for people to act according to it .
- Goal ambiguity may not be a bad thing in all cases.
- Goal clarity may not be a good thing in all cases, and may be a bad thing in some cases.

Goal clarity may not be possible anyway, beyond some general level of abstraction. Our first generalization may be either more seductive or sensible than it first appears. It is seductive in so far as principals believe the current writing about the "principal as instructional leader" without understanding some of the difficulties and requirements that lie behind that sort of role. Research (Martin & Willower, 1981) suggests that, in reality, principals do not do much of the "instructional leadership" role. But if principals believe they must, and if they act as if they must, and if they do not know how to do what they think they must, disaster may not be far behind. The generalization is also pretty sensible. The public wants to believe that they are spending money on something that makes sense. They want to believe that someone is in charge. They want to be able to call for leadership in the expectation that someone will stand up and claim the role. Thus, current writers and the public seem to be demanding that the principal "not just stand there, but do something." And, we suspect, the something ought to look as though it is justified in an organization mission.

More than a few superintendents and principals have foundered on the shoals of organization missions that were sufficiently different from what their public believed was desirable. We do not have to look far for examples: year round schooling, school desegregation, and open campuses were all seen as important correlates to a mission of liberating young minds in an environment of equal opportunity. But in each example, the public balked and administrative heads rolled. We have already seen the extent to which the public is ambivalent about what it really wants from schools. While complicating the lives of principals, the ambivalence need not immobilize. However, the wise principal is advised to sniff the wind a bit to see how the mission can be stated in ways that do not outstrip public expectations.

The third generalization, that some are more equal than others, is a fact of administrative life. Some members in the organization simply have more to say about it than others. A set of goals, by definition, directs the organization to accomplish some things and not others and excludes the goals that have not been adopted. Some of those goals are dear to someone. Politics, by definition, is the "authoritative allocation of values" (Easton, 1965) and goals are political statements. In a world of limited resources, some people get favored and some do not. In the main, those with more power are more likely to have their values attended to than are those with less power. It makes sense, then, for a principal to give some attention to those who are used to having attention given them.

Probably it is axiomatic in the literature that in order to give people a sense of contribution to the organization they need to have a sense of how what they do fits in with what is going on in the organization. To do that, there needs to be some public statements of what the organization is doing. This corresponds to the "roughly west" metaphor already mentioned. People may not always agree with the general direction, and they may not always devote their energies to going in it, but at least they have a reference point. Subsequent deviation becomes a matter of choice, not of ignorance. In the same way, resource allocation may not always be connected to goal attainment, but resource allocation in the absence of general direction is subject to the rawest forms of political infighting or to administrative caprice and whimsy. Neither condition appears desirable on the face.

The popular literature (Bennis & Nanus, 1985) and some of the more serious discussions (Clark & Astuto, 1988) suggest that leaders in successful organizations ought to "leap before they look" on occasion. They are not suggesting, of course, that organizational leadership is some sort of drunken ballet. They are suggesting that unforeseen opportunities arise, that successful leaders are alert to forces in the environments of the organization, that too much analysis can paralyze, and that timing, sometimes, makes all the difference. Consequently, leaders need some degrees of freedom to play hunches and to act opportunistically. The rationalistic perspective, as we have seen, views goals as concrete guides to action. Goals are to be used to determine alternatives at choice points. But opportunities for growth and improvement may not present themselves in terms of stated goals, if the goals are stated in unambiguous terms. That suggests, then, that some degree of goal ambiguity is desirable, in so far as the ambiguity provides leadership with an opportunity to make bold moves that might otherwise be questioned as outside the declared mission. These moves may become mission-changing after the fact, but that is part of the reason that leadership exists. March (1986) argues that

> many administrators recognize the political nature of rational argument more clearly than the theory of choice does. They are unwilling to gamble that God made clever people uniquely virtuous. They protect themselves from cleverness by asking others to construct reasons for actions they wish to take. (p. 26)

In much the same way, goal clarity may not be a good thing in all cases and may be a bad thing in some cases. March (1986) makes the case quite succinctly when he argues:

> For example, there are good reasons for moderating an enthusiasm for precise performance measures in organizations. The introduction of precision into the evaluation of performance involves a trade-off between the gains in outcomes attributable to closer articulation between action and measured objectives and the losses attributable to misrepresentation of goals, reduced motivation for development of goals and concentration of effort on irrelevant ways of beating the index. (p. 25)

The wisdom of March's remarks need be examined only against the games principals and teachers play with norm-referenced, standardized, national achievement testing as a measure of school success. As March concludes, "there is likely to be a difference between the *maximum* [emphasis in original] clarity of goals and the *optimum* [emphasis in original] clarity" (p.25). Finally, let me suggest that goal clarity may not be possible anyway, beyond some general level of abstraction. Organizational life is a multivariate world, with multiple causes and multiple effects. Each of you has seen good work trivialized by an insufferable insistence that the effort be articulated in excruciating detail. What seemed noble at the start, becomes silly in the stating. It is hardly the stuff as dreams are made on. Specificity and detail interfere with commitment, at least if the object of the commitment is something more than putting eggs in cartons. The language of mission, at least as expressed in English, ought to be elegant enough to gain attention of powerful actors; however, that level of abstraction may not be precise enough to provide direct correspondence with objectives, subobjectives, and the like.

Intervention Strategies

The readers of this volume are going to have to do things. Each one will be responsible for making sense out of the buzz and confusion of activity associated with urban schools. Urban schools are busy and hectic, and not places in which calm reflection is the order of the day. Nevertheless, the principal continues to be responsible. "In short, decision makers in an organization are floating in the stream, jostled capriciously by problems popping up, and finding anchors through action at a given time in a given place" (McCall & Kaplan, 1985, p. 6).

What is suggested in this chapter is that one of the anchors might well be a reasonably stated mission. The mission ought to provide some guidance for future direction and sufficiently motivate members to do a bit more than they would have done otherwise in order to achieve a higher level of performance than they might have thought possible. These seem not unreasonable expectations for a mission statement.

Mission statements are constructed, not revealed, although intuition and inspiration may have something to do with them. The principal is the only person in the school who has the full-time responsibility for thinking about the whole school and how it could develop. As a consequence, the principal probably ought to be in charge of developing the mission statement. That does not mean that consultants and many other sorts of persons cannot be or should not be involved. On the contrary, they should; but the principal is the one without whom the process does not occur.

Perhaps the most important underlying factor in successfully developing a mission/goal statement is that the persons who are involved believe that the process of developing such a statement will have consequences. That is, they must believe that the goal statement will affect their lives in important ways. There is no formula for getting the key actors in an organization to believe that what they are being asked to do will make any difference at all to their lives. At the heart of the process is the general credibility of the person who is asking them to do it. If the principal is not credible in general, the process will not be taken seriously. A new principal will have to work to establish some initial basis of credibility before asking a staff to engage the process.

A second prerequisite for beginning a process of establishing missions/goals is that the principal has a very clear idea of what she or he wants out of the process. This is not to suggest that what the principal wants is what will emerge, but that the credible principal's sense of the good and the possible is going to be very persuasive for a large percentage of the actors. Someone has to have an idea and what the principal thinks is important.

A third prerequisite is that the principal know the school. This may be patently obvious, but any process of mission development is contentious and one of the favored ploys of those who resist such efforts is to claim that "we are already doing that." If the principal is unable to answer the claim with facts that refute it, the claim will stand, even though the principal "knows" that the claim is false. Thus, a principal must have at hand an enormous amount of information about the organization, including details of its processes and evidence of its outcomes. Without such facts, the principal is not in a position to be as persuasive as she or he might be.

A fourth precondition for deciding to start the process is that the principal believes in it sufficiently to be willing to put into it a great deal of time and energy. These processes are not often easy, nor can they be done effectively some Wednesday afternoon when things are slow.

Finally, a principal's decision to engage a school staff in serious discussion about what the school stands for and hopes to achieve ought not be held without some very clear understandings with the superintendent of schools. By implication, mission statements have resource consequences. If the consequences are unacceptable to the superintendent, then it is probably best to wait until some other time. In addition, if the superintendent does not favor fairly high levels of school autonomy it is probably not wise to do very much more than "refine" the mission statement of the district, if the district has one.

If the five prerequisite conditions of credibility, clear personal focus, extensive knowledge, willingness to commit time and energy, and permission can be met, then the principal is in a position to start a process. From here, there is no magic formula, no simple, recipelike set of steps. The rest is simply good administrative work;—planning, process, affirmation, and institutionalization.

Goals are value statements and, as such, tend to elicit serious debate. By expressly stating goals, some units are going to get favored and some are not. By definition, then, goal-setting is a political process, not a technical one. Planning of a political nature is the right sort of planning. The principal must know the political landscape of the school and must think hard about how that political landscape will influence what will be possible. For example, because the principal has a good idea of how she or he wants the mission statement to look (precondition number two) and a good idea of the implications of that for resource use in the future, the principal knows before beginning who is likely to be favored and who is not. Another planning question is "Whose values are sufficiently like mine that he or she or they can be counted on to support the direction I think we should go?" Yet another question is, "Where might the resistance arise and what resources (internal and external) are available to those who resist?" Another question is, "How does information move around in this organization, and how can I assure that my message is being heard loud and clear in the halls, lounges, and classrooms?" These questions, and others like them, are political questions, and their answers are to be found only in the particular political context of the school. Although external consultants are both advantageous and disadvantageous, such persons can be helpful in working with the principal to make sure the right questions are being asked. In addition, a consultant may be able to nose around the organization sufficiently to help the principal answer some of the planning questions.

The choice among processes is wide. Schmuck and others (1977) offer as helpful a collection of possibilities as is available in education. Each of the processes, though, has essentially three phases: entry or problem definition, data gathering, and feedback. A principal faces a critical point in deciding how to define the problem (entry). Perhaps three general strategies are available. In the first, the *rational*, the principal approaches the issue as a problem requiring a solution. In its most simple form it looks like this, "Folks, I've been thinking, and it seems to me that we need a better sense of what we are doing around here." This may be followed by a set of reasons (falling achievement test scores, changes in local demographics that are producing different kinds of students, data on what happens to graduates, and the like). Such a problem definition is unlikely to get very much attention, except in a school in which the professional norms of the staff are very high and where staff members have become quite used to dealing with one another around questions of educational outcomes. Such a school, by the way, is already likely to have an operating mission statement.

A second strategy of problem definition is a *political* one, in which the principal declares that an emergency exists in the form of external threat. In its simplest form it looks like this: "Folks, the superintendent (school board, parent group, or whatever) is hopping mad about what we are doing over here. We have three months to come up with a concrete school improvement plan. If we don't, she or he is going to take serious (unspecified, of course) action to straighten out the mess here." That strategy may gain the initial attention of the group, but is subject to erosion as people begin to calculate what actions really could be taken by the superintendent and decide that they are willing to risk it given the alternative of modifying current practices. Further, the group might come quickly to the realization that the only real consequence is that the principal will be let go, a consequence that some, at least, might favor.

The final problem-definition strategy, the *selfish*, is to define the problem in terms of collective, long-term self-interest. This strategy has two tactics. In the first, the self-interest is the promise of reduction of pain brought on by current circumstances. This tactic depends on the identification of real issues that cause pain for sufficient numbers of people in the organization. It might take the form, "Folks, none of us is feeling very good about the fact that (real issue causing real pain). It is evident to me that we might be able to do something about this if we sat down and talked about it as part of a general discussion about what we are trying to accomplish." The crux, obviously, is to identify an issue of sufficient difficulty and magnitude that it cannot be dismissed by referring it to the assistant principal. The second tactic is the high-road tactic of appealing to the staff's sense of what they might become. This is the tactic that typically gets mentioned in discussions of vision. It is not a bad tactic. But for a cynical, or jaded, or tired staff it must be used very carefully, and then only after sufficient numbers of informal tests with the power structure of the school to give some assurance that allies can be found. It must also be presented as a tactic that will lead to highly desirable changes for many people. Altruism is not a solid base on which to build an exercise of this sort.

No research exists to allow a definitive statement about the relative probabilities of success of each of these strategies. However, it is probably true that self-interest is a reasonable enough human emotion with which to begin (Argyris, 1957). Most people do want to gain some satisfaction from their work. If they can be convinced that cooperative activity will enhance their sources and levels of satisfaction they are likely to test the proposition (Barnard, 1938).

The second stage of the process is information gathering. The critical information to be gained is what people want and what they might be willing to do to get what they want. Some people will want the process to go away, but most will not. They will want to say something about themselves and their interests. Schmuck et al. (1977) discuss numerous information gathering techniques, as do Beckhard (1969), Owens (1970), Firestone and Rosenblum (1988), and Spencer (1989). All these techniques will work and the choice among them is as much a matter of logistics and the principal's preference as anything else. Perhaps a rule of thumb is that the more contentious the faculty the less should be used, in the early stages, techniques that rely on group meetings and other forms of personal interaction. This is not always true; a skilled outside consultant might suggest such a meeting in these circumstances. The purpose would be to surface all of the agendas and to craft an overarching mission. But even that strategy is likely to be accompanied by various forms of distancing, in which small groups might work together, or in which the prior use of questionnaires would have occurred. The major criterion to be met in this stage is that all the salient actors are given ample opportunity to say what they need to say. This is the first part of an ongoing political litmus test, in which people decide whether the process is authentic.

The third stage is that of information feedback. People want to know what other people have to say and what other people want. Themes will emerge; people will discover that they want what others want. They will discover that what they and others want does not seem impossible to fulfill. They will craft a statement of mission that meets the criteria described earlier. A thoughtful principal will easily see how the themes connect and how the connections can be used to develop a powerful statement of purpose. Educators believe that children and youth can experience joy and success in schools. Educators also believe that they can construct environments in which joy and success are possible. Because they believe those things, they will provide a principal with the language they want to hear that reaffirms their own beliefs. Only the most cynical will resist.

The next stage is one of affirmation and celebration. People need a chance(s) to affirm that what is before them is what they want and to celebrate their accomplishment. They need to be able to say to themselves and to others that they have done a good thing, a thing that will make their lives and the lives of others better. The affirmation/celebration stage is not to be taken lightly, because it serves as the foundation for changes in the culture of the school. If it has meaning, the mission statement will be the foundation for changes in personal behaviors, in procedures, in processes, in interaction patterns, in influence patterns, in social statuses, and in a host of other forces that people have learned to take for granted. People must be allowed to feel very good about the mission statement, because it may mean a great deal of change later.

The final stage is to institutionalize the mission statement. What this means is that the principal must do something that confirms the mission statement as important for the school. Some obvious actions are to tell people outside the organization what it is, to remind people inside the organization what it is, and to begin to model it in his or her own behavior. If the mission of the institution says something about insuring that all students will have an equal chance to succeed and the principal continues policies that clearly limit the chances for some children, the mission statement becomes quickly and publicly a lie.

A more subtle form of institutionalization occurs as the principal takes actions that please people and justifies them in terms of the mission. That suggests that the principal ought to find opportunity to take actions that please people. It also suggests that the first actions taken under the rubric of the mission statement ought not to be ones that displease people. In addition, as persons within the organization begin to propose changes in the way things are done, and to justify them in terms of the mission, the principal must be quite careful in the choice of the ones to deny. If a part of the mission is to increase student participation in learning and the principal clamps down on a noisy classroom or refuses a request for unorthodox materials, the principal may be sending a message that the mission is not to be believed. What is at issue, obviously, is the degree to which the principal's behavior changes in response to the mission. Without change in the principal's behavior, change from others is unlikely.

Conclusion

We have had much discussion of excellence, of site-based management, and of self-renewing schools (Duttweiler 1988). Each of these discussions begins with some form of the admonition that a key function of a modern leader is to help the organization establish and maintain purpose. Although the associated processes are not simple, nor is it abundantly clear that school missions are free of contention, it *is* abundantly clear that leadership and purpose are inextricably tied. Samuel Butler said it in *The Way of All Flesh*:

> It is not by what a man has actually put upon his canvas, nor yet by the acts he has set down, so to speak, upon the canvas of his life that I will judge him, but by what he makes me feel that he felt and aimed at. (Butler, p. 5)

References

Argyris, C. (1957). *Personality and organization.* New York: Harper.

Baldridge, J. V., & Deal, T. (1975). Eds. *Managing change in educational organizations.* Berkley, CA: McCutchan.

Barnard, C. (1938). *The functions of the executive.* Cambridge, MA: Harvard University Press.

Beckhard, R. (1969). *Organization development: Strategies and models.* Reading, MA: Addison-Wesley.

Bennis, W., & Nanus, B. (1985). *Leaders: The strategies for taking charge.* New York: Harper & Row.

Bidwell, C., & Friedkin, N. (1988). The sociology of education. In N. Smelser (Ed.), *Handbook of sociology.* Newbury park, CA: Sage.

Blau, P. (1956). *Bureaucracy in modern society.* New York: Random House.

Boyan, N. (Ed.) (1988). *Handbook of research on educational administration.* White Plains, NY: Longman.

Bredeson, P. (1985). An analysis of the metaphorical perspectives of school principals. *Educational Administration Quarterly, 21.*

Briggs, P. (1987). *Phoenix: An urban city.* Tempe AZ: College of Education, Arizona State University.

Burns, J. (1978). *Leadership.* New York: Harper & Row.

Butler, S. (n.d.) The way of all flesh. Books, Inc. New York. Art-type edition.

Clark, D., & Astuto, T. (1988). Paradoxical choice options in organizations. In D. Griffiths, R. Stout, and P. Forsyth (Eds.), *Leaders for America's schools.* Berkeley, CA: McCutchan.

Corcoran, T., Walker, L., & White, J. (1988). *Working in urban schools.* Washington, D.C.: Institute for Educational Leadership.

Drucker, P. (1974). *Management: Tasks, responsibilities, practices.* New York: The Free Press.

Duttweiler, P (1988). *Organizing for excellence.* Austin, TX: Southwest Educational Development Laboratory.

Easton, D. (1965). *A systems analysis of political life.* New York: Wiley.

Etzioni, A. (1961). *A comparative analysis of complex organizations.* New York: The Free Press.

Firestone, W., & Rosenblum, S. (1988). Building commitment in urban high schools. *Educational Evaluation and Policy Analysis, 10, 4,* 285-299.

Goodlad, J. (1984). *A place called school.* New York: McGraw-Hill.

Hoy, W., & Miskel, C. (1982). *Educational administration: Theory, research, and practice,* 2nd ed. New York: Random House.

March, J. (1986). How we talk and how we act: Administrative theory and administrative life. In T. Sergiovanni and J. Corbally, (Eds.), *Leadership and organizational culture.* Urbana, IL: University of Illinois Press

Martin, W., & Willower, D. (1981). The managerial behavior of high school principals. *Educational Administration Quarterly, 17.*

McCall, M., & Kaplan, R. (1985). *Whatever it takes.* Englewood Cliff, N. J.: Prentice-Hall.

Morgan, G. (1986). *Images of organization.* Beverly Hills, CA: Sage.

Myers, J. (1990). *The relationship between administrator ideology of pupil control and school discipline effectiveness* Unpublished Ph.D. dissertation. Arizona State University. Tempe, AZ.

Owens, R. (1970). *Organizational behavior in schools.* Englewood Cliffs, N. J.: Prentice-Hall.

Parsons, T. (1956). Suggestions for a sociological approach to the theory of organizations. In A. Etzioni (Ed.), *Complex Organization: A Sociological Approach.* New York: Holt, Rinehart & Winston.

Parsons, T. (1969). Suggestions for a sociological approach to theory of organizations. In A. Etzioni (Ed.), *A Sociological reader on complex organizations.* 2nd ed. New York: Holt, Rinehart & Winston.

Schmuck, R., Runkel, P., Arends, J., & Arends, R. (1977). *The second handbook of organization development in schools.* Palo Alto, CA: Mayfield.

Sedlak, M., Wheeler, C., Pullin, D., & Cusick, P. (1986). *Selling students short*. New York: Teachers College Press.

Sills, D. (1969). The succession of goals. In A. Etzioni (Ed.), *A sociological reader on complex organizations*, 2nd ed. New York: Holt, Rinehart and Winston.

Sills, D. (1970). Preserving organizational goals. In O. Grusky and G. Miller (Eds.), *The Sociology of Organizations: Base Studies*. New York: The Free Press.

Spencer, L. (1989). *Winning through participation*. Dubuque, IA: Kendall/Hunt.

Spring, J. (1986). *The American school 1642-1985*. White Plains, NY: Longman.

Stout, J. (1981). *The enculturation of new school board members: A longitudinal study of seven school districts*. Unpublished doctoral dissertation. Arizona State University, Tempe, AZ.

Tallerico, M. (1988). *The dynamics of superintendent-school board relationships*. Unpublished doctoral dissertation, Arizona State University, Tempe, AZ.

Thompson, J. (1989). *Bridge to the future: How elementary principals share their vision*. Unpublished doctoral dissertation. Arizona State University, Tempe, AZ.

Thompson, J., & McEwen, W. (1969). Organizational goals and environment. In A. Etzioni (Ed.), *A sociological reader on complex organizations*, 2nd ed. New York: Holt, Rinehart & Winston.

Vaill, P. (1986). The purposing of high-performing systems. In T. Segiovanni and J. Corbally (Eds.), *Leadership and organizational culture*. Urbana, IL: University of Illinois Press.

Weick, K. (1985). Sources of order in underorganized systems: Themes in recent organizational theory. In Y. Lincoln (Ed.), *Organizational theory and inquiry: The paradigm revolution*. Beverly Hills, CA: Sage.

Name Index

Subject Index